When Desperation Cries

by

Erin B. Cummings

ISBN: 1-932047-01-8

Printed in the United States of America.

Dedicated to all of Ruthie's Children

Prologue

No one knew why it happened, but in that city of Demopolis, Alabama, a lot of the chickens developed sores on their heads. It seemed that one day they were healthy, but the next day they were sick.

The sun's rays beamed down on the chicken coop, waking the sleeping chickens to a new day. One white hen with sores on her head stood up from where she was resting and wobbled around erratically. The chicken was feverish. Her head hung close to the floor. She hobbled about until she managed to stumble out of the open door and fall on a patch of grass. White pus seeped from one sore on her head above her right eye. The pus, thick and mingled with blood, fell upon her feathers and quickly dried into a crusty mask over her right eye, closing it tightly.

Struggling to open her eye and losing the battle, the poor chicken continued to wobble off the small patch of grass searching for relief from her pain; she was now near blindness. Soon another sore on the chicken's head burst open and the pus seeped into her left eye. The sun's hot beams hastened the drying effect. Now both of her eyes were sealed shut. The chicken went into a frenzy. Not only was she in pain but now her sight was completely gone. The helpless creature ran squawking, the pain and fright unbearable. She came to an halt by the well in front of the shack, resting for a moment. Suddenly a banging noise penetrated the air, confusing the chicken even more. A man had opened and slammed the door to the shack he called home. The startled chicken leaped, flapping her short wings and landing on the ledge of the well. There she sat momentarily, swaying her head from left to right. She tried to stand but stumbled like a drunken man. Missing her mark, she plummeted into the depths of the well. A faint splashing noise was heard. The man looked toward the sound of the splash but quickly dismissed it. He had a hatchet in his hand. He stepped off his porch and started his journey toward the chicken coop. Walking in long strides he kept his eyes focused straight ahead with a mixture of determination and sadness showing on his face.

The chicken struggled violently. Her squawks reverberated in the shaft causing her to panic even more. Her wet feathers dragged her down further into the cool water. She gasped one last time for air to fill her lungs, but only water entered her tiny beak. The splashing came to a halt. Her fight for survival ceased.

The man went into the coop looking around for the white hen with the sores on her head. His plan was to take the chicken out of her misery and bury her in a shallow grave. His tall figure searched the coop but the chicken was not there.

"Where the hell is that chicken?"

He left the coop and went into the yard. While looking around he suddenly remembered the splashing sound he had heard a few moments earlier.

"Oh hell, naw, not the well!"

He started running toward the well. He reached it and looked inside. With disgust, he threw the hatchet to the ground.

"Damn chicken done fell in the well! Now I gotta get her out!"

He sighed as he headed back toward the shack. "Flo told me ta kill that old sick chicken before now. I know she gonna be mad."

CHAPTER ONE

Everyone gots a story to tell. Mines begin seventy-seven years ago. My hair weren't gray then and my skin weren't wrinkled. It all started wit a girl who mind weren't strong. She my mama. They tell me she almost kilt me when I was a little baby. They say she fourteen when she git pregnant wit me. The man what git her pregnant, didn't wanna marry her. He already married.

They tell me that one day my mama took a cardboard box and punch a small hole in it. She was jus a hummin as she put a long string in the hole and tie it to the box. The other end she helded in her hand. I was only four months old when she took me and the box and went outside. She walk up a hill that wasn't far from the shack she live in. She put the box on the ground at the very top of that hill, wit me in it. She grab hold of the other end of the string and went tearin down the hill. They say the box fell over and I tumble out. I was a rollin down the hill when my grandmama look out the door and saw me. She dash out the door like a bolt of lightning, runnin to that hill. She grab me jus afore I roll on some rocks at the bottom. They tell me I was badly bruised and screamin my head off. My grandmama took me from my mama that very day and gave me to Aunt Flo, my mama's oldest sister, and her husband Roy, who had no chillins of they own. They say my real mama didn't protest, she jus sat on the step of the porch hummin to herself and rockin back and forth as Aunt Flo passed her holdin me.

When I turns six years, old Aunt Flo told me that she was gonna take me to see my mama. Aunt Flo say my real mama was well now.

"Was she sick Aunt Flo?" I look up at my aunt wit a question on my face.

"Yeh, she was kinda sick. She had to have somebody take care of her. Now she can take care of herself."

My mama live in my grandparents' house. Grandpapa had builted that house when he young. He and Grandma had to live wit his parents until it finish. They raise fourteen chillins in the house, six girls and eight boys. All of dem move out the house cept for my mama. My grandmama and grandpapa was dead. Aunt Flo said that I seen dem afore but I don't remember. I guess I was jus too young.

I didn't wanna go to see my real mama. *"Maybe she gonna put me in a box again and go down a hill wit me in it,"* I thought. *Maybe this time I jus fall out the box and die."*

I remember Aunt Flo wakin me up that Saturday mornin and dressin me in my blue dress wit the little red flowers on it. Aunt Flo made that dress for me to wear on Sundays. That day I had to wear it to see my real mama. Aunt Flo put my hair in three braids, one at the top and two in the back. She tie a white ribbon on each braid. I wore my black patent leather shoes and white socks wit little ruffles on top.

Aunt Flo tell me, "You look real purty. Don't git dirty 'cause I want you mama to see you lookin you best."

"Yesum, Aunt Flo."

Aunt Flo left me standin in the kitchen as she went in the bedroom. I stay in one spot, afraid to move. I reckon if I move, some dirt jus might jump on me. I jus stood there by the table lookin around and thinkin about seein my real mama.

I look at the old brown cabinet in the right corner. The paint was a peelin off it 'cause it was so old. That cabinet helded flour, sugar and dem other things that came in bags for cookin, plus our plates, forks, spoons and knives. The table that sat in the middle of the room was large, wit four chairs made of rushin. Papa paint the table and chairs a dark brown jus like the cabinet. I traced the sun's ray that was lightin up the table, back to our shutters which covered two neatly cut square holes directly across from one another. We had no glass in dem. We opened the shutters every mornin for light and fresh air, and closed dem at night no matter how hot it git in the house. The reason is we feared dem snakes might climb up the side the house and enter in.

Our stove was wood-burnin. My aunt always kept one pot on it at all times. She washed the others and hanged dem on nails on the wall. This was a practice that her own mama did. Aunt Flo was fond of sayin that if you kept a pot on the stove, no matter how bad things git, that one pot would always manage to git somethin in it for cookin.

The kitchen floor was wooden, and Aunt Flo swept it twice a day. Once in the mornin and once at night by candle light. I heard that some people had lights that come on when you put you fingers on a little thing that stuck out the wall called a switch.

I 'member when I was five years old I asked Papa about electricity. I couldn't say electricity. Jus couldn't form the words right. So I said e-lect-wristy-a tee. Every time I say the word, it make Papa smile. I asked, "Why the lights comes on and you don't have to light no candles, Papa?"

"That's electricity. You has to pay for you house to be wired for electricity. Then every month you has to pay you electric bill." Papa was a sittin on the porch in a chair chewin tobacco when he said that. He spit a wad out on the ground.

I pat him on the knee. "Where e-lect- wristy-a- tee come from Papa?"

"It come from electricity poles. Dem poles is as tall as dem there trees up yonder."

"So poles is really trees."

"Yeah, Ruthie." Papa spit out another wad of tobacco and wipe his mouth wit his hand. "Poles is trees wit no limbs, wit wires a comin out the top." Papa look at me and smile.

I lift my arms and hump my shoulders. " Why ain't no poles nowhere round here, Papa?"

"Most colored folks can't afford electricity. Papa lean back in his old creaky chair, stretch out wit his toes pressed on the porch to keep him from fallin.

"Is that why we don't have no e-lect-wristy-a-tee, Papa? Is we like most colored folks?"

Papa kinda smile. He raise his eyes and looks at me. "First thang is, we rent this here house and it ain't wired. Even if we had our own house, I can't afford to have it wired. Jus like the rest of dem colored folks."

Right then, my aunt come out the room all dressed up in a pink and white dress wit black shoes and a hat wit a big rose on the front. She look like she a goin to church. My Aunt Flo was a short small-frame woman wit skin was the color of pecan; rich and vibrant. Her hair short and black, and she keep it black by dyin it once a month like a religious practice. It was like she afraid of lookin old.

When we leavin the house, Papa, who really my uncle, was standin by the well a lookin down in it. He had a water bucket in his hand. By the look on his face, you could tell that he was tryin to figure out how to do somethin.

Papa was a tall dark-skin man. He had the most stern eyes I ever seen. He was medium built but his face was round as a melon. His skin on his face was full of small holes like the ones you see in the dirt when it's dry and you sprinkle water on it. The holes didn't go in far, jus indented his skin a bit. His hair was as gray as the sky when it storms. Papa didn't smile or talk much. He look like he didn't take nothin from nobody.

"We a goin now." Aunt Flo walked pass Papa a smilin like nothin didn't matter.

"Ain't gonna do you no good." Papa stood there wit one hand on the bucket and one hand on his hip.

"Jus git that dead chicken out like I told you, man. Have my water on that there stove when I git back." Mama grab hold to my hand.

Papa put the bucket over the well and let it down. He must have let go the handle that helded the rope 'cause I heard a splash. "Like I said, it ain't gonna do you no good."

I reckoned that somethin was wrong wit Papa to say that to Aunt Flo, but I knew better than to ask why. That was grown folk business and chillins knew better than to git into grown folk business. Git you mouth slapped right off if you asked questions about they business.

It was a scorchin hot day wit the sun strong and piercin. Aunt Flo and me was walkin along the long dusty road. I kept lookin back at Papa. Mama was lookin back at him like she was gonna go back and say somethin else. She stop us for a second and then it seem like she was a changin her mind. We continued walkin down the road. I thought about havin to drink that water from the well.

I also thought about the chicken in the well—my pet chicken, Sugar. I name her that 'cause she white as sugar and sweet as could be. Papa didn't say which chicken fell in the well but I knew. I knew 'cause Sugar wasn't outside when Aunt Flo and I left the house. Sugar was always outside in the mornin after Papa would spread the corn for the hens to eat, but not today. I hoped that Papa would git drinkin water from the neighbors. If Papa made me drink that water from our well I knew I would throw up. I couldn't bear the thought of drinking water that Sugar died in.

It seem like it took forever to git to my real mama's house. I had never seen my real mama. I wondered if I look like her. I wondered if my aunt would make me stay wit her. I look up at Aunt Flo.

"Aunt Flo, I don wanna leave you to stay wit my real mama."

"You ain't gonna stay wit her Ruthie. You jus gonna see her."

"Good, 'cause I love livin wit you and Papa, Aunt Flo."

Aunt Flo jus look down at me and smile. I look up at Aunt Flo wit questionin eyes.

"Aunt Flo, does my real mama loves me? Or does she jus wanna kill me?"Aunt Flo stop walkin and look down at me.

"You real mama loves you very much. She don't wanna kill you."

"That's good, Aunt Flo, that she loves me and not jus wanna kill me. If she tried to kill me this time I would jus run away. If she loves me, I is gonna love her too." Aunt Flo smile at me and we continued walkin.

When we finally gits to the house where Aunt Flo say my mama live, I could see a lady facin us, ironin. She look at the both of us, frowned and stopped ironin. She was shorter than my aunt, and wit long black hair. Her hair look like it hadn't been combed in a while. Small pieces of white stuff that look like cotton was all mingled up in it. She look much younger than my aunt. She wore a dress that had lots of different colors in it. The sleeves seemed like they had been torn off. My aunt motioned for her to come to the screen door.

"It ain't locked." The lady eyed my aunt.

My aunt open the screen door and push me in. "I brought you daughter. I thought you might wanna to see her. Ain't she purty?" My aunt lift my chin. "Jus like you when you was her age. Say hi, Ruthie."

I was sort of shy. A thin child, but tall for my age. I stood there beside my aunt lookin at my real mama.

"Ruthie, I said say hi to you mama." I didn't wanna move. My aunt push me toward my mama.

"Hi Mama," I say in a low tone as I look up at her.

I was expectin my real mama to do somethin since I was her real daughter and all. I was thinkin that maybe she would give me a hug or a kiss. Aunt had said that she really loves me, but she didn't do nothin. She jus went back to ironin. She didn't even look at me. She jus kepted a lookin at my Aunt Flo like she was mad. I didn't feel like she heard me, so I said hi again.

"Hi girl!" Her tone of voice was mean. It made me cry.

"What do you want, Flo? Why you bring her here? She ain't mine!"

"Ruthie, go outside and sit on the porch!" Aunt Flo took my hand and led me to the door. I went on out and sat on the porch wit my hands over my eyes, cryin. Aunt Flo stay inside and talked to my mama.

"She is you daughter, Mattie! Why you keep sayin she ain't!" I heard my aunt talkin but I didn't hear my mama saying nothin. "What is wrong wit you?" Still no words was spoken by my real mama. "Mattie, answer me!"

"I ain't got no chillins, Flo. Don't you know that? You all say that I tried to kill that little girl out there. I ain't never tried to kill nobody. Why y'all keep a sayin mean things like that about me?"

When I heard my real mama say dem words I started cryin harder.

Aunt Flo came out, look at me cryin, and took a deep breath. She took my hands from my face, reach in her pocket, and pull out a handkerchief to dry my tears. She bent down and look me in the face.

"Girl, stop that cryin!"

"But my mama didn't talk to me. She say that I ain't her's. She don't love me!" I stammered.

"I love you." My Aunt Flo hand me the handkerchief. Her shoulders was slumped now. All the happiness had left her face. Now she looked tired.

"Dry you eyes, girl. I don wanna see you cry no more, you hear!"

I dried my eyes. My aunt took hold to my hand and we started for home.

"Aunt Flo, does I have to see my mama again?"

"Naw, we ain't a comin here no more." Aunt Flo's voice dragged.

"Good, 'cause I don't wanna see her no more either."

As soon as we reached the house and my aunt opened the gate, I ran to the well. The water had risen up in the well almost to the top. The chicken was gone. I left the well and followed my aunt up the stairs to the porch of the house.

When we gits to the door, Papa open it for us. He took one look at my aunt's face and knew what happen. "Told you, Flo."

"I was sure she would be different by now. Well, I reckon I better git these here clothes off me and that girl, and git supper ready."

Me and Aunt Flo went into the bedroom. Aunt Flo took my Sunday dress off me and put it on a hanger that she hung on a nail on the wall. She help me put on a old dress. She took off her own clothes and put on her workin clothes. I took off my shoes and socks 'cause I like walkin barefoot on the wooden floors. The wood felted cool on my feet, and I liked the slappin sound my feet made walkin across it.

When we git through dressin, I ask Aunt Flo if I could help make supper.

"You can help by puttin the dishes on the table when I tell you to. Right now you jus sit down at the table." Papa came in the house wit a brown-feathered chicken in his hand. The chicken head was a swingin lifeless from side to side. Papa hand it to Mama. She put the chicken in the pot of water on the stove, which by now was at a boil. Mama dip the chicken in the hot water. Took it out again and started pullin it feathers off. I went over where Mama was, to take a look at the chicken. The smell of hot chicken feathers was foul. I put my fingers to my nose.

Papa had sat down at the table. He took a pipe out of his pocket and was tappin it in his hand to remove the old tobacco.

I went over to Papa. "Where that dead chicken you took out the well?" "I buried her in the back yard."

"We don't have to eat her, Papa?"

"We ain't a eatin her 'cause her body was poison."

"I is glad we don't have to eat poison chicken, Papa. You sure it wasn't Sugar?" Papa don't say a word. He jus gits up and goes on back outside. I went to the bedroom and gits a book and my doll Pattie. Aunt Flo had made the doll out of a old sock and stuff her wit cotton. Pattie had black buttons for eyes and a black button nose. Aunt Flo had sewed a smilin mouth on her wit red thread. Her arms and legs was stuffed wit cotton too. Pattie's dress was blue and white. Her hair was black yarn that Aunt Flo had sewed on her head. I liked puttin her yarn hair into braids. Whatever style Aunt Flo put my braids, I put Pattie's in the same style. I loved Pattie.

I put Pattie in a chair beside me and play like I's a teacher and she the student. I had a book wit me that I brought out the bedroom. My book was about a rabbit and a fox. I couldn't read yet, but Mama had read it to me so many times I remember the story. I pretend like I's a readin it to Pattie.

Soon the house smell of boiled chicken, onions, cinnamon and apples.

Aunt Flo call to me. "You can help me put the dishes on the table now, Ruthie."

"Yesum, Aunt Flo." I took Pattie and my book back to the bedroom and laid dem both on my bed so I could go back to the kitchen and help Aunt Flo wit the dishes. When we finish settin the table, Mama call Papa in. Before we ate, Papa say the blessin. We never ate any food without sayin the blessin.

I ate my supper a smackin my lips and lickin my fingers.

"Ruthie, use you fork."

"Yesum, Aunt Flo." I use my fork for a little while, but I still ended up usin my fingers to pick out the pieces of chicken. After I eats my chicken and dumplin, Aunt Flo give me a slice of pie. I ate the crust off the top first. It taste of butter, apples, sugar, and cinnamon. I smile at Aunt

Flo. "Mmm. Aunt Flo, this here pie sure nuff is good." I stuck my fingers in the pie, pulled out a slice of apple, and stuffed it in my mouth.

"Why thank you, Ruthie." Aunt Flo smile at me.

"I is thirsty, Aunt Flo."

"I'll git you some water."

Aunt Flo gits up from the table and walk over to a bucket. She dip a jar in the bucket and brung it to me. I look in the jar. "Is this here water from our well, Papa?"

"Yeah, Ruthie."

I stare into the glass. I hated that old well. No matter what fell in it we had to drink the water. Papa said we would never git sick from it, 'cause we live a stone throw away from the Tombigbee River, and the waters from the river run under the well, filterin it. Once a day the water would rise up in the well, and spill up over the top onto the ground. The water from the well was so clear it sparkle. So cold, that if you drunk it too fast it made you brain freeze. I kept a lookin at my jar of water. It was crystal clear. But I kept thinkin that it was poison.

"Drink that water, girl." Papa stop eatin but he still held his fork.

"Papa, that poison chicken fell in the well. Ain't the well water poison too?"

He put his fork down. "The Lawd done blest it. He done got rid of all the poison. Come a few hours and the well be overflowed wit even more clean water." Papa took his jar of water, turned it up and dranked every bit. "Good water. Nice and cold." He put his jar down and look over at me still starin in the jar.

"Drink that water, girl."

"Okay Papa." I drunk a little of the water. "I think I is gonna be sick, Papa. I can feel the throw up." I put my hands to my mouth, ran from the table, and heaved.

I looked around at Papa. He had stood up from the table and was pointin his finger at me. "You better not throw up or you will be eatin that throw up jus like dem dogs eat they own."

Suddenly, I don't feel sick no more.

After supper when my Aunt Flo gits me ready for bed I hug her as hard as I could around her waist.

"Why is you huggin me so hard? You almost took my breath away, child."

"I jus love you so much, Auntie."

"I love you too." She smile, huggin me back. "Now git into bed,

Ruthie." Aunt Flo release the hug and I let go too.

"I ain't said my prayers yet. Can't git in the bed without prayin." I git on my knees beside my bed, put my hands together and close my eyes.

"Dear Lawd, thank you for everythin. Please bless Auntie and Papa. Please Lawd make my real mama not hate me. I ain't done nothin to her. In Jesus name I pray. Amen."

"You real mama don't hate you, Ruthie. She jus kinda crazy-actin sometimes." Aunt Flo pulled the covers back, took hold of one of my hands and help me in the bed.

"She act like she don't care about me at all. You love me don't you, Aunt Flo? You and Papa?"

"Yeah I really do. Even before the day my own mama gave you to me." Aunt Flo put the covers on me. Suddenly I git an idea.

"Auntie, can I call you Mama from now on?"

"Yes you can, honey." She kiss me goodnight and left the room.

I looked over at Pattie's smilin face, and took her in my arms. "Guess what, Pattie? Aunt Flo is my real mama now. I is gonna pretend that she had me. Not my real mama. Aunt Flo wouldn't never tried to kill me. You know why, Pattie? 'cause she loves me. I smile and hug Pattie tighter to my chest. All the Angels in heaven couldn't been more happier than me that night.

CHAPTER TWO

It was nineteen thirty-three; I jus turned eleven. It was summer and school was out. They was the Depression goin on in the whole world. They tell me that a lot of rich people kilt demselves 'cause they had lost all they money. The Depression didn't bother us much 'cause we was already poor. Didn't have nothin much to lose.

It was expected that I help out around the house. Papa work at a cement plant. But he still didn't bring home much money. "They don't pay much for a man what jus sweeps the floors," Papa said.

Mama said we were blest that Papa had a job. Most colored folks in the South didn't have no job cept for being hired out to pick cotton. Most of the factories had closed, and if there was a job openin, they usually hire a white man. She say a colored man was the last one hired and the first one fired.

We had a garden in our back yard. I didn't like workin it 'cause snakes and bugs would be in it sometimes. We had a few chickens and that was about all. I needed a new pair of shoes and Papa couldn't afford to buy dem for me.

Mary Ann, a girl at school, said that all the girls in Demopolis was gonna be lookin for a job that summer. I wanted a job jus like dem other girls. Besides I wanted to save some money for college, so I could be a teacher when I grows up. Mary Ann had once told me that if I want to go to college I better start savin for it now. I decided to ask my mama if I could git me a job.

Mama did clothes for some white folks for extra money. She did the washin and ironin in the mornin and the sewin after supper. I watch her tryin to thread a needle, and went over and sat on the floor next to her. "Mama, you wouldn't have to work so hard if I git me a job." I looked at her wit my eyes raised like a little puppy dog. I hoped that she wouldn't tell me that I had to work around the house again the summer. Mama ignored me. As she git close to the needle eye wit the thread she miss her mark time and time again. She finally gave up.

"Thread this here needle for me, Ruthie."

I threaded the needle and handed it back to her. "All the other girls is gonna be workin this summer, Mama. Jus think, you could buy a new washtub. You won't have to work so much; jus relax sometime. I need a pair of new shoes. I could buy dem instead of Papa."

"My eyes sure ain't what they use to be." She place the button on the shirt and started sewin.

"I started feelin frustrated. Mama wasn't listenin to me. I took a breath, put one of my hands on my aunt's knees and shook it. "Mama please."

Aunt Flo stopped sewin. "I got to ask you Papa."

"Okay Mama, you ask Papa and see what he say."

I went in the bedroom, close the door and pray silently that Papa would say yes. After I git through prayin, I walked over to my bed and pull out one of my old books that was under it. I was jus bout to read it when I heard Papa come in the house. I could hear him and Mama talkin through the wall.

"Roy, Ruthie jus ask me to ask you if she could git a job this summer."

"I guess so. If the girl could bring in some extra money we sho nuff need it. I hear some chillin in the big cities work in factories twelve hours a day. Chillin got to work since the Depression. Yeah, let the girl work."

My heart leaped for joy. I ran out the room. "Thank you, thank you!" I kiss dem both.

"You been listenin to our conversation, girl?" Papa winkle his forehead like he mad.

"Couldn't help it, Papa. Don't be mad. You gonna be so happy when I bring in some money to help out."

Papa didn't say nothin. I didn't care. I was gonna git me a job.

Early that next day I went a lookin for a job. The day was clear, bright and promisin. In my mind I knew that I gonna git me some work even if it was jus babysittin. I walk up the road toward the house where Mary Ann live. When I git there, she was already gone.

I look up the road and seen a bunch of colored girls walkin toward the white folks part of town. I ran and caught up wit dem. Mary Ann was there.

She look at me. "I know you mama not lettin you work. You too young."

"I's jus as old as you is."

Mary Ann kind of laugh. "Girl, stop tellin stories, you know you is only eleven. I is fourteen! Some of these here girls are even older than me. I hear some of dem are even grown."

"Don't matter. Somebody gonna hire me!"

I walk wit dem until we git to the white part of town where we split up. Everybody went from door to door askin for work. Some of the girls git hired right off, bein they was grown and all. Mary Ann git a job afore me.

I thought to myself. "If Mary Ann could git a job, I can too." I was determined to git those new shoes and money for college.

I walk on down the road to jus about the last house on the street. It was a purty house. White, wit a white picket fence. As I open the gate, I seen flowers on both sides of the walkway to the porch. They was grass in the yard, cut down low and neat like a rug.

We didn't have any grass in our yard. Papa always kilt it. Papa say that he didn't want any grass in the yard. He said if we had any we wouldn't be able to see the snakes. Papa could see the snakes if there were jus dirt there. He would git the shovel and kill every last one of dem.

When I gits on the porch of the house I noticed they had a swing. I imagine sittin on that swing on hot nights, drinkin lemonade. "White folks has it good," I thought.

I knocks on the door and a tall, thin-framed woman wit brown hair and brown eyes open it. She was wipin her hands on an apron that she had tied around her waist. She stopped wipin dem and look at me, both hands on her hips.

"What you want, little colored gal?"

I cast my eyes to the ground and said shyly. "I is a lookin for a job, ma'am."

I was careful not to look in her face. I remember Mama sayin to me once, "Never look in white folk faces, especially not in they eyes. They don't like it. They say we be disrespectin dem if we look in they eyes."

Papa voice warn, "White folks don't want colored folks to look in they eyes 'cause we might see the Devil in dem." Devil or not, I wanted me a job.

"What can you do? I know you can't be no more than ten!"

"I is eleven, ma'am. I can wash, iron, and scrub floors real clean. I can babysit and cook a little. You won't be sorry if you hire me, ma'am."

"Maybe I won't be sorry, but you might!" She laughed. "Let's see how good you can wash."

The lady told me to follow her to her back yard. When we git there I notice two wash tubs and a scrub board that was layin against a old tree. Her scrub board was a little bigger than Mama's.

"I ain't got many clothes to wash. You stay here. I'll be right back."

"Tis gonna be easy," I thought until she come back. She kept goin back and forth into the house bringin out clothes until she had a pile that was taller than me.

"Okay, git to work."

"Yesum. Where is you well, ma'am?"

"I don't have a well. We git our water from the kitchen sink."

The lady took me into her kitchen and show me how to turn on the water from her sink. She gave me a bucket, and I filled it wit water. I took the water outside, makin trip after trip until I filled both the tubs. One of the tubs was for washin; the other for rinsin. The lady git me some soap and a bag of clothespins. I started sortin though the clothes and saw that some of dem was already clean. I wonder why the lady got clean clothes to wash.

I dip the dirty clothes in one tub wit the soap, scrub dem on the wash board, rinse and hung dem up to dry. I was gonna jus dip the clean clothes in the rinse water and hang dem up. But I had to scrub dem too 'cause the lady got a chair and sat down and watch me. I felted strange wit the lady watchin me like that . She also kept askin me questions like, "What's your mama and papa's name? Where's your school? What's your mama look like?"

"I told her I lived wit my aunt and uncle. She started askin me questions about my real mama.

Finally the lady gits up from her chair, walks over and touch my hair. I had it tied together wit a ribbon in the back. It reach almost to my waist.

"Never thought colored folks had such soft hair. Thought it would be hard as barb wire."

I turned real quick and look at the lady. She kinda chuckles, went back to her chair and sat down again. I went on back doin the clothes, but I thought to myself, "After today I ain't a comin back here."

When I finish wit the clothes, the lady git up out of her chair. "I hope that you don't think that I was too hard on you. I jus wanted to see if you were a hard worker like you said. Here is your money. Come back tomorrow. You won't have to wash nothin."

I looked at the money. She gave me three dollars. My eyes widen. Most colored girls had to work all week for two dollars. She had give me three for one day's work.

"Thank you ma'am!" I put dem dollars in my pocket.

"You better be gettin on home now."

"Shouldn't I be a takin down the dry clothes, ma'am?"

"I'm gonna do that." She motioned for me to leave.

I walked to the front of her house. As I was about to open the gate, the lady suddenly call me back. I went back hopin that she wouldn't remember how much everyone gits paid and take my three dollar back.

"You know we have talked all day, and I never asked your name."

"My name Ruthie, ma'am," I said, wit relief.

"Please to meet you Ruthie. I'm Miz Williams."

She walk wit me back to the gate, still askin me questions. She even ask me the size of my shoe. I told her.

"You be back here tomorrow, Ruthie."

"I will ma'am." I walk out the gate down to where Mary Ann work. It must have been around six or seven when I left Miz William's house 'cause when I went to the door where Mary Ann was hired, the lady say Mary Ann had been long gone. I start walkin home.

On my way I decided to stop at Mary Ann's house to show her my three dollars. I gits to where Mary Ann live and knock on the door. Mary Ann answered it.

"Girl, don tell me that you is jus leavin those folk's house." Mary Ann was lookin at me wit a frown on her face.

"Yeah, but looka here. She gave me three dollar and I jus work one day." I was feelin right proud of myself.

"Three dollars!" Mary Ann eyes open wide. Let me see. "That's more than anybody git unless they work a whole week."

I reach in my pocket and took out the three dollars and show dem to her. "See, she gave it to me 'cause I is a good worker and all."

"What did she have you to do?" Mary Ann eye my money.

"I jus wash a few clothes."

"What took you so long?"

"It took me so long 'cause after I git through we sat down and ate cookies and drank tea." I laughted.

"You tellin lies." Mary Ann stop lookin at the money. She wrinkles up her forehead. "What really happen?"

"She give me so many clothes that it took me this long to wash dem. I could swear some of dem was already clean but I scrub dem anyway. She watch me the whole time. I wasn't gonna go back no more 'cause I kinda felted funny wit her watchin me. But then she gave me this here three dollars. She can watch me cleanin. I ain't gonna feel funny if she gonna keep givin me three dollars every day. Anyway, she said that she ain't givin me any clothes to wash tomorra."

I should have have gone to her. She must be crazy to give so much money."

"She ain't crazy. She jus like to watch you, Mary Ann."

"You better git on home fore you mama come here after you, Ruthie."

"Yeah, I know it late. Bye, Mary Ann, I be comin by to git you tomorra. We can walk together."

"Okay Ruthie, you git on now." Mary Ann went back in and close the screen door.

I ran home. Sure enough, Mama was a waitin by the door. "Girl, what took you so long?"

"Mama, I found a good job. Looka here at how much money I got." Mama smile as she eye my money.

"Is she gonna pay you that every day? Most folks git two dollars a week. If she give you three dollars a day, you is gonna be makin fifteen dollars a week!"

"She didn't say, Mama. She jus give me this here money."

I hand the money to my mama. That's what all the chillin did after they git paid. They mama and papa took what they want and then give you what they want you to have. "Mama, can I have fifty cent of that there money?"

"You sure can, honey."

Mama gave me fifty cent outta her own pocket. I was thrilled. I took the money, found a jar and put the fifty cent in it. I close the lid and place the jar under my bed. After I buy my shoes, I thought, then I is gonna save for my college education. One day I is gonna be a teacher. When I come out of bedroom, Mama aske me again why I was so late gettin home.

"I stopped by Mary Ann's house, Mama after I left Miz William's. I jus had to tell Mary Ann bout all the clothes she had me wash."

"You ain't no stranger to washin a lot of clothes, Ruthie." Mama was sittin in one of the kitchen chairs. She had a bowl of white potatoes that she was a peelin as she talked.

"I know Mama, but some of dem were clean. I had to wash dem

anyway."

"The lady jus want to see if you was a hard worker."

"That is jus what Miz William's said. I guess that I better help you wit supper now, Mama."

"Naw, you go wash up Ruthie."

I took a bucket and went outside. I tied the bucket handle wit a rope that was always hangin from a hook on the well, drew some water out the well, and dip my hands in the water, feelin the coldness of it. I quickly splash some on my face. It was still warm outside, but the water made me shiver. I wash my hands, pour out the remainin water, and went in the house. Later Papa came home, smellin of sweat. His clothes was dusty. His eyes droop like he sleepy.

"Hi Papa."

"Hi Ruthie. You git a job?"

"Yessir."

"Good."

Papa sat down at the table. I put the plates and forks on the table, then sat down at my usual spot. Mama put the food on the table, and Papa say the prayer as usual. We all started eatin. Mama and I talk about what we was gonna do wit the money I made. Papa was quiet. He jus kept shovin mashed potatoes wit gravy and fried chicken in his mouth. He didn't even look at us at all.

Mama and I was still talkin after supper while we wash the dishes. When we git through, Mama told me to take a bath. Papa left the house like he always do when the lady folk took a bath, 'cause all baths were taken in the kitchen. The same tub we use for washin clothes we use for takin baths. We kepted the tub by the cabinet.

Mama heat some water on the stove and pour it in the tub. I git out the lye soap, took off my clothes, and git in the tub. I scrub down good. I wanted to be really clean when I git to Miz Williams house the next day. When I git through I put on my bed clothes. When I's dressed, Mama call Papa. He come in and eased hisself in one of the kitchen chairs. I walk over to him and kiss him on the jaw. "Night, Papa."

"Night, girl."

Mama was a standin by the stove. I went over to her and kiss her on her jaw too. "Night, Mama."

"Night, Ruthie."

I went in the bedroom, leavin dem in kitchen.

We all slept in the same room cept we slept in different beds. Mama and Papa slepted together. I slept in the smaller bed. We had a rope wit a blanket across it hidin my bed from theirs. If I had to git up in the middle of the night for anything I had to say, "I be gittin up." That was for respect.

I always say my prayer before I go to bed. That night I was so tired. The best I could do was say thank you Lawd as I layed down in my bed. Then I was fast asleep. I slepted until Mama woke me up the next day.

CHAPTER THREE

When Mama woke me up it was past seven. She let me sleep a little later since I was so tired the night before. When I woke up I put on my shoes and walk to the outhouse. All the colored folks had one. They tell me that some poor white folks have dem too. A outhouse look like a small house. Inside is jus a hole in the ground wit some boards around. It's built up so you can sit on it like a bench and git comfortable. I always looked around when I gits there. Jus the thought of snakes brought shivers down my spine.

Mary Ann told me a story once about snakes, a old man and a outhouse. The story was about her neighbor, Old Man Riley. One day he had to go to the outhouse real bad; he had the runs. Mr. Riley had a newspaper wit him but he never git the chance to read it. They was a big old rattlesnake down in that hole that Old Man Riley didn't see. He jus sat right down and did his number. His number fell right on that snake, Mary Ann said. The snake must not have like that, so it jump right up and bit Old Man Riley backside. Old Man Riley ran in the house yellin, still doin his number. His wife was in the kitchen. He plead for her to suck out the poison. She look at his backside wit his number all over it. Real pitiful-like she say, "Honey. What suit you wanna be buried in?" He died right there in his kitchen.

Anyway, when I git through doin my business I went back in the house to wash up for breakfast. I wash my face wit the water from the jar in the kitchen. Mama was in the kitchen gittin things ready for breakfast. I went into the bedroom to change into my dress. It was clean and press. Mama must have washed, starched, and ironed it that night while I was sleepin.

I stay in the bedroom a few minutes longer jus sittin on the bed wonderin if Miz Williams was gonna be askin me more questions. I hear Papa git up out the bed and head for the kitchen. I knew I had to cook so I headed for the kitchen too, but when I git in the kitchen Mama had already cooked. I felted bad. "I's sorry, Mama. I was jus in the room thinkin. I didn't know it was so late. You want me to put the dishes on the table?" I started for the cabinet to git the dishes.

"Go on child. I is gonna put the dishes on the table." Mama walk in front of me to the cabinet. "Go and sit down. I ain't mad at you. You is a workin girl now. The only thing I want you to do is eat you breakfast."

I went to the table, and Mama put the dishes and the food on the table in front of me and Papa. Mama had made biscuits, salt pork with honey on the side, jus what I liked. I was surprised. She was looking at me so proudly like I had won me prize or somethin. I look over at Papa. I thought that he would say somethin about me bein a workin girl, but he didn't say nothin. He jus kept eatin his honey and biscuits.

Mama sat down at the table. "I hope that lady gives you another three dollars today. If she does I can buy me another wash tub. My old one ain't lookin too good."

"I don't know, Mama. She a nice lady; maybe she will. What does you think, Papa?"

Papa stop eatin, sat back in his chair. "If she does, it's a trick to it. I don't trust her, and its best for you not to trust her. Don't sound right her givin you that much money on the first day."

We all went back to eatin, not sayin a word. Mama waited until I finished, then told me to come in the bedroom. When we git in there she whispered to me. "Don't pay Papa no mind child. There is some good and bad in any race. Maybe she one of the good ones. Don't be a tellin you Papa that I told you this. Hurry up now, tis almost eight thirty. You don wanna be late for work.."

"Yes ma'am." I kissed her and went in the kitchen and kissed Papa.

When I left, Mama said bye but Papa groaned. He never looked up at me.

I walk to Mary Ann's house, a swingin my arms and smilin from ear to ear. Everybody I see I say, "Mornin." When I git to Mary Ann's house she was a waitin outside.

"What took you so long? Girl, you is gonna make me late!"

"You has a special time to git there?" I said, as I walked to her side.

"Yeah. Dem white folks don't want you a comin to they house any old time. They wanna be gittin a decent day's work outta you."

"Well, Miz Williams didn't give me no special time. I come any time I want." After those words Mary Ann and I walk witout sayin a word.

Mary Ann started walkin fast. I couldn't keep up and found myself runnin out of breath. "Mary Ann, you don't has to walk so fast, girl!"

"Didn't you hear what I said? Ruthie, I got to git there before nine o'clock. If you wanna keep you job, you better git a runnin."

"Well didn't you hear me? I don't have to run. Miz Williams didn't tell me no time; she jus say, 'come here tommora.'"

"She will, jus wait if you be late gittin there today. She'll tell you what time to be there tommora. If you keep bein late, she gonna fire you for sure. Git herself another girl to work for her."

I thought about what Mary Ann said and we both started runnin. Finally, we reach the house where Mary Ann work. We was both out of breath, and we stop for a moment to rest before Mary Ann open the white picket gate. She turn around, folded her arms, frown at me, and raise one eyebrow.

"Hurry up and finish you work today so you can leave on time. If you is too late comin here I is gonna leave you. Remember that."

"I is gonna remember."

I went on down the road a bit until I come to Miz Williams house.

I knock on the door, and Miz Williams let me in. She was wearin a white apron, a white dress, wit white shoes. I thought to myself, *"She sure like white a lot."*

"Morning Ruthie, come on in. I want you to meet my husband and my little girl."

She led me down a narrow hall into her kitchen. Her husband and daughter was sittin at the table eatin breakfast. Mr. Williams was a tall man wit curly yellow hair. His daughter had the same color hair. I look up at his face and seen his blue eyes; he had a kind smile. Quickly, I cast my eyes to the floor.

"Mornin Ruthie," his voice real pleasant. He stood up from his chair takin his daughter by the hand causin her to stand up too. "This here is Susie."

"Hi. I'm six. How old are you?"

"I is eleven. Be twelve come October."

Susie walk away from her papa over to her mama and whisper in her ear, but it was loud enough for me to hear.

"Is she here for me to play with, Mama?"

Miz Williams smile at Susie. "She is here to work. Ain't that right, Ruthie?"

"Yesum." Susie went back to the table and finish eatin her food.

"You want somethin to eat, Ruthie?"

"No ma'am. I jus ate, but I thank you ma'am."

"Well tomorrow you jus come here and have breakfast with me and my family."

"Yesum, Miz Williams."

I hear that people you works for did give you breakfast and lunch. If I had known that Miz Williams was gonna feed me, I wouldn't had to listen to Mary Ann argue.

"Martha, I got to go." Mr. Williams walked over and kiss Miz Williams on the cheek.

Miz Williams walked him to the front door. She hug and kiss him again, "You have a nice day, Billie Roy."

Mr. Williams left. Susie git up from the table and put her plate in the sink, but her mama say, "Susie you don't have to do that anymore. Ruthie will do it."

"Can I go out and play then?" Susie asked.

"Yes, you can."

Susie went down a hall and came back wit a red ball in her hand. She kiss her mama and go outside.

Miz Williams lead me into a room that had a long chair. Two tables sat on each end of the long chair. A longer table was in front of the long chair. A regular size chair sat jus a few feet from one table that was beside the long chair. The sofa and chair color was a light green Her tables was made out of wood and shined like glass.

"That sho nuff is a long chair, Miz Williams."

"That isn't a chair; that's a sofa. Don't you folks have a sofa?"

"No ma'am. This the first time I seen a sofa. Everybody I know jus has chairs that they sits in around the table."

Miz Williams jus smile at me. "Ruthie, these tables needs dusting. Let me go git you a rag."

Miz Williams left the room. I stood in the room jus lookin around. I look in the corner of the room and seen a cabinet made of brown wood. The front of the cabinet had a door that was mainly glass. Inside the cabinet was little figures of animals, mostly black or brown horses. The horses all stood on four legs wit their heads down, cept one. That horse stood on it back legs wit it front leg up as if it was posing for a fight. That horse color was as white as a sheet. I was staring at the horses so hard I didn't hear Miz Williams come into the room.

"That's called a curio."

"I ain't never in my life seen anythang so purty, Mrs Williams. Dem horses look so life-like."

"My grandfather whittled all those horses. I like the white one more than the rest. That's why he is on the top shelf. I got another figurine I want you to see later."

"Yesum."

I took the rag that she gave me and started dustin her tables. She stood in the middle of the floor and watch my every move as I dust her lamps. Finally she told me to stop. I put the rag down. Miz Williams left the room and came back wit a figurine. She shoved it in my face. It was a of a colored man wit a white man standing over him wit a raised whip. The colored man face was all frowned up. His mouth was open like he was in a lot of pain. He was on his knees tied to a post. His carved shirt was torn wit red marks on it, the color of blood. I whisper, "I don't like this one."

"I love it. This here is the best he ever did," she said it, all proud-like.

I felted sort of bad inside, like when you is somewhere you ain't suppose to be. I didn't wanna work for Miz Williams no more. I hung my head down. Miz Williams look at me and chuckle at my reaction.

"What's the matter, Ruthie? You look all sad."

"Nothin, ma'am."

"I know what can cheer you up." She left the room, and came back wit a purty dress that she hand to me. "I brought this for you yesterday after you left. I really would like you to try it on, Ruthie."

My eyes is wide wit surprise.

"Thank you, Miz Williams. Thank you so much." I hug the dress to my chest. It was green and black checkered wit short sleeves and a white collar. It look almost like the one that I had for my paper doll, Elizabeth. I knew Mama could never afford to buy me anythin like this. Everythang I wore, my aunt made it for me. This was my first store-brought dress. I tried it on. She told me to look at myself in the mirror, and I seen that the dress made me look purty. "I just knew that dress would be perfect. If you keep workin for me, Ruthie, I will buy you pretty things just like this. You could dress better than any of your friends. That's if you don't quit."

"I ain't gonna quit, Miz Williams. I is gonna be back here tommora. That if you want me to come tommora."

"Yes, I want you back here tommorow." Miz Williams was smilin.

I took off the dress and put my workin clothes back on. Miz Williams put the dress on a hanger and laid it on the sofa.

"Come on, Ruthie, you don't have to clean anymore today. I wanna make some cookies. Do you like cookies?"

"Yesum."

"How about peanut butter cookies?"

"I sure does like me some peanut butter cookies."

"Then peanut butter cookies it is."

I followed her in the kitchen. "Ruthie, do you ever wish that you was white?"

"No ma'am. Mama said that God make us all, the way he wanted us to be. If he made me colored that all right wit me."

"Where does your real mama lives, Ruthie?"

"She ain't far." I really didn't know where my real mama live. I hadn't seen her since I was six.

"You know, Ruthie, when I was a little girl my mama used to make peanut butter cookies and put raisins on them. Let's put some raisins on top of these."

"Yesum."

"Ruthie, you get the raisins from the bottom shelf in the corner cabinet."

"Yesum." I went over and git the raisins. I had a good time wit Miz Williams that afternoon, makin cookies, laughin and tellin jokes. When dem cookies got done, I ate dem warm until I couldn't eat no more. When it was time for me to go, Miz Williams said that she had somethin to ask me.

"Did the figurine bother you?"

"It make me feel bad for the colored man."

"It's just a figurine, Ruthie, for heaven sake." Miz William chuckled.

"But it make me feel real bad, ma'am."

"Well I am gonna put it away so you can never see it again. Here's your pay, Ruthie." Miz Williams reached in her pocket and pulled out some money.

"Thank you ma'am."

I eye the money in my hand. Miz Williams give me three dollars that day too. I couldn't wait to tell my mama. I thought that this lady must be rich.

"Let me go git you dress."

She went back into the sittin room and came back wit the dress. She hand it to me and walk me to the door.

"Make sure you come back tomorrow. Don't you eat breakfast at home 'cause I want you to eat with us here."

"I won't, Miz Williams. I is gonna be back here tommorra." I walked off her porch down her walkway to the street where Mary Ann work, my dress in hand and three dollars in my pocket. When Mary Ann saw me wit the dress, she grab my arm.

"I hope you didn't steal that!"

I snatch my arm away, "No I didn't steal it! Why you say somethin like that? Miz Williams give it to me. She brought it yesterday."

"Why would a white lady buy a colored girl a dress? Did she pay you?"

"Sure did." I wave dem dollars in her face.

"I know that lady not gonna pay you again, come tommorra."

"Yes she is. The same thang, three dollars."

"No, she ain't. She payin you in advance, and she not gonna give you nothin at the end of the week."

"What is that word 'advance,' Mary Ann?"

"That mean before. She payin you before you work."

I thought about what Mary Ann say, and it didn't make no sense to me. "No she won't. I work there every day, and she pay me after. You know what Mary Ann? You is jus jealous."

"I ain't jealous."

"Yes you is."

Mary Ann and I argue all the way to her house.

CHAPTER FOUR

When I git home Mama was talkin to one of the ladies that she wash clothes for. Both of dem was at the front door. The lady was pickin up her clothes. I had seen her give my mama two dollars. The lady look around and saw me.

"She sure has grown, Flo."

"She sure have. Almost as tall as me, and she only eleven."

"She's eleven now?"

"Sho nuff is."

"Can she come and work for me now? I'll pay her two dollars a week."

"Ruthie already got a job, but I sho nuff thank you for askin."

"Well if she's free later on, remember she can come work for me."

"I is gonna remember that Miz Jones."

Miz Jones took her basket of laundry and put it in her car.

"I'll be back next week, Flo with another basket."

Miz Jones git in her car and took off down the road.

"What you git, Ruthie?"

"Miz Williams bought me this here dress."

I hand it to Mama. She held it up in front of her to see it better.

"Ooh ain't it purty. Looks like it fits you too."

"It does Mama. I try it on at Miz William's house and it fit real good."

"Ain't that nice of her. But I hope that she don't git the notion to pay you in clothes."

"She pay me too, Mama. Looka here, three dollars."

"Oh thank you, Lawd," Mama look up to the sky.

"I suppose you be wantin that fifty cent again."

"Yes ma'am. I is a savin for college."

I hand Mama the three dollars. She reached in her pocket and took out fifty cent and gave it to me. I put the fifty cent in my pocket.

"So you savin for college."

"Yes ma'am."

"What you wanna be when you get outta college?"

"I wanna be a teacher."

"Good. It's gonna be nice to have a teacher in the family."

Mama and I went into the house. I went into the bedroom and hung the dress on a nail by my bed. I gits on my knees and looks under my bed for my jar. When I finds it, I I open the lid and put the fifty cent in it. After I put it back, I git up off my knees and went in the kitchen.

"Supper gonna be late. I've been too busy washin and ironin all day. You make the hot water for corn bread, Ruthie, while I fries the chicken."

"Yesum Mama."

Mama git the chicken ready for fryin. I put a small pot of water on the stove. You had to use hot water to make the cornbread. I turn and notic that the table had a bowl of red olives on it.

"Mama, did you pick dem olives for me?"

"Sure did. You can have dem after supper for dessert."

"Thank you, Mama."

I love red olives. There was a olive tree in the neighbor yard and some of the branches hung over the fence. The neighbors made money from that tree. They would pick the olives when they was green and sell dem, but they didn't come over the fence to git the ones that was on our side. Dem olives would continue ripenin. When they turns red, they was sweet, and when you bit into dem they was smooth. The favor was between a cherry and a olive. As fast as I pick dem I would stuff dem in my mouth. Since I been workin for the last two days, I didn't have time to go and pick none. I was real happy that Mama pick dem for me.

"Mama, Miz Williams had me help her cook today. We made peanut butter cookies. Jus me and her."

"She really like you. You keep cleanin her house real nice. Make everythang sparkle. She'll keep you. Next year after school you can go to her. You won't have to go door to door lookin for work."

"Yesum, Mama. I will."

As soon as we finish cookin, Papa come in the house. He look at me and Mama. He spoke to the both of us. "Hi Hon. Hi Ruthie. You help you mama cook?"

"Yesum, Papa."

"Sure smells good."

Papa took a chair and Mama put a plate of chicken, collard greens, and hot water corn bread in front of him. Most our meals we ate chicken.

Mama was real creative wit chicken. Fried, baked, or boiled, we knew it was gon be chicken for supper.

Papa said the blessin, and we all started eatin.

"Papa, Miz Williams gave me a dress."

Papa look up from his plate at me. "Did she pay you?"

"Yesum, Papa. She pay me."

"The same amount?"

"Yesum, Papa."

"Good." Papa went on back eatin. When supper was finished, Papa went outside and sat on the porch. Mama and I wash the dishes. While I swept the floor, Mama went outside wit Papa. When I git through sweepin I brought out one of the chairs from the kitchen and place it on the porch beside Mama. They both was jus lookin around not sayin nothin. The rockin chair moaned as Mama rocked. It started gittin dark. Fireflies gather together not far from the porch. The light from their bodies lit up and then went out, again and again, as they dance to the melody of the warm air. I watch dem without blinkin until they finish their act and disappear into the night.

"You can stay out here for a little while, Ruthie; then you git ready for bed, you hear?"

"Okay Mama." I look at her face, lit up only by the moon light. I is hopin the fireflies would come back, but after a few minutes I git sleepy.

"I is goin in now Mama."

"Okay. I knew you would be tired."

I was up early the next day anticipatin the breakfast that Miz Williams was gonna make. The smell of Mama's homemade biscuits, salt pork and eggs filled the house. The food was temptin, but I membered what Miz Williams say, so I sat down like I was gonna eat and took one bite of a biscuit.

"Mama, I ain't hungry this mornin."

"Wrap that up, Flo, so the girl could have it for lunch."

"Mama, you don't have to do that. Miz Williams gonna give me lunch," I protested.

"Wrap it anyways, Flo. You needs a decent lunch, girl."

Mama found a clean white cloth and wrap the meat, eggs and biscuit like a sandwich and gave it to me. Papa look at me from across the table. His fork in his hand. "You know you gonna quit working when school start. School is more important than work for a girl your age. Make sure you let your lady know that, you hear?"

"I will, Papa. Mama, did you tell Papa that I wants to be a teacher when I grow up?"

"Naw, I didn't, Ruthie."

"I is a saving for college, Papa. Every time I git paid I put fifty cent in a jar for my college learnin. I know that it would take a while and hard work.."

"That's good, but you hurry on now. You don't want be late."

"Okay Papa."

I ran out the door leavin my sandwich on the table, and was a runnin down the road when I hear my mama call me. I figure that she want me to come back and git the sandwich. I kept a runnin to my job. I decided not to stop by Mary Ann's house, but go straight to Miz Williams. When I git there, I was all outa breath, and Miz Williams was a standin at the door waitin for me. I thought I late, wit her waitin like that. It turn out, she happy to see me. "Hello Ruthie. Guess what I made special this mornin?"

"I don't know, ma'am."

"Pancakes, and lots of them. I hope you haven't eaten 'cause there's plenty for you."

"Thank you, ma'am."

When I enters the kitchen I seen that she had made more than pancakes. She had sausages, ham, eggs and sweet milk to go wit it. There is a door from the kitchen that led to the back porch. I stood there by the table waitin for her to fix me a plate so I could go outside and eat on that porch.

"What is you waitin for, Ruthie? Help yourself."

"Thank you, ma'am." I went to the kitchen sink and wash my hands, then I took a plate and fill it wit sausage, pancakes, ham, and eggs. I git a glass of sweet milk, pour syrup on my pancakes, and headed for the back door. Miz Williams stop me.

"Where in the world are you goin, Ruthie?"

"Outside ma'am, so I can eat."

"Why you wanna go to the back porch to eat, child, when I have a table for you to eat on?"

"I thought colored folk weren't allowed to eat at white folk table."

"In my house, you eat at my table. Now come on back here."

I went back and put my plate on the table. I sat down in one of her chairs and start eatin. "This sho nuff is good, ma'am."

"Thank you Ruthie. Let me see where Susie and her father are. If they don't hurry up their food is gonna be cold."

As soon as Miz Williams said that, Susie and her father came in the kitchen. They both look at me real funny like.

"About time you two come in here. I was about to come and get you," Miz William said. "Why are you both lookin at Ruthie like that? I told her to have breakfast with us from now on."

"That's fine with me, Martha," Mr. Williams said.

"Mama, is it all right now for colored people to eat with whites at their table?" Susie asked.

"No, it ain't, but I is gonna let Ruthie eat at our table 'cause I like her."

Susie smiled at me and sat down in a chair that was close to where I was sittin.

"Ruthie, when you git though cleanin, wanna play a game wit me?" Susie asked.

"Ruthie is here to work Susie. I told you that before. She's gonna be busy for the rest of the day. When she gets through it will be time for her to go." Miz Williams put a plate down in front of Susie.

Mr. Williams and Miz Williams started talkin. I didn't listen to their conversation 'cause Susie and I was too busy playin like our food was animals. As we bit our food the animals were beggin for us not to eat dem. When we was through eatin, Mr. Williams left for work. Susie went outside to play, and I clean up the kitchen.

Everythang in Miz Williams kitchen was white cept the curtains, floor, and pots and pans. Her curtains was green. They hung at the two glass windows in the kitchen. She had a linoleum floor that was green wit white specks in it. Miz Williams didn't want anythang out on her counters. When I finish the dishes I had to put everythang away. She stay in the kitchen watchin me. Only when I was through did she leave. I waited for her to tell me what she want me to do next.

When she return, Miz Williams had the same clean clothes that I had jus wash the day before and they was still folded. "Here's some clothes for you to wash, Ruthie."

"Yesum."

I took dem on outside and started washin. It seem like the same amount that I had done before. Miz William came outside and watch me wash again. When I was finish we both went in the kitchen. I look at her clock; it was time for me to go.

"I got somethin for you Ruthie," Miz Williams said. "I wanted to give it to you when you were ready to go." She left the room and came back wit a bag. Inside was a pair of black patent-leather Mary Jane shoes.

"For me?" My eyes widen.

"Yes, for you, Ruthie," Miz Williams was smilin.

"Thank you, Miz Williams. These sure is some fine lookin shoes."

"Try them on."

I tried dem on, and they fit. "They is the most nicest shoes I ever had. I sure thank you again."

"And you are welcome, again. Make sure you come here again tomorrow. From now on you will be eatin breakfast with me. I don't want you to be afraid to sit down at the table like you were today, you hear?"

"I won't, Miz Williams, and I thank you, ma'am."

I put my old shoes in the bag. I walk home a swingin the old bag of shoes and from time to time lookin down at my new ones. When I git home Mama reaches out her hand for the money, and I remember that had I forgot my pay for that day.

CHAPTER FIVE

H e had the biggest eyes and lips that I ever see on a colored man. He always wore a black suit and wide brim black hat no matter how hot it git. One of his legs must have been shorter than the other 'cause when he walk, you could see his body go up and down. That was our insurance man, Mr. Verney.

Every month he would come by our house to collect a dime for the insurance policy. Mr. Verney didn't have no wife. I hear Mama and a lady say that he beat his wife and she left him. He had four chillins. I heard Mama and a lady say that Mr. Verney was always flirtin at women folk tryin to git hisself a new wife. But no single women in the town wanted Mr. Verney 'cause he was so mean.

I was in the garden, helpin Mama pick a few strings beans for supper. Papa was still at work. I look up and seen Mr. Verney a comin up the road.

"Mama, here come Mr. Verney."

Mama stop pickin the beans and put the few she had picked in the little basket. "I better go git that man's money."

"You want me to go tell him that?"

"Naw, jus tell him that I is in the house."

"Okay, Mama."

Mama went on in the house through the back door. I went to the front of the house and met Mr. Verney as he open the gate.

"Evenin, Mr. Verney. My mama gone in the house to git you money."

Mr. Verney look at me and frown, then he started walkin toward the house.

"You can go on in, Mr. Verney."

Mr. Verney kepted walkin. When he reaches the porch Mama come to the door and open it for him. "Come on in Mr. Verney. Sure is a nice day, ain't it?"

"It sure is. It sure is, Flo."

Mr. Verney went in the house, and Mama close the screen door. I went back to the garden and finish pickin green beans.

I believed that Mr. Verney was still mad at me 'cause of what I did to Jimbo, his son. Jimbo was my age. He sat a few desks over from me in school. He told the other kids that I was sweet on him, but I didn't like Jimbo like that. He was all right for a friend, but not a boyfriend.

He thought I like him after we share a candy bar. It happen like this: My

Mama would give me a nickel on some Friday mornins before school. After school on those Fridays, I would run to the store to buy a candy bar called "Damn If I Know." The candy bar was about five inches long. It was thick wit chocolate and peanuts wit a caramel center. All the chillins love to buy that candy bar. Not jus 'cause it was so good, but sayin it name gave dem a chance to cuss.

One Friday, my mama had given me a nickel. I put it in my pocket not knowin that the pocket had a hole in it. After school on that Friday, I went runnin to the store like the rest of the chillins. Even the chillins that didn't have a nickel went to the store hopin to git a piece of they friend's candy bar. If they didn't git a piece of candy, at lease they git a chance to hear the other chillins cuss and watch Mr. Burns'—the man what owned the store—face turn red.

I went in the store that day and stand by the counter. They was several chillins in front of me. When Mr. Burns ask what they want, the chillins git pleasure out of sayin, "Damn If I Know." Each one had they own special way of sayin it. One boy lean on the counter wit one hand on his hips and the other one on his cheek and said, "Huh, Damn If I Know."

The other chillins laugh. Mr. Burns' face turn red, and he git the candy bar and slam it on the counter.

"A nickel, boy!" He demand as he helded out his hand for the money.

The boy give him the money, take the candy bar, and move over to the side of the counter. A girl took the boy's place. The girl stand there not sayin a word. Mr. Burn act like he didn't want to wait on her when he ask what she wanted. The girl put both hands on her hips and in real sassy say, "Well, Damn If I Know."

It went on and on like that until it was my turn. I had to come up wit another way to say the name, wit actions different than the other chillins. Mr. Burns ask me what I want. I hump my shoulders, casted my eyes up to the ceilin, and said.

"Damn If I Know." The chillins giggled.

By this time Mr. Burns was steamin; he threw the candy on the counter.

I reach in my pocket to give him his nickel, but it wasn't there. My fingers felted a hole. I had lost it.

"A nickel, I said." Mr. Burns reach out his hand.

I kept searchin in my pockets over and over again like that nickel was gonna show up. I felted warm. My throat felted dry. I felted scared not knowin what Mr. Burns might do if I didn't give him his nickel. Jimbo was in the back of me waitin his turn. He must have notice that I didn't have my nickel for the candy bar, 'cause he marched up to the man and said, "Here is her nickel, sir."

The man took Jimbo nickel. I grab the candy bar and move out the line. The man ask the next one in line what he want, and the next kid said, "Damn If I Know."

Jimbo and I went on out the store.

"Thank you, Jimbo. This here candy bar is yours."

"That's all right. You can have it."

"I is gonna pay you for it come next Friday. Mama always gives me a nickel on Fridays."

"I don't want you to pay me for it. I tell you what. If we share it, then you won't have to pay me for it. Next Friday, when you git you money we can buy another candy bar and share that one too."

Sound good to me. We broke the candy in half. He took one half and I took the other. Since his house was pass mine, he walk wit me until I git home. While we were walkin I couldn't help noticin his big eyes and lips. They was jus like his papa.

The next Friday when I git my nickel, I bought the candy bar and share it wit Jimbo. Next thing I knew was the girls was sayin that I was sweet on him. Every day in school when he caught my eye he would throw me a kiss.

I told him on many occasion that I didn't like him, but the fool kept throwin me kisses and tellin the other chillins that I was his sweetie.

"When school gits out, I'll be rid of him," I said to myself.

I was right about that. But one day, when I was a walkin home from work I hear somebody behind me callin for me to stop. I look around; it was Jimbo. "Oh no, not Jimbo," I thought. I start walkin faster. "Jimbo disappear, please disappear," I repeat to myself over and over.

He start to walkin faster too. I start runnin. He start runnin. I ran faster.

"Hey Ruthie," he yell, "I got somethin for you."

He repeat it until I jus stop runnin so he could stop yellin like a fool after me. When he caught up wit me he was smilin like a possum.

"What you got for me? No matter what it is, I still don't like you."

"It don't matter if you don't. You gonna love me one day."

"You makin me mad, boy. I is already tired, and I don't feel like being bother wit you. So go away."

"You tryin to be mean to me , but I knows you like me, Ruthie."

Jimbo stood there lookin at me wit his hands in his pockets like he was up to somethin.

"I don't like you, boy. Hurry up. I don't have all day."

"Jus give me a little time. It kind of hard to depart from it."

"If you don't show me what you got for me quick, fast, and in a hurry, I is gone. And you better not follow me." I put my hands on my hips and poke out my lips so he know I mean business.

"I heard my pappy tell Mr. Smithy he need a workin gal, a Ho. Mr. Smithy said that he knew one named Lula Bell. Pappy went in his dresser and git two whole dollars. Pappy was smilin and sayin that he was gonna make that gal happy. Then he went to town. He gave me a nickel before he left, and I figured that if two dollars could make Miss Lula Bell happy, a nickel might make you happy."

"What's a Ho? What kind of work she do? Does she clean up houses?"

"I don't know." Jimbo scratch his head. "But it sure made Pappy anxious. Here, take this here nickel."

Jimbo shoves the nickel in my hand. I give it back to him.

"Don't want your old nickel. You keep it. I got me some money, boy."

"Oh come on, Ruthie. Take this here nickel, please. I want you to have it."

I looks at his face beggin like a puppy dog, and decide I would take it if it would make him leave me alone.

"Give it here, Jimbo. I is gonna give it to my mama. Maybe she can use it."

I helded out my hand. He put the nickel in it, then he put his right arm around my neck, pullin my face close to his and gave me a quick kiss on my cheek. I yell and he turned me loose. "I hate you! Why you has to kiss me?!"

I wipe my face where he had kiss me. He was lookin at me real proud.

"Cause I really like you, Ruthie, and I wanna make you a happy Ho."

"I is not happy, Jimbo. Right now, I is mad."

"You gotta be happy. You got my nickel! If the nickel won't make you happy then give it back."

He helded out his hand for the nickel.

"I ain't gonna give you nothin. I is keepin this here nickel 'cause you kiss me and this pays for the damage you did to my face."

"Okay. You keep the nickel, but will you be my Ho? Pappy and Mr. Smitty talk like a Ho is a special workin lady. You is special to me, Ruthie."

"Naw Jimbo! Leave me alone."

I start walkin. He walk beside me, still beggin.

"Please Ruthie."

"I ain't gonna be your Ho, boy!"

"I is gonna tell everybody anyway that you my Ho."

When he said that he made me so mad I ball up my fist and punch him in his mouth as hard as I could. He fell on the ground wit his lip busted wit blood ran down it. I left him there and went home. I wasn't home long when Mr. Verney came to the house a bangin on the door. Mama went to the door and he ran in like a madman a shakin his finger in my face and demandin me to give him back his son's nickel.

Mama was taken back wit him runnin in her house like that. "What wrong wit you, man? Don't you be a talkin to my Ruthie like that." Mama put both hands on her hip as she talk but he didn't pay her no mind.

"Give me back Jimbo's nickel, girl!"

"I ain't givin him back this here nickel. It rightfully mine. This is my pay for him kissin my jaw."

"Git away from her!" Mama step between me and Mr. Verney. She had a skillet in her hand now. She had raised it up. "I is a warnin you, Verney. If you don't git away from my Ruthie, I is gonna bop you so hard you gonna see stars before dark!"

Mr. Verney moves away from me and Mama. "This girl is sassy, Flo. You all ain't raisin her right. She ain't suppose to talk to grown ups like this. She need her behind whupped."

Mama frown at Mr. Verney, the skillet still raised. "I ain't whupping Ruthie over no nickel."

Mr. Verney looks around at me wit his lips stuck out. His eyes lookin even bigger. "Make her give it back, Flo!"

Mama brought the skillet down to her side. "Ruthie, give him back that damn nickel!" I gave him the nickel.

Mr. Verney took it and shove it in his pocket. He put one hand on his right hip, lean to his right side and look at Mama. "You better git all you can out of her right now, 'cause before she turn fifteen she gonna be a Ho or done kilt a man and in jail. If I was you, I wouldn't send her to no school. I would jus make her work."

"You don't tell me what to do wit mines! You jus raise your! Mama raise her voice. "You better git outa here now! You got your nickel."

Mama and I watch Mr. Verney go out the door to the gate. He walk fast goin back down the road, his shoulders and hips movin up and down like pistons of a car.

"The nerve of that man comin in my house like that. He wouldn't have done that if Roy was here. If Roy walk through that door while he was here actin like a fool, I don't even wanna imagine what would have happen." Mama left the door and went on back to cookin. I jus standin at the door thinkin about Jimbo and all the trouble he 'cause me.

"Come on over here Ruthie. Help me finish supper and tell me what happen between you and Jimbo."

I told her the whole story, even about me leavin him wit his mouth bleedin.

Mama chuckle. "That's the funniest story I ever heard. You shoulda beat the crap out of him for asking you to be his Ho."

"What's a Ho, Mama?" I ask

"Right now you don't need to know what a Ho is. What I can tell you is that you were right not lettin that boy call you that. Jimbo's pappy should watch what he say in front of his chillins. One day I is gonna tell you what a Ho is."

After that day Jimbo didn't come around me no more. I finish pickin the beans and went in the house through the back door. I hear Mr. Verney talkin to Mama.

"Your sister ain't nothin."

"Don't say that about my sister, Verney"

"You know this right, Flo. She still floppin around wit married men. Havin babies left and right. I would have made a good woman out of her. You know that, Flo. But no, she had to..." Mr. Verney stop talkin as soon as he saw me comin in the kitchen. He was sittin at the table wit a small book and pencil in his hand, and Mama was standin on the other side of the table facin Mr. Verney.

"Here's dem beans, Mama."

Mama took the beans and put dem in a pot of water and washed dem. Mr. Verney git up from the table, all the while eyein me.

"This here gal sure look like her mammy." Mr. Verney said as he put his pencil in his pocket.

"She sure does. I told her mama the same thing last time I seen her." Mama said, while smilin at me. She took the beans out the water and hand the pot to me. "Pour the water out this pot outside, Ruthie."

"Yes ma'am."

I took the pot to the front door of the kitchen, went out over to the steps and pour the water out on the ground. While I was pourin the water out I heard Mr. Verney talkin to my mama again.

"You better git all you can out of her right now. 'Cause if you don't, come fifteen that gal is gonna be jus like her mammy."

"Time for you to leave now, Verney. Your talkin is beginnin to strike a nerve wit me."

I came back in the kichen and hand the pot to Mama.

"Jus remember what I said, Flo."

"Bye Verney."

Aunt Flo turn her back, not even lookin to see if Mr. Verney was leavin. He went to the door. I look at him and said, " Bye Mr. Verney."

Mr. Verney jus look at me not openin his mouth. He went on out the kitchen door. Mama and I finish cooking supper.

CHAPTER SIX

The amount of money Miz Williams gave me git less and less. The first week she gave me thirteen dollar. The next week she gave me seven. By the third week I was give three dollars for the whole week. Every time she gave me my pay she would remind me of the money she jus spent on me.

"You see Ruthie, I want you to have nice things jus like my Susie. I had to use some of the money that I was gonna pay you to buy your clothes. I think that that is fair. Don't you?"

"Yes ma'am," I would say, feelin disappointed.

Mama told me not to git upset. "You is still gittin paid more money than a grown woman gits, and new clothes too."

"But I want the money, Mama."

"Jus be grateful, child. God's chillins should always be grateful. Take the clothes and money wit a smile."

So even though I was disappointed from not gittin the amount of money she gave me at first, I smile every time she give me my pay and new clothes.

Summer was almost over, and I couldn't wait to go back to school. I had made fifty-one dollars over the summer. My aunt had let me keep fourteen for my college education. I felted proud of myself every time I look in my jar. Mama had a new dress that she bought from the money I made. And Papa had a new pair of pants, whether he want dem or not. They was a few new things bought for the house. I hoped I could still work on the weekends for Miz Williams when school started. Mama was happy about the idea, but as usual, Papa wasn't.

I went over one day to Miz Williams to work, but a woman that look the image of Miz Williams, jus older, was at the door wit one eyebrow raise and her mouth tight lipped. She gaze down at me.

"Git away from here!"

I back away from the door. "Does Miz Williams live here?" I said, wit my voice shakin.

"Didn't I tell you to git away from here?" the woman said, raising one hand in a tight fist.

"Yes ma'am!" I turn and ran off the porch, down the walk to the gate. I stop when I hear Miz Williams call.

"Ruthie stop. Come on back here!"

I stop runnin and turn around. Miz Williams was on the porch standin beside the older woman. "You didn't tell me that you had a niggard workin for you."

"Mama, I didn't think about it at the time. She's been workin for me since the beginnin of summer."

I reach the porch and spoke, "Mornin Miz Williams."

"Mornin, Ruthie."

I look at the older woman. "Mornin, ma'am."

"Hum," The woman turn her head and went in the house.

Miz Williams followed behind her. I was the last to go in. Miz Williams talk as we walk in the house about what she wanted me to do for the day. "Ruthie, after you eat, I want you to wash clothes and help me pack up some things."

"Yes ma'am." I wonder why she want me to pack things. I went to the kitchen sink and wash my hands. The older woman was sittin at the table watchin me. Miz Williams was by the stove takin a pan of biscuits out the oven.

"They sure smell good Miz Williams." I breathed in the aroma of hot buttermilk biscuits.

"Thank you Ruthie." She took the pan of bread and put it on top of the stove. When she ask me, I went over and git a bowl out the cabinet and gave it to her. The woman was still watchin me. Mr. Williams and Susie came to the table.

"Mornin Grandma." Susie went over and hug the woman.

"Good morning, baby." The woman hug her back, but kept her eyes on me.

Susie sat down in her usual chair.

"Mornin, Ruthie"

"Mornin, Susie." We both smile at each other.

Mr. Williams came in the kitchen. "Good mornin Mother Ann. Mornin, Ruthie," Mr. Williams then took a seat.

"Mornin, Mr. Williams."

I help Miz Williams set the table. I set a chair by Susie. All the while, the woman eye me. The family gits their meal. I sat down by Susie. The woman jumps up out her seat and shout.

"This is enough!"

"Mama, what is the matter?"

"That niggard is sittin at the table. You know better than that, Martha!"

"Mama, sit down. I will take care of this." Miz Williams took a breath. "Ruthie, git your food and and eat on the back porch."

I look at Miz Williams confused. "But you said that..."

"Ruthie, do as I say!" Miz Williams sounded upset wit me.

"Yes ma'am."

I git a plate and fill it wit the meal of the mornin, and went out to the back porch. My stomach felted like it was tied into knots making it impossible to eat much. I wonder how long the woman was gonna stay. I waited until I was sure that the family had finish eatin and brought my plate in. Only Miz Williams was in the kitchen.

"Ruthie, wash the dishes. After you are through with them, take these here boxes and put them on the table. I have to figure out what I want packed up for now."

I took my plate over to the trash can and scraped out the food that I had left in it. I was about to put the plate in the sink wit the rest of the dishes when Miz Williams stop me. "No Ruthie, don't put your plate in the sink. Wash those that are already in there first. Then wash yours."

"Yes ma'am." I wonder why she want me to put my dish aside and wash it last. The sink wasn't full wit dishes. Afterward we start packin up some of her pots and pans. I wondered what was happenin.

"You movin, Miz Williams?"

"Yes, in about two weeks."

"I is sorry to hear that, ma'am."

"I won't be needin your help anymore after I move, Ruthie, unless your folks let me borrow you for two weeks to help straighten out the new house."

"I don't know if they let me go, wit school startin in a few week ma'am."

"Tell them that I am gonna pay you well. I was thinkin of about fifty dollars."

"Fifty dollars!" I shout. "That a lot of money. But I still don't know if they let me go 'cause school is almost a startin. Papa and Mama wouldn't want for me to miss school."

"Well, tell them what I've just told you. It's only two weeks. A smart girl like you could make up those two weeks in school after you git back."

Miz Williams left the kitchen leavin me to the packin. Susie came in after her mama left. She walk up to the table and picks up one dish that I had wrap wit newspaper and put it in the box.

"That lady you saw is my grandma."

I look at Susie. "I figure that."

"She be leavin this afternoon. Right now she said that she was gonna stay in my room in my bed until she leaves."

"Hum huh." I said, not lookin at her.

"She's really not mean, Ruthie."

"I didn't say that she was mean, Susie. I jus said, hum huh."

"We will be leavin soon. Mama said in two weeks. We're gonna to be livin in Birmingham. That's far away from here."

"She told me, Susie."

Susie begin talkin about how she had seen her new house and how much she like it. The more she talk, the worse I felted. I was a thinkin, "After they move I ain't gonna have me a job." I was only half listenin to Susie.

Miz Williams came in the kitchen. "Susie go help your grandma git her things ready." Susie ran out the kitchen toward her room.

"Ruthie, I got the clothes ready for you to wash. They are layin outside by the back porch. You go and take care of the washing. I am gonna finish packin."

For the rest of the day, I wash and iron clothes. I didn't even know when Susie's grandma left; I was too busy to see her leave.

When I git home that day I didn't tell my folks about Miz Williams movin. I walk in the house, not sayin much. Seem like Mama notice I was actin different. "What the matter, child? You actin like the world has jus dump all its problems on you."

"Nothing wrong wit me, Mama. I jus tired." I was feeling real bad inside like somebody had my heart and was tearing it apart. I want Mama and Papa to have nice things, and now I had let dem down. Come school time I wouldn't have no job. I help Mama finish supper as usual, but I didn't feel like eatin. I ask if I could skip supper and go to bed.

"You can go on to bed, but it sure is a mite early."

I went to bed anyway. I wasn't sleepy, so I jus star up at the ceilin until I fell asleep. The next day when I went to Miz Williams house she ask me if I spoke to my folks about me helpin her for two weeks.

"Mama ain't gonna let me leave, bein that school is about to start."

"Well, I'll see about that."

I didn't wanna go to Miz Williams new house wit dem. But I jus couldn't tell her. I felted if I told her I didn't wanna go it might hurt her feelin. After all, she had been nice to me. I knew that Mama would tell her no, anyway.

I git through wit my work for that day, and went to where Miz Williams was packin up some more items. When I come in the room she stop what she was doin.

"Ruthie, I am gonna be ready to go with you in a minute."

"Go where, Miz Williams?" I ask.

"I am goin to your house to ask your mama if you could help me with the move. I told you that earlier."

"You don't have to go home wit me, ma'am. It all hot and the road is sho nuff dusty where I lives. You might git you clothes all dirty. I ask her again and tell you what she say tomorra."

Miz Williams ignore me, as she call Susie to go wit her. Miz Williams had on a white dress, but this time she put on a pair of white gloves. I walk behind Miz Williams and Susie all the way to my house. She jus ask me directions.

"Which way do you go, Ruthie?"

"Down this road, ma'am."

"How much farther, Ruthie?"

"Not much farther, ma'am."

Susie start walkin in back of her mother wit me, but Miz Williams turn around. "Susie, you walk beside me."

"Mama, I wanna walk in the back wit Ruthie."

"No, you walk up here in front wit me." Susie went back walkin beside her mama.

When we git to my house Miz Williams didn't go in. Instead she told me to go tell my mama to come outside. I went on in the house. Mama was hand sewin a button on a shirt. She look up and see me. "You don't have to help me fix supper today, Ruthie. It almost ready. You was so tired yesterday, I thought I give you a break."

"I is okay, Mama. Miz Williams outside to meet you."

"The lady you work for? Let me go and meet her and tell her how much I appreciate the nice things she done for you." Mama put her sewin in a basket and went outside. "Hello there. I is Ruthie mama."

Miz Williams reach out her gloved hand for Mama to shake. "And your name is?" Miz Williams asked.

"My name is Flo."

"Well, Flo, my name is Miz Williams, and this is Susie. Say Hi, Susie."

"Hi Flo." Mama spoke to Susie, then she look back at Miz Williams. "I wanna thank you for being so nice to my Ruthie."

"Well thank you, Flo. Then I guess you won't mind me takin her for a few weeks to help me move."

"Taking Ruthie? What you mean, takin Ruthie to help you move?" Mama jerk her head and widen her eyes. She look puzzled.

"You see, I am movin in two weeks. Didn't Ruthie tell you?"

"No ma'am, she didn't tell me nothin."

I was was in the back of Mama. She turn around and look at me.

"Ruthie, why didn't you tell your mama?" Miz Williams sounded disappointed.

I walk to the right side of Mama and hump my shoulders. "I don't know."

"Well, I came over to ask you about her comin with me to help me with the new house for two weeks. I'll pay her well, as I have all summer."

"I don't know. School is a startin in a few days. We don't want her to miss the first days of school."

"She'll make it up when she gets back," Miz Williams said, quite pleasantly. "Ruthie is such a smart little girl."

Mama shook her head. "I don't know. I never let her spent a night away from me."

"It's only two weeks. If it'll make you feel any better I'll put her in the colored school there for those two weeks. "

"My Ruthie is smart. She only eleven and in the seventh grade here. Will they be willin to put her in the seventh grade there?"

"They'll do what I tell them."

"You sure you is gonna have her back in two week?"

"Yes I will, unless Ruthie started doin so well in the other school that she wanna stay." Miz Williams laughed. "Sometime, I hear that they give money to colored chillins to go to college."

"That hard to believe. The government don't hardly wanna feed colored folk. Give dem money for college? That really hard to believe.

Anyway, you is jus gonna keep her for two weeks. Don't make sense to put her in school for two weeks there."

"I didn't come here to discuss that. Will you let her go?"

"I guess so. Like you say, it only two weeks. After all, you been real nice and we needs the money."

"Then that's settled Have her at my place on movin day."

"Yes ma'am."

Miz Williams turn and start for the gate wit Susie at her side.

"Where is you movin to?" Mama asked.

"To Birmingham." Miz Williams said, and opened the gate.

Mama and I watch Miz Williams and Susie as they disappear down the road. "I don't wanna go to Birmingham to help her, Mama. I wanna start school on time."

"She gonna pay you well child. You can stand to miss two weeks of school."

"But I don't wanna miss two weeks of school."

"She really need the help. She promise to send you back, Ruthie. You can make up those two weeks when you git back."

"Mama please!" I put both of my hands to my chin like I was a prayin. "Don't make me go." Mama start walkin toward the door. I kept pleadin until she turn around.

"You wanna go to college, don't you?"

"Yes ma'am."

"Well the only way you is ever gonna git to college is to work. We is poor, girl. You know that. I would feel so proud if you went to college to be a teacher. You be the first one in our family to go. Girl, most of us haven't even finish grade school. You is gonna make it through college."

"Will fifty dollars pay for my college, Mama?"

"No, but it a start."

I went in the house behind Mama. I felted that Mama was right. I could make up those two weeks after I got back.

When Papa came home from work the day, tired and hungry as usual, Mama told him about Miz Williams. "The lady that Ruthie work for came by here today."

"What she want?" Papa said, as he pull up his chair for supper.

"She want Ruthie to help her when she moves.".

"Where she movin to?"

"To Birmingham."

"Birmingham! What you tell her?"

"I said that it okay for her to go."

Papa sat down in the chair. "Ruthie shouldn't be goin so far from us to help anybody, Flo."

"She seem like a nice lady, Roy. Anyway we needs the money. You know Ruthie wants to go to college. The lady said she gonna pay Ruthie real well. Fifty dollars for jus two weeks work." Mama cut up some bread and hand it to Papa.

"Why she need some little colored girl? Ruthie don know how to set up a house. Why can't she git somebody to help her that grown?" Papa lift the bread and dip it in some gravy.

"Jus eat your supper, Roy. We'll discuss this later on tonight." Mama glance over at me.

"Why can't she git somebody when she git there?" Papa sound annoyed.

"Roy, jus eat your supper. We is gonna discuss this later on tonight, I said."

Papa ate his supper witout sayin another word. When supper over Mama and me clean up the dishes, and then I went to bed. When Mama and Papa came to the room I pretend to be asleep; I want to know what they was gonna say. Mama pull back the blanket that divid our beds, and shook me. I didn't stir.

"She asleep. We can finish what we was discussin."

"You done already made up you mind. I don't know what else they is to discuss." Papa sound annoyed.

"She ain't ours. That is the reason why I is lettin her go. I don't want her to turns out like her mama. Maybe they is a reason why Mattie acts like that."

"You know why your sister acts like that. You jus don't wanna accept it. Ruthie ain't like her. You don't know what this girl is gonna do when she grow up. You jus keep listenin to old Verney. Sometime I feel like beatin the hell out him!"

"I ain't a thinkin about old Verney. I is a sayin that maybe somethin happen to Mattie. Mattie git three more chillins and never git married. I don't know why she keep a doin that. Ruthie wanna be a teacher. I feel it best to keep her workin for what she want."

"I ain't a sayin that she shouldn't work for what she want. I is a sayin that we shouldn't let her go so far away wit somebody we don't know."

"That Miz Williams seem to be all right Roy. You gonna see I is right."

"Do what you wanna do." It sound like Papa turns his back away from Mama.

I felted bad about the things Mama was sayin. I wonder who were those three other chillins my real Mama had. I thought to myself, "I bet that she didn't put dem in a box like she done to me. I bet she wanted dem and kept dem. My real mama don't love me, even say that I wasn't hers. Now Aunt Flo want me to go too, and I don't know why. I is a good girl. Why nobody want me?" My heart felted heavy. I didn't sleep all night.I jus laid there and let the tears roll down my face.

CHAPTER SEVEN

Miz Williams told me to stay home for those two weeks before her move. One day when I was out walkin wit my friends Jessie May, Bessie, and Hattie I spot some white gloves in the mulberry bushes. I look closer and seen they look jus like the gloves Miz Williams had worn that day when she shook Mama's hand. I pick dem up. I reckon she lost dem. Then I couldn't decide if they was hers or not. I wonder why someone had throwed dem in the mulberry bushes. They was a perfect pair of gloves.

"That's sho nuff a nice pair of gloves you found there, Ruthie. I wonder who dem belong to," Bessie said, as she touch the gloves.

"Don't know. But I wonder why someone would throw somethin this nice in dem bushes."

"You gonna keep dem for youself, Ruthie?" Hattie asked.

"I don't want dem. I was jus thinkin that these here gloves jus might belong to Miz Williams."

"Who that is, Ruthie?" Jessie May asked.

"The lady I work for. She came by the other day wit some gloves on that look jus like these here."

"She must didn't want dem. Can I have dem?" Jessie May reach out her hand, and I give dem to her.

She put the gloves on, held her head up like she was a queen. "Lookie here. I is a lady." She point one gloved hand at us. We all giggle.

"Let me try dem on," Hattie begged.

Jessie May hand the gloves to Hattie who helded her head up and looked down on us, walking wit one hand on her hip and the other gloved hand touching her chest. "All you poor colored persons git out my way."

Bessie grab her hand. "Let me try the gloves on, Hattie."

Hattie draw back her hand wit a disgusted look on her face. "Oh no! A colored person has touched my hand. I must burn these here gloves."

We all laugh, but I thought about the horse in Miz Williams curio. *I hoped the gloves wasn't hers.*

Friday morning I was suppose to meet Miz Williams at her house. She was gonna be a movin that day. I git up earlier than usual to pack my little belongins. Mama woke up and look at me.

"So you is up."

"Yes ma'am." I stood by her bed, rubbin the sleep out my eyes.

"Well, let me git on up wit you. I wanna make sure you don't forget nothin that you might need for those two weeks."

Barefooted, I went in the kitchen and lit a candle. I git the wash bowl, put it on the kitchen table, and fill it wit water. We always left a big jar of water in the kitchen at night, and used it for washin up in the mornin. After being in the kitchen all night it felt warm. I splash some on my face. Mama came in the kitchen, her blue and white gown almost draggin the floor. She had her hair rolled up with paper strips made from a brown paper bag. The ends were twisted and pointin up. It made Mama look like she had little pieces of trees on her head. I smile as I look at her head.

She went over to the stove and put a few pieces of wood in it. "Put on you shoes and go git me some water. I wanna cook you somethin to eat before you go."

Papa usually gits the water in the mornin, so I stood there half asleep, wit water drippin from my face, not quite understandin what she meant. She handed me a towel to dry my face.

"Hurry up chile.Go git the water. You don't wanna make the lady late."

"She ain't gonna be late Mama. White folk don't git up early as color folk."

"And how you know that?"

"Miz Williams told me."

Papa came in the kitchen dressed in his long johns. He was barefooted jus like me and Mama. Yawning, he blink his eyes and sat down in one of the old brown kitchen chairs. He motion for me to come to him, and when I did, he put one of his hands on my shoulder.

"I know that you only gonna to be gone for two weeks, but you write to Papa you hear? As soon as you gits there."

"I will Papa."

I put on my shoes, then went on outside to the porch. The mornin air was warm. The sun was a comin up, givin the sky a yellow, red, and orange color. The smell of the air told me it was gonna rain. I look around for snakes. "Snakes if you out here, it time to go home. Sun a coming up and you know it gonna burn you."

Mama came to the door wit the bucket.

"Who you talkin to, Ruthie?"

"Nobody Mama."

"Here the bucket. You can't git no water witout the bucket."

Mama hand it to me and went back in the house. I tiptoe to the well, being extra careful where I step. I hear a rustle. Drawin in a quick breath, I look toward the sound. My heart was a racin, but it was jus a small possum.

"Go on home, possum," I said in a low tone. "You almost scared me to death."

The possum look back at me then run off. At the well, I tie the rope to the bucket handle, and let the bucket quickly down until I hear the splash. Still a holdin on, I loosen the rope so the bucket could tilt over and fill up wit water. When it was filled, I pull it up and put it on the edge of the well so I could untie the rope. I didn't notice a big brown spider a sittin next to it. It ran down the brick, and I jump, knocking the bucket back into the well.

"I hate you well!" I scream. "Now I got to draw water again."

Back at the house, Mama grab a cup and dip it in the bucket. Then she open up the shutters and throw the water out the window. She seen me looking at her. "It was jus a bug, Ruthie."

Now I don't wanna eat breakfast knowin that a bug was in the water. Instead I went and got dressed.

When I came back out, Mama spoke. "Ruthie, you be a good girl while you away, and do what Miz Williams tell you."

"I will, Mama."

I took my plate and put a forkful of eggs on it, one piece of salt pork, and one flapjack. Mama look at my plate. "You not hungry, Ruthie?"

"No ma'am, I ain't hungry. I keep a thinkin about missin school."

"Seem to me she could have got herself somebody grown to help her," Papa said, as he stacked his flapjacks on his plate. He took a bite of his fried salt pork.

"It only two weeks, Roy." Mama hand him the bowl of sugar for his coffee.

"School is startin today and this here girl is gonna miss it. That Miz Williams wouldn't keep her girl outta school to help some colored folks. I bet you she wouldn't." Papa shovel a fork full of flapjacks in his mouth.

"Roy we needs the money. Ruthie is a smart gal. You watch and see. She will be back bringin home good grades jus like she done before. What is two weeks of missed school work to Ruthie? Nothin. Right Ruthie? She been made that up in no time."

I didn't say nothin.

Papa finish eatin his breakfast in silence, but I couldn't eat at all. After breakfast, Mama told me to git my things. In the bedroom, I put four dresses, two slips, panties and socks in a sack. Suddenly two weeks seem like a long time.

Make sure you take your rain coat. It sure look like it gonna rain."

"Yesum, Mama."

"I got to go to work Ruthie," Papa said. "If I didn't have to, I would walk down there wit you to see you off."

"Yesum, Papa. I know you would have."

When I is finished, I carried the sack out to the kitchen. Mama stood up. "Ruthie. I is gonna walk you to the gate."

"I is gonna go to the gate wit you too. Jus let me git my pant and shoes on."

After a few minutes, Mama came out the bedroom wearin a dress and shoes, and Papa came out wearin a brown pair of dusty lookin pant and wore-out shoes turned up at the toe.

"Roy, why don't you put on clean pant?"

"Woman, leave me alone!"

"Ruthie don't want her Papa walkin her to the gate wit dirty pant on."

"Ruthie don't care what I wear to walk her to the gate. Anyway, I is gonna go to work after I see her off and these here pant gonna git dirtier." Papa slap his hands on his pants and dust comes off like a little cloud.

"Stop that, Roy! Not only is you pant dirty, but you gonna make my house dirty too.

I was sure gonna miss Mama and Papa fussin, even though it seem silly to me.

When we gits to the gate, I open it. Tears well up in my eyes. "I is gonna miss you."

"It's only two weeks, chile. Your gonna be back here before you know it, wit money for you college," Mama said.

"You is gonna be okay, Ruthie. Papa don't want you to go. But you Mama here said it gonna be okay. So I hope it will."

"Stop talkin like that, Roy. You know that Ruthie is gonna be all right. Give me a hug Ruthie." Mama helded out her arms, and I went into dem.

"Give you old Papa a hug too."

"I is gonna be back soon, Papa."

Turning Papa loose, I close the gate and head to Miz Willams house. They got smaller each time I turn my head to look back. Then I turn down another road and they was gone. I kept thinking, *I is gonna be back down this old road in two weeks*. I never thought that it would take me six years.

CHAPTER EIGHT

When I git to Miz Williams house, they almost ready to go. She was directin two colored men how to load the rented truck. She didn't smile when she saw me. "It's about time you got here. I thought I might have to come and git you."

"I was jus sayin goodbye to my folks ma'am. I is sorry I is late."

"Mornin Ruthie." Mr. Williams was carryin a lamp in his hand. "You can sit up front wit us."

"Yes sir."

I slung my little sack of clothes in the back of the truck and watch as the men put the canopy over the back of the truck. I glance up in the sky. The clouds was a comin in. It was gonna be a storm. I remember how Mama told me to not to forgit my raincoat, but when I open my sack to git it, it wasn't there. I scurried up to the door of the truck, and waited until Miz Williams and Susie got in. Miz Williams didn't notice me standin in back of her. She was about to close the door when she seen me.

"Why are you standin there?" She raise one of her eyebrows.

"Mr. Williams told me to sit up front."

"There's no room for you up here. Git on in the back with the furniture.

"There's room for her up here, Martha. She don't have to sit in the back." Mr. Williams said as he step in the truck.

"I told her to sit in the back." She looked at me wit a frown on her face. "Now git, gal!"

"Yesum." I let go the door of the truck and ran to the back.

The two colored men were sittin on the floor of the truck. One of dem look at me and shook his head. "Where you goin? You can't sit back here, little girl. Go on back up front and sit wit dem folks."

"I can't sir. Miz Williams told me to sit back here."

He shrug. "Well, stand there for a moment so we can fix a place for you to sit. Come on, John. Let's move this here furniture."

The men stood up and started pushin the furniture closer together. They drag the sofa off to the side. "I hope that lady don't mind you sittin on her sofa." The man named Pete chuckled.

The men got out the truck, and John lifted me into the back. He git in after me, and Pete closed the gate, climbing over the top to git in.

"We in. Start movin!" Pete yelled.

Mr. Williams started the truck to rollin. I studied the two men sitting on the floor in the spot they had fixed for demselves. John was shorter than my papa. He was sort of a heavy man wit light-colored skin and brown eyes. His lips were thick wit small cracks on dem, and he had a few slight freckles on his face. Pete, on the other hand, was the color of dark molasses. He was tall but skinny. I don't know how he even lift that sofa without fallin over. He look like the mild summer wind could blow him away. He had a tiny mustache that seem as if it had trouble comin out his face. It was so uneven, it had spots of baldness in between each hair.

"Little girl, why is you goin with dem? Don't you has any folks?" Pete asked.

"Yes sir, I got a mama and a papa. I jus be goin wit dem for two weeks to help straighten out they house. Then Miz Williams is a gonna send me back home. She told my Mama that she gonna pay me real good. She gonna give me more money for two weeks work than Papa makes in three months," I bragged.

"Do you mama know that woman is mean, makin her little girl ride in the back wit furniture when there is plenty of room up front wit dem?" John questioned.

I jus look at him. I didn't know what to say.

"Little girl, if I was you, when they gits to they destination and we git through unloadin this here truck, I would go back home. We got to take this truck back, and you is welcome to ride back wit us." Pete said.

"I can't do that sir. I promise that I would help her out for two weeks." I made myself a pillow wit my little sack of clothes and laid down.

"What kind of mama you got anyway, sendin a little girl off like this? I wouldn't do that for nothin in the world." John shook his head.

"Miz Williams is nice. She jus be mad about somethin so she put me back here. Anyway, I git the whole sofa to myself."

I laid down on the sofa and put my head on the pillow I had made. The motion of the truck rock me to sleep. When I woke up I need to go to the bathroom and I was hungry. Mr. Williams had already stop the truck.

They must have needed to go to the bathroom too. Pete and John had left out the truck. I look up and seen Miz Williams and Susie hurryin toward a buildin that looked like it might be a bathroom. I git out the truck and ran up to her.

"I got to go to the bathroom, Miz Williams."

"Well go on around the back. There is a colored bathroom around there."

Miz Williams and Susie went into a door that said "Whites." I went on around the back and saw a door that said "Colored." When I open the door, the smell of old pee hit my face and pierce my nose like acid. I helded my breath and went in. The toilet was yellow wit urine stains, and the floor was filthy. There was no toilet tissue and nothin to wipe you hands on. The sink had a film on it and the knobs was broken, so a tickle of water ran out.

I had to go real bad so I tried not to think about how filthy it was. I wish I had jus peed in the bushes. I wouldn't have had much privacy but at least the bushes was cleaner. I helded my breath as long as I could, but then I had to let it out and take another one. It felt like the air was drench with pee too. I could taste it wit every breath I took. I hurried and peed, pushin it out as fast as I could. There was no soap to wash my hands so I let the water from the sink run over dem and dry dem on my dress. When I git outside I took in a long deep breath of air to clear my lungs. I walk around and seen Miz Williams and Susie walkin to the store not far from the bathrooms. I caught up wit dem.

"I is real hungry ma'am. Can I please have somethin to eat?"

"Didn't your mama pack you somethin?"

"No ma'am. I left too early; she didn't have time."

"Well I am sorry. I don't have any money to buy you nothin."

She continue walkin to the store wit me followin behind. When she git inside she orders some sandwiches. She reach in her pocket and pull out some money. A white man in the store told her to tell me to go outside.

"Go back to the truck, Ruthie," Miz Williams said.

She looked at the white man and smile. "I'm sorry. I didn't know she was behind me."

He handed her three sandwiches and three sodas. I walk out the store, back to the truck. She walked pass me standin by the truck and didn't even look at me. She and Susie jus went to the front and got inside. I look up in the truck. Pete and John was there eatin they sandwiches. They both see me.

"Little girl, you ain't eatin," Pete said, as he took a bite.

"Ain't got nothin to eat." I hump my shoulders.

"That lady won't buy you nothin?" John drank some of his soda.

"No sir, she say she ain't got no money."

"Let me have twenty cent, John." Pete held out his hand to John.

John laid his sandwich down beside him, reach in his pocket and gave Pete some coins. Then he reach back in his pocket and pull out another coin.

"Here another dime, Pete. Buy her a soda too."

Pete got down out the truck and help me git back in. Then he head toward the back of the store.

I sat down on the sofa, and watch John wolfin down his sandwich. I wonder if he might get choked eatin so fast. When he finish the sandwich, he wash it down wit soda. Pete return wit a ham sandwich and grape soda. He hand dem to me, then he sat down and start eatin his own lunch.

"Thank you Mr. Pete and Mr. John."

"You is welcome."

I bow my head in prayer. "I thank you Lawd for this here sandwich and soda. Amen." When I look up, both of the men were lookin at me. I felted I should say somethin. "I always says a prayer over my food sir."

"Don't pay us no mind," John said. "We should have prayed over our food too. It a good thing that you folks taught you to pray. Pete here don't know how. His folks didn't teach him nothin except here the food; let's eat."

"Why you be lyin like that in front of this here little girl?" Pete said.

John chuckle. "You know it true. When you family at the table, you better grab what you can and eat it fast. They acts like that the only meal they is gonna git for the rest of they lives. Those negros ain't gonna stop to pray. Too many of dem. Fifteen in all, and eat like dogs." John slap one hand on his thigh and gave out a hearty laugh throwing his head back so it land on a cloth chair.

"You better stop laughin at me and keep your old nappy, greasy head off that lady chair. If you gits it greasy, she ain't gonna pay you one dime."

John stop laughin and move away from the chair.

"Little girl, you sure you don't wanna go back wit us?" John wipe his mouth wit his shirt.

"No sir. But I thank you. Miz Williams gonna send me back after two weeks. She really a nice lady. She use to buy me things when I work for her in Demopolis. And she still gave me my pay." I pick up my sandwich and took a bite.

"You should be in school." Pete took another bite of his sandwich..

"My mama said that I be a goin to school as soon as I gits back. She real proud of me. She said that she know that when I gits back I is gonna make up for those two weeks real fast. I is eleven and in the seventh grade." I took another bite of my sandwich. Pete and John jus chuckle and shook they heads.

When Pete got through eatin, John got out the truck and close up the gate. He climb back in and yelled, "Gate a closin!"

Mr. Williams start up the truck again and we was on our way. It start pourin down rain. The rain didn't touch me 'cause of the canopy, but I got cold, and started shiverin. I laid down on the sofa and ball myself up in a knot holdin on to my shoulders to keep warm.

"Didn't bring a coat huh?" Pete said.

"No sir, I forgot it."

He got up and look around the truck to where Miz Williams had packed her blankets. He git one out and hand it to me.

Grateful, I wrap it around myself. No one talk for a while. I laid there listenin to the rain. It sound like popcorn poppin in the skillet as it fell on the canopy.

It was nightfall and still rainin when we git to Birmingham and Miz Williams house. Pete and John quickly unload the truck, settin the furniture in the different places in the house where Miz Williams want it. After about an hour, the rain finally stop.

When Pete and John git through unloadin the furniture they call me over to the truck. " Little girl," Pete said, "We gonna ask you one more time if you wanna go back wit us."

"I don't know sir. Miz Williams might git mad if I go back wit you."

"She don't seem to care what you do. We can take you back home to you mama and papa."

"She's ain't goin nowhere!" Miz Williams shouted. She was a standin by the truck. "Yes ma'am." Both Pete and John said, in a low tone wit their heads bowed.

"Can we bid her farewell, ma'am?"

"Go on and hurry about it."

John bended his head down by my side and whisper, "Write you folks as soon as you can. Tell dem to come git you. You hear?"

"Yes sir."

"Take care of youself and hurry up and git back home."

"I will sir."

They both went to the front of the truck, and I watch it pull away headed back toward Demopolis.

"Ruthie, come on in this house and get yourself ready for bed."

"Yes ma'am."

"Go git some cover to put on the sofa."

I went over to the bag in her sittin room. I reach inside and got a pink blanket. A pillow was inside the bag too. I put dem both on the green sofa. When I finish spreadin the blanket Miz Williams left for her own room. I put on my gown, got on my knees, and said my prayers. When I finish wit my prayer I laid down on the sofa. When my head hit the pillow I fell asleep.

CHAPTER NINE

I felted a hand shaking me. "Ruthie, it's time to git up."

I sat up on the side of the sofa, wipin the sleep out my eyes. I look up at Miz Williams.

"Hurry up. It's mornin. We have to get this house together today. Not tomorrow."

"I got to go to the bathroom."

"Go on and wash up. Don't take too long." Miz Williams puts on a apron. "Breakfast will be ready in a few minutes."

"Yes ma'am."

I git up off the sofa, grab hold to my sack of clothes and headed to the bathroom.

"Wait a minute."

I turn around. Miz Williams was a lookin in a bag. "Here is a washcloth."

I went over and got it. I passed Susie bedroom on the way down the hall, and Miz Williams' room was across from the bathroom. The bathroom had towels and wash cloths in it already. Miz Williams must have put dem there, I thought. The bathroom had runnin water jus like the one they had in Demopolis. I use the toilet, flush it, and watch the water go around. The room smell clean and fresh like flowers, 'cause the window was open. Lookin out, I could see purple flowers with petals that look like little bells outside the window. I took a deep breath. "Dem flowers sure smell good." I said to myself.

"Ruthie, hurry up." Miz Williams shouted through the door.

"Yesum."

I took the washcloth she give me and wash up wit it. When I was through, I dress quickly, left the bathroom and went down the hall through the sittin room to the kitchen. Miz Williams was a cookin some oatmeal. She turn around and look at me.

"Ain't it a nice house, Ruthie? I think we are gonna be very happy here."

"Yes ma'am." I stood there for a moment not knowin what to do.

"Well don't jus stand there. Set the table. Today oatmeal, tomorrow a feast." Miz Williams chuckled.

I went to a box on the floor, lookin for the bowls and spoons.

"They are over in that box." Miz Williams point to a box close to the stove where she cookin.

I went over, open the box, and pull out the bowls. The spoons was in another box that was sittin by the kitchen table. While I was settin the table, Miz Willims went to get Mr. Williams and Susie. Susie came in to breakfast dressed in a short-sleeve, pink gown.

We all ate together that day at the table jus like we did back in Demopolis. When we git through eatin, Susie went back to her room to git dressed. I wash the dishes. Mr. Williams and Miz Williams start arrangin furniture in the sittin room. When they was through, I help Miz Williams put up her white lace curtains.

Later, Susie and me put up the dishes, pots, and pans. We made a game out of it, pretendin each pot was a fat general. The top of the pot was the generals' hat. Miz Williams wanted all her pots to have the tops on. We gave each pot the funniest name we could think of. The one I like most was General Mack-Fat-boil-in. It was the biggest pot Miz Williams had.

Susie and I name all the plates and saucers too. We gave all the plates names like Lady Hilton and Lady Gevalia. The saucers was given chillins names. We didn't have time to name the bowls and cups 'cause Miz Williams said for us to hurry up. After Susie and I was through wit the dishes, I mop the sittin room and kitchen floors.

The sittin room floor was made out of wood. After I wash it, I had to wax it. When I was through, it shine like glass. I wax the kitchen floor too. It was white linoleum wit gold sparkles. Miz Williams had me wash and wax the wooden hallway floor too.

Miz Williams was very happy wit what I had done. She pat me on the shoulder. "Good job, Ruthie. I don't think that I could find anyone that does a better job than you."

"Thank you, ma'am." I was feelin proud of myself.

"Come on now; let's get ready for supper."

I was happy Miz Williams was actin nice to me again. When the night came and it was time for me to go to bed she hand me a blanket and I head toward the sofa.

"Where are you goin?" She was standin in the sittin room wit her hands on her hips.

"To the sofa, ma'am." I helded the blanket tight to my body. By the sound of her voice, I felted like I had done somethin wrong.

"You are not sleepin on my sofa no more."

"Where is I gonna sleep, ma'am?"

"On the back porch. I jus gave you a blanket. You can spread it out on the floor and sleep on it."

"Yesum."

I walk on back to the back porch wit Miz Williams behind me. The back porch was jus off the kitchen. It was square with a rickety floor. It had sides around it and a roof, but the wood had separated in some areas, letting air in. It had two doors. One door from the kitchen. The other door led to the back yard.

Mr. Williams came in and look at Miz Williams and me spreadin out the blanket. "Is she gonna be all right out here?"

"She's gonna be jus fine." Miz Williams turn to her husband. "You can go on to bed now, Billy Roy."

"You sure she's gonna be all right?"

"I said she is jus fine." She frown.

"All right, I'll see you when you come to bed. Night Ruthie."

"Night, Mr. Williams."

"Hurry up and lie down. You better be up early tomorrow, so we can go shoppin. I don't have nothin for breakfast except oatmeal and I know that nobody wants that again."

"Yes ma'am." I laid down in the middle of the blanket, gatherin up the ends and pullin dem over my body. Miz Williams stood there watchin me. Then she left through the door to the kitchen, closin it behind her. The room was pitch black. It was so dark that when I put my hands in front of my face I couldn't see dem. I felted somethin crawlin on my face. I jumped up and brush at it, but it fell back on my face. I knew what it was this time. It was my own hair. Layin back down, I felted scared and all alone. I miss my own bed, and I miss my mama.

I said my prayer. "Dear Lawd, please bless Mama and Papa. Please bless Mr. and Miz Williams and Susie. Lawd, why Miz Williams want me to sleep on the porch? I don't like it out here by myself. Anyway, Lawd still bless her. Amen."

I tuck the blanket in tighter around me, and kepted a tellin myself that it was jus for two weeks. I said that over and over until I felled asleep.

CHAPTER TEN

The next day was Sunday. Miz Williams had forgotten that on Sunday the stores was closed, so we had to eat oatmeal again. But on Monday, Miz Williams and me went shoppin. I had to trot along behind her. Sometime she stop to introduce herself to a neighbor who happen to be outside. She saw a lady workin in her yard. Miz Williams went right into her gate and up to where the lady workin.

Miz Williams reach out her hand to the lady and say, "Hello, I am your new neighbor, Miz Williams."

The lady got up from workin, took off her gloves, and shook Miz Williams' hand.

"Well hello, Miz Williams. It's nice to have you as a neighbor. My name is Mae."

"And your last name is?"

"Walker. Miz Mae Walker."

"I am pleased to meet you Miz Walker. This here is Ruthie. My little niggard that I brought with me. She is a real good worker. Cleans my house until it shines."

That woman look at Miz Williams kind of funny-like and say, "That's wonderful."

Miz Williams smile and say, "Well I got to go now. I must git to the store. Ain't got nothin for breakfast this mornin. I'll be back around to introduce you to my husband and my little girl, Susie."

Miz Williams and I continue walkin on down the road. She introduce me, to every person she seen, as her little niggard. Every time she did that I felted smaller and smaller. We finally got to the neighborhood store, wit wooden shelves reachin up to the top of the ceilin. Each shelf was fill wit bags of sugar, flour, grits, bakin soda, lard, and can goods. They was some meats on the counter like hot dogs, bacon, and bologna. I guess the other meat was kepted in the back in a ice box. They was a barrel by the door filled wit pickle pig feet. Breads of different kinds was on the counter too. Two men was puttin some can goods on the wooden floor, right in the middle of the store. The cans was pile high in a cone shape. Potato chips was on a stand. The store smell of cinnamon and allspice. They was everythin you would wanna buy for eatin, in that store.

A old white woman was shoppin, and a man stood behind the counter smilin at us as we came in the door.

"Well hello there," the man said. "I ain't seen you around. You must be new."

"Are you the owner of this here store?" Miz Williams ask as she walk up to the counter.

"Yes, I am."

"Well I am Miz Williams; I just moved here. This here is Ruthie, my little niggard."

Mr. Gray was a short, slumped-over white man wit gray hair. He look kind of old and chubby. He wore wire frame glasses that really let you see the bags under his eyes. He look tired, but he seem kindhearted.

"I will be sendin my little niggard here to the store from time to time for groceries."

"Okay, Miz Williams. You can count on me to fill the orders right."

"Well, I'll be a needin a few things today."

Mr. Gray seen as if he pull up some energy when she said that.

"Can I go outside while you buy grocery, Miz Williams?" I ask.

She didn't mind, so I went outside and sat in a chair that was in front of the store. I was happy to git away from her even for jus a few minutes. I sat there thinkin about how we colored chillins used to sing a little song about niggards. We would pat our hands together while singin it. I hum it in my head. "I'm not a niggard; I'm a ne-ga-ro. When I becomes a niggard I'll let you know."

I was hummin that song when the old white lady came out the store, her bag full of groceries. She was strugglin like it was too heavy for her, and she drop her purse. When she reach down to git it, some of her groceries fell out the bag. She straighten up, sighed, and look over at me and smile.

"Little girl, could you help me?"

"Yes ma'am!" I hop out that chair and pick up the old lady's groceries. I was happy to do it 'cause she call me a little girl. Not a niggard, but a little girl. I start talkin to her, while I pick up her food, about how I didn't mind helpin her, and if she ever need anymore help, I was glad to do it.

I was talkin so much that I didn't hear Miz Williams callin me. She came out the store and seen me helping and chatterin away. She grab me by the back of my dress and snatch me up.

"You come when I call you, you hear me!"

I drop the lady's food and my lip trembl. I manage to say, "Yesum."

"I'm sorry Miss, don't be so rough on her," the old lady said. "She was just helpin an old woman."

Miz Williams turn around and look at that lady. Her lips curled; her eyes narrow.

"This is my niggard. If you need help, git your own niggard!"

The lady's shoulders jump a little, and her eyes blink.

"Get in there and get those bags!"

She turn my dress loose and I went on in the store. I hear Miz Williams and that lady exchange words. I felted sorry for the old lady.
Why Miz Williams had to do her like that? She only need a little help. She wasn't takin anythin from her. I volunteer, I thought, as Mr. Gray hand me the bags.

When I gits out the store, the old lady was gone. Miz Williams took one of the bags from my arms, and we started walkin to the house. She didn't say a word to me on the way back. When we git back, Mr. Williams and Susie was up and talkin at the kitchen table. Miz Williams said "hi" to dem both real sweet like nothin happen. Mr. Williams went back to his bedroom, and Miz William start cookin breakfast. She told me to wash my hands and help her set the table. I wash my hands in the kitchen sink, and Susie ask her mama if she could help me.

"Yes you can, honey." Miz Williams said, very sweetly again.

"Ruthie, I is gonna miss you when you leave." Susie put the forks on the table.

"I is gonna miss you too, Susie."

"Won't you ask your mama to let you stay wit us a little longer?"

"I would like to stay wit you, Susie, but I got to go to school. You got to go to school too."

"You can go to school here, Ruthie. Mama said that they have a colored school here."

"I miss my mama, Susie."

"While you're here let's be best friends, Ruthie."

I smile, and we started makin funny faces at each other, jus a gigglin and laughin so hard.

"You two stop playin." Miz Williams sound like she a little upset.

"Yes ma'am," we both said. But we kept makin faces at each other and tried not to laugh out loud.

"Breakfast is ready. Go get your papa, Susie."

Miz Williams had cook bacon, eggs, and pancakes for breakfast. I sat there wit dem and ate at the table that day. Though I had to sleep on the back porch, at least I was still welcome at the table. After breakfast, Miz Williams told Susie she would be startin her in school come the next day. She told me to clean up the kitchen, and she never mention takin me to school. Susie ask if she could help me clean up the kitchen and Miz Williams say yes. After we git through, I remember that I need to write my Mama. Miz Williams was in the sittin room readin a magazine. She look up at me.

"Miz Williams, may I have some paper and a pencil?"

"What do you need them for."

"I promise Mama and Papa that I would write dem as soon as I got here, ma'am. It been three days now and I ain't wrote."

"I suppose you'll need an envelope and a stamp too."

"Yes ma'am."

"Well I guess I can manage that."

She got up and left the sittin room. Susie and I went into the kitchen and wait. We was lookin out a window when Miz Williams came in the kitchen. She hand me a few sheets of paper, a pencil, and a envelope.

"Thank you ma'am," I said, as I took the items.

"Sit at the table and write your mama." I sat down.

"What you gonna write?" Susie asked, as she sat down next to me.

"I is jus gonna tell my mama that I miss her and I will be home in a week and a few days."

Miz Williams left the room.

"Can I help you write it?"

"I got to write the letter all by myself, Susie. Maybe next time you can help me."

I started writin my letter wit Susie looking over my hand at it.

Dear Mama,

I miss you and Papa. I didn't write you the first day 'cause I was so tired. I have almost finish helpin Miz Williams git her house together. I miss school, Mama. I miss my own bed. Miz Williams said that I have done a good job to the neighbors here. I know that it will be a week and a few days before the two weeks are over but I wanna come home now. Please Mama, come and git me. I will tell you why after you bring me home. I love you and Papa.

Ruthie

I put the letter in the envelope, address it, and seal it up. Then I took it to the porch and put it in my little sack.

"I'll ask you mama for a stamp when I gits ready to mail it later today."

"You ain't gonna mail it now?"

"I is gonna mail it later. You wanna walk to the mail box wit me when I go to mail it?"

Miz Williams came to the porch. "Have you finished writin your letter?" Her voice was as sweet as pie.

"Yes ma'am."

"Let me have it. I will mail it for you."

"Ruthie and I can mail it, Mama."

"You don't have time to go to the mailbox. Ruthie has work to do. I have to go to the mailbox myself. I'll mail your letter when I mail mine."

I got the letter from my sack and hand it to Miz Williams. She put it in the pocket of her dress and left the room.

"I sure hope she don't forget to mail it."

"She won't forget, Ruthie. Mama don't forget nothin."

"Well I got to go find out what you mama want me to do next."

"If she wants you to wash clothes, I'm outa here. I'll help you do anythin but wash them there clothes." Susie said.

We found her mother gatherin some clothes for me to wash.

The next day, Miz Williams put Susie in school. A week later, she left the house to walk Susie to school. When she return, she had a letter in her hand. It was from my Mama. Miz Williams open the letter and read it to me.

Dear Ruthie,

I is glad that you are havin such a nice time. Miz Williams is such a nice lady. May God bless her. You stay there and be a good girl. Do what she say like you always have. Mama is very proud of her little girl. Papa is too. I will see you in two weeks. Mama miss you.

Love, Mama

"Can I read the letter, Miz Williams?" I asked.

"You most certainly can."

She handed it to me, and I read it. It read jus like Miz Williams had said. I was hurt. Mama didn't even mention about comin to git me. She jus want me to be good.

"Come on Ruthie. Put that letter up now, you hear, and git on back to work."

"Yes ma'am." I gits to cleanin again.

That day, when Susie came home from school she want to talk to me, but I didn't feel like talkin 'cause I was feeling too sad. She left me to my work and went outside.

When the two weeks was over, I told Miz Williams that it was time for me to go home.

"Why Ruthie, I thought you was happy here."

I was too scared to say that I wasn't happy. "I is happy here, ma'am, but it time for me to go home."

"I want you to stay wit me a little while longer, Ruthie. I need you."

"I needs to go home, ma'am. I be missin too many days of school. Mama will be lookin for me."

"You can make it up, Ruthie, when you git back. A smart girl like you can always catch up in school. I want you to write your Mama a letter tellin her that you would like to stay two weeks longer. I'll go git the paper and a pencil."

She left out the sittin room and came back wit some paper and a pencil. Then she had me write that I was having a nice time and that I want to stay a little longer. She told me to tell my mama that she was gonna put me in the colored school. She told me to write that Mr. Williams was gonna give me more money if I was allowed to stay. Maybe even a hundred dollars. I didn't wanna tell my mama that. What I want to tell her was that I want to git home quick, fast, and in a hurry. But I couldn't write that 'cause Miz Williams was lookin over my shoulders all the time when I was writin. When I finish the letter, she even read it.

I was hopin my mama would say to git home now, no matter how good a time I was havin. But when the letter came the next week, mama told me to go ahead and stay for two more weeks. Miz Williams read the letter before I did. In fact, she hand it to me open. My heart sunk upon readin it, and I wonder how I ever gonna let my mama know that Miz Williams sometime treat me like I wasn't nothin.

Miz Williams wrote my Aunt again. She told me about it after, claimin that the letter had come. But I never seen it. She told me that my Aunt Flo said for me to stay as long as she need me. I told Miz Williams that I really want to go home. I miss my Mama and Papa so bad that I felted like jus goin home on my own. Miz Williams thought I sayin that I wanted to run away from her, and she told me that if I ever ran away she would hide all of her jewery and tell the police I stole dem. After that I started bein scared of her.

I ask Miz Williams, a few days later, if I could write my mama again. She said that my aunt should write me instead of me writin her; she was tired of usin up her stamps. Months passed, but Mama never wrote me after the last letter I sent her.

CHAPTER ELEVEN

One day, after I been there for a month, Miz Williams had a visitor. I hear her come in the house. Susie and me was eatin lunch at the table and playin a game of tic-tac-toe. The woman and Miz Williams was jus a talking about how nice the house was when they walk into the kitchen and the woman stop dead in her tracks. She stare at me. It was Miz Williams' mama. Susie git up, ran to her grandma, and hug her around her waist. But the woman jus stood there, not touchin Susie. Not even lookin down at her. I got up from the chair, swallow hard, wonderin what she was gonna say now.

"What's the matter, Mama?" Miz Williams asked.

"Why is that niggard eatin at your table? Git away from that table, niggard!"

I look at Miz Williams, wonderin what I should do next.

"Take your food and eat it on the porch, Ruthie." Miz Williams said.

"Yes ma'am." I pick up my sandwich and went on outside and sat on the steps of the porch. Miz Williams shut the door behind me.

When Miz Williams open the door I seen her mama kiss her and Susie. Then she came out the door and walk past me sittin on the porch. She act like I wasn't there. Miz Williams call me in the house. "I need you to go to the store for me." She had this solemn look on her face that let me know I was in for trouble.

"Seems like I have been feeding you wrong, Ruthie. I is gonna change that now."

She gave me a nickel and told me to buy two pounds of navy beans.

"I can eat what you eat, Miz Williams. It don't bother me, ma'am."

"Jus go to the store like I told you."

I ran down to the store. When I git there, Mr. Gray was outside sweepin the front of his store. It was a hot day and he was sweepin like he could barely make it.

"Hi, Mr. Gray."

He stop sweepin, look at me and said, "You that gal that helped Miz Green pick up her groceries. She brought somethin here and told me if I seen you again to give it to you."

Mr. Gray laid the broom aside and went in the store wit me followin behind him. He walk behind the counter and brought out a box of hard candy. My eyes lit up like a Christmas tree.

"Why thank you, sir!"

"Don't thank me. Thank Miz Green. Now what can I do for you?"

"Miz Williams wants two pounds of navy beans."

I took out a piece of candy and put it in my mouth while he got a bag and started fillin it wit the white hard stuff.

I felted sorry for him, being he was so old and had to work so hard. "Mr. Gray, I'll sweep the front of the store for you. You might pass out. Hot day like this."

"What's it gonna cost me?" he said, smilin.

"Nothin sir. I jus wanna help you 'cause you needs it."

"Why thank you. You know where the broom is."

"Yessir." I went out the store and got the broom. I swepted the front, being careful to git all the dirt. Mr. Gray came out his store when I got through and said I did a good job. He offered me a penny, but I wouldn't take it. I was happy to help him. He seem like a nice old man.

Mr. Gray hand me my candy and those beans, and I made my way back to Miz Williams' house. She standin in the front yard waitin for me.

"What took you so long?"

"It hot, ma'am. I don't walk so fast when it hot."

I didn't think it was smart idea to tell her that I had swept Mr. Gray's store for him. I was afraid she might git mad like she did wit Miz Green. She spot the box of hard candy.

"What you got in your hand?" She grab the box..

"Mr. Gray gave it to me. He said that white lady that I help, left it for me.

"Don't you be acceptin anything from nobody, you hear?" Miz Williams screamed. "Git on in here. I got a job for you." She motion to me wit her hand to go in the house.

When I git inside she had a bucket of water, a scrub brush, and some lye soap by the table for me.

"What you want me to scrub, ma'am?"

"I want you to scrub that chair that you been sittin on and the table. I can't afford to buy another one, and I don't want me nor my family catchin any niggard germs."

I started scrubbin the chair all the while thinkin, *Well, a niggard, as you called me is scrubbin your table and chair. If there was any germs on dem they would git right back on.* I scrub until she said that they was clean. Then she told me to scrub down the bathroom, and she watch me clean it. I had to use the toilet, so I put the brush down.

"What you doin? I told you to scrub this bathroom."

"I got to use it."

"You can't use my bathroom."

"Where is I gonna do it at?'

"I'll give you a jar. You can go in the garage."

I had to hold it while she look around in the kitchen for a jar. I shook, but held it until she found one and hand it to me. Then I bolt for the garage with the jar in hand. When I got there, Mr. Williams was workin in it.

"Please, please Mr. Williams. I got to use the bathroom. Miz Williams told me that I can't use the bathroom in the house no more, she told me I had to use it out here. Could you please go out for jus a second, so I can do my number sir, please?"

"Why did she tell you that?" Mr. Williams said as he pick up some tools.

"I don't know sir, but I got to pee bad." I was a shakin. "Please sir. I is about to pee on myself."

"I got to see her about this." He left in a huff.

As soon as I got my panties down, I put the jar up under me but the floor caught most of it. I was ashamed. Mr. Williams was gonna come back in the garage, smellin the pee and seein it on the floor. I pull up my panties, took the jar to the backyard, and pour the yellow liquid out over the bushes. I brought the jar back into the garage and set it on one of the shelves. Then I went to the faucet in the front yard and wash my hands. I dried dem on my dress. As I was walkin back to the house I wonder what I was gonna do if I had to do the number two, since I couldn't use her bathroom no more.

When I git back, Miz Williams was in the kitchen. I don't know where Mr. Williams was. But he didn't eat supper wit his family that night. Miz Williams was cookin roast chicken, potatoes, and peas wit apple pie for desert. She also had a pot on the stove wit beans. She didn't season the beans except wit salt. She made a pan of cornbread to go wit it. She gave the meal to me and told me to eat it on the porch where I slept. I did as she said.

I thought that she was jus gonna be gittin beans for that one day. After supper I went up to her and ask. She was puttin up the leftovers in bowls when I went to her.

"Miz Williams. Do I have to eat these here beans again tomorra?"

"Was I not understood? I told you I was feedin you wrong. From now on, that is your everyday meal. You should be glad to git a meal. I hear that a lot of niggards are starvin."

"Yes ma'am." I left her side and started washin the dishes. I didn't like beans. Especially lima beans. I hope she never made those. I wonder why her mama tell her to feed me jus beans.

Miz Williams spoke to me. "I am puttin up these leftovers for my family. I know how much is in every one of these here bowls. You better not take any or I'll know, and I'll punish you for that, Ruthie. I really will."

"Yesum," I said and turn back to finish washin the dishes. I was about to put my dish in the water to wash when Miz Williams stop me.

"Ruthie, don't put the dish in there with the rest of my dishes."

"Where is I gonna wash it then, Miz Williams?"

"Outside. Run the water outside and wash your dish under the faucet."

I took my plate outside and wash it. When I brought it back inside she gave me a rag to dry it and show me where it was to stay on the shelf away from the rest of her dishes.

She cook for me once a week. Whatever beans she cook that week had to last me until Monday of the next. I ate beans for breakfast, lunch and supper. Susie felted sorry for me, and she came up wit a plan to git me some of the family's food.

I was in the sittin room dustin tables when Susie came into the room. Miz Williams was watchin me dust. Susie went over to her mama.

"Mama, can I have nickel?"

"What you want it for?"

"I want to buy ice cream today while I'm outside playin wit my friends."

"Okay. I'll be right back."

Miz Williams left to git the money. Susie came over to me.

"I have a plan to feed you." I stop dustin and look at her.

"How Susie?"

"When Mama goes to town, I am gonna take some of the food in the ice box and give it to you."

"But she never goes to town. Anyway, she's gonna think I stole it and punish me."

"No, she won't. I'm gonna tell her that I took the food."

"She's comin back!"

Susie sat on the sofa, and I went back to dustin. Miz Williams came over to Susie and hand her the nickel. "You can buy your ice cream now."

"Thanks Mama." Susie went outside. I felted excited, thinkin about me gittin some food when Miz Williams goes to town. But it didn't happen until two weeks later.

After supper one evening, Miz Williams told me that from now on I had to keep my clothes in the garage. I was to bathe in the garage and dress in there. I was only allowed to sleep and eat on the back porch. She didn't want Susie and me to play together no more, and I couldn't talk to any of the colored girls that work for any of the other white people that live around there. I didn't even know there were any colored girls workin around there.

Mr. Williams didn't like the idea of me using his garage as a bathroom. I hear him say one day while I was sittin on the porch where I slept and ate, "Why can't she use the bathroom in the house, Martha?"

"Cause she's a niggard and it ain't right for her to be usin a white person's bathroom."

"It's not right for you to make her use the garage either."

"Well she's got to go somewhere."

"I don't know what is going on with you. You are getting impossible, Martha." Mr. Williams storm out the door.

Mr.Williams start workin nights. He would leave early in the afternoon. I hear him tell her that he had to catch more than one bus to git to work; that why he had to leave so early. That made Miz Williams mad. He also start comin in later and later in the mornin.

One day when Miz Williams sent me to the store to git my ration of beans for the week, Mr. Gray notice I was gittin a little thin.

"What's the matter wit you, gal? You sick?"

"No sir, I'm jus tired of eatin beans sir. Sometimes I can only stomach a spoonful a dem."

Mr. Gray studied me for a moment. "Tell you what, Ruthie. If you can come to the store and sweep it up every day, I will let you pick somethin to eat for your pay."

"Can I start today, sir?"

"You certainly can."

"Well I'm gonna sweep you store real nice and clean. Can I have a ham sandwich, sir?" I said.

"I'll make it for you right now."

He hand me the broom. I went to sweepin. I swept out every corner he had in the store. I was gonna finally git some food other than beans. When I gits through, he hand me the beans and the sandwich. He had a thick slice of cheese on it wit a load of ham. He hand me a soda. "Do I have to pay for the soda, sir?"

"No, it's free."

"Thank you, sir. Can I eat it outside your store?"

"You sure can."

The two other men that work for Mr. Gray look like they didn't like what he was doin, but they didn't say nothin.

I took that sandwich, ran to the side of the store, and ate it like they was no tomorra. I was so happy to be eatin. When I was jus about through, I seen Miz Williams comin up the road to the store. I tried to hide the rest of my meal, but she seen it.

"Where did you git that sandwich?" Her eyes narrow at me.

"I didn't steal it; I work for it." I started shakin like I had to pee, but I was jus scared.

Mr. Gray came out the store when he heard Miz Williams.

"She worked for me and earned that sandwich, ma'am."

"Don't you be feedin my niggard!" she screamed.

"The gal looks like she could use some food. She is powerful skinny."

"Nobody feeds my niggard but me. Do you wanna be known as a niggard lover, Mr. Gray? May I remind you that this is the South."

By that time, the two men that was in the store came out. Mr. Gray look at dem. "Ain't nothin to see here. Go on back in the store."

"Where're those beans?" Miz Williams ask me.

I had laid dem on the sidewalk. I walk over and pick dem up.

"Here they is, ma'am."

"Now git on home."

She made me walk in front of her all the way to her house. She didn't send me to the store after that for a long time, but finally one day she sent me again. I went in the store, and gave Mr. Gray the grocery list that Miz Williams had made out. On the top of the counter was a few slices of bologna and two slices of bread. My mouth water as I gave Mr. Gray the list. He must have been gittin ready to make somebody a sandwich. I had a pocket on my dress, so when he turn around to git some things off the shelves, I grab the bologna and the bread and put dem in my pocket. One of the men that work at the store turn around and look at me jus as I was stuffin the food in my pocket. My heart start beatin fast. My mouth felted dry. My whole body trembled. *Oh God.* I thought, *I know this is wrong but please don't let dem send me to jail. I promise you that after today I won't steal no more.*

The man turn his head and said nothin. Mr. Gray fill the order and gave me the bags. I gave him the money that Miz Williams give me and bolt out the store. On my way back, I ate the meat and bread that was in my pocket, and thank God for the food, promisin him that I was gonna to be a good girl.

But the next time I went to Mr. Gray's store, I stole a bag of potato chips that was lyin on the counter. Mr. Gray seen me jus as I put the bag in my pocket. It was so big I couldn't git it all down in my pocket. Mr. Gray looked down at my pocket of potato chips, and I said the same prayer. He turn his head, like he didn't see nothin. I walk back to Miz Williams house feelin bad that I had stole from Mr. Gray again. I ate the potato chips, but I didn't enjoy dem this time even though they was fresh. I decid to pray to God again. I walk and prayed.

"Lawd, please help me not to steal anymore. I know that I is you child and I shouldn't be stealin. I know that those beans is what you made for us to eat. But I is tired of eatin beans. Lawd, please make a way so that I can git somethin else cept beans to eat. Thank you Lawd. Amen."

CHAPTER TWELVE

A cement road was bein builted on the street where Miz Williams house was. Every day I could hear the trucks a rollin and men shovelin. Every day, I would try my best to git to the front gate and watch dem. They was diggin, layin down something that look like little rocks. Then they would pour cement. One of the men would go to a different person's house each day and git buckets of water.

As the road progress, they got close to the front of Miz Williams' house. I was so happy when that happen 'cause that way I could see dem men working up close. I tried my best to git outside and watch dem. If I couldn't, then I would watch from the window.

One day, a tall, slender white man wit curly brown hair came to the house. He was the one that gits the water. He had jus open the gate and was headin toward the faucet in Miz Williams' yard. He had two buckets in his hand. I grab a rug that I was intendin to beat and head out the door with it. Jus as I is a comin out the door, the man saw me. He stop walkin and look at me like he ain't never seen a colored girl in his life. Eyes jus a starin up and down at me. I stood there wit the rug in my hand a lookin at the man wonderin what was wrong.

Finally he spoke. "You look like desperation."

I had never heard that word. "What is desperation, sir?"

"It means that you looks like you need some help."

"I don't need no help, sir. I can handle this here rug all by myself."

"Your folks must be awful poor, can't buy you no shoes or feed you, huh?"

I look down at my feet. I had jus cut the toe part out 'cause the shoes were gittin too small. I curl my toes up in shame.

"I is doin okay, sir."

The man shook his head and went toward the faucet. I laid the rug down on the ground and follow him. "Why you need all dem buckets of water sir?" This time I remember what Mama said about not lookin the white man in his face.

"I is the water boy. I gits the water for the men. A man can git mighty thirsty workin in the hot sun." He turn on the water and fill his buckets.

"You work here, little girl?"

"Yessir. And I been a livin here for a year now. When I came here, I was eleven; now I is twelve."

"Why you livin here? Where are your folks?"

"They lives in Demopolis."

"Your folks want you to stay here?"

"No sir. Miz Williams jus ain't sent me home yet."

The man finish fillin his bucket and turned off the faucet. "I got to git back now; tell your Miz that I said thank her for the water."

"Yessir, I'll tell her."

I watch him as he fade away into the crowd of men. Then I went on back in the house to git the rug beater. I could hear Miz Williams in the bathroom. It sound like she was throwin up. She was doin that a lot lately. When she git through, she came out the bathroom and told me to clean up the mess she had made. I gits a bucket and rag and went on in the bathroom. Most of the vomit was on the floor. I remember what the white man had said about me. Curiosity took over, and I look into the mirror at myself. My plump jaws had disappeared. Under my eyes was dark. I look like those old people that was tired all the time.

"That can't be me." I stare at myself. Finally I took myself away from the mirror and started cleanin up the vomit. As soon as I git through, Miz Williams calls me.

"Go to the store. Here is a list of things I want you to git." She handed me a list and the money to buy what she need.

When I gits to the store, Mr.Gray was workin behind the counter.

"Hi Mr. Gray. Remember me?"

"What in the hell happen to you gal? You been sick?"

"No sir?"

"You're as skinny as a stick. Lookin pitiful this time."

I look down at the floor, feelin sorry for myself. "Miz Williams wants you to fill this order for her." I hand him the list.

He read it and start gatherin up the things. He also slice up some bologna and put it on the counter. "You know, I don't see too well these days. My workers don't either. If somebody were to take something from me, I probably wouldn't see them take it."

I look at Mr. Gray, wonderin why he said that to me.

"If I were to turn my head, I wouldn't see if somebody was takin this here meat from me." He turn his head. I stood there waitin for him to finish the order. He turn back around. He took a few pieces of meat and hand dem to me.

"Thank you, Mr. Gray." I shove the meat in my mouth, smilin as I chew.

Mr. Gray went on back to gettin the order together. When it was ready he gave me the bag of things; I gave him the money, and ran out the store.

"Hope you feel better soon, Ruthie," he yelled.

"Thank you, sir."

Miz Williams felted sick in her stomach most of the time. So when she need something from the store, I was the one that had to go. I was happy to go to the store 'cause it got me away from her. I felted free. Also when I came to the store, Mr. Gray would leave potato chips or a soda or bologna on the counter for me to eat while he got Miz Williams' order together.

The man what gits the water usually went to a different house each time he need it. After that day that he seen me, he fancied Miz Williams house. He would come by, and if I was outside he would talk to me. He told me about his chillins. He told me about a rusty-colored dog he had that like to chase possums. He talk to me until his buckets was filled wit water. I stood there a listenin, soakin up every word. I start feelin comfortable around him and look forward to seein him.

One day Miz Williams told me to git the weeds out her flowerbed that was in the front yard. I was jus a pullin weeds when I hear a voice. I looks up from my job.

The man came over wit his buckets in his hands.

"Little girl, I been meanin to ask you name."

"My name Ruthie, sir."

"Well, I'm Mr. Oscar Collins."

"Please to meet you sir."

I gave my head a little nod as I spoke to him.

"Wanna see a picture of my family?"

"Yes sir."

I stood up. The man took out his wallet and hand me a picture of his family. My eyes get wide. He had a picture of a dark-skin woman wit a lot of little light-skin and dark-skinned chillins all around her.

"That my wife and all my younguns."

I couldn't answer him. My eyes were fix on the colored folks in the picture in disbelief. I had never heard of a white man marryin a colored woman.

"You think I is white, don't you girl?"

"You sure do look white." I lift up my head and look him straight in the face. His smile was wide. His eyes was gray. I stare at his eyes. I had never in my life seen a colored man wit gray eyes.

"Most people think I is white, but I is a colored man. It easier to git a job when folks think you white, especially at times like these." He wink at me. "Little girl, you looks like you ain't been treated right. Why don't you come home wit me? My wife would be glad to have another little girl livin wit us."

"I don't know, sir. Miz Williams might git mad."

"You think about it. We be finish wit this road in a little while. When we gits finish, I'll come here and take you home to my wife, if you want."

"Yes sir. I is gonna think about it sir."

He put his wallet back in his pocket and fill up the empty bucket.

I thought about what the man say, but I wasn't sure about leavin. I didn't know if his wife or chillins would like me or not.

Mr. Oscar came into the yard the next day. He was a swingin his buckets as he made his way to the faucet. Miz Williams was in her bedroom. She had told me that she was gonna be in there layin down for a hour or so. When I seen Mr. Oscar, I jus walk out the front door. He turn his head and look at me.

I put one of my feet over the other to hide my toes. I put my hands in my pockets. My head was bented down but I cast my eyes up at him. Mr. Oscar start talkin as he fill his buckets.

"You know I has a little girl 'bout the same age as you is." He told me about her, and when he was through he bid me farewell and said that he would be back tommora.

The next day came. I went outside as I spotted Mr. Oscar comin up the road wit his buckets swingin. I ran to the gate. He was whistlin a tune. He seemed to be in a very good mood. He passed by the other houses in the neighborhood to git to Miz Williams house. When he gits to the gate he smile at me. I had never noticed that Mr. Oscar had winkles in his forehead until he smiled that particular day.

"Hi little girl. Won't be long before we git through wit tis here road. Has you thought about what I was tellin you? I talked to my wife and she said that she wants you to come on home wit me. She said that she would be mighty proud to have another little girl livin wit us." He open the gate and walk in the yard.

"I wanna go sir. I won't be no trouble. I promise." I had a rag in my hand for I was dustin Miz Williams' lamp before I came outside. I was a twistin the rag wit both of my hands.

"Good. I is gonna be comin back here to git you as soon as we is finish this last stretch of road, jus up yonder." He start walkin toward the faucet. I walk behind him. This time my feet felted light. I wanted to shout "yahoo!" Instead, I jus smile from ear to ear. Mr. Oscar started whistlin again. Neither one of us seen Miz Williams come out the house.

"Why are you comin all the way down here to git water?" Miz Williams sound agitated.

"Jus like talkin to this little girl here, ma'am."

"Well I don't want you talkin to my niggard." Miz Williams stomp off the porch and went straight up to the man. "I heard you tell my niggard that you were a niggard too. I heard you ask her to go home with you. You ain't takin her nowhere. Furthermore, I have a mind to tell your boss that you are a niggard."

Mr. Oscar stood there wit his mouth gaped open and his eyebrows raised . He tried to say something, but no words come out.

"You won't have a job. Then how your gonna feed you niggard family?"

Mr. Oscar skin color turne red. Beads of sweat started comin down his face. He looked scared.

"Now take those buckets and git out of here!" she screamed. "I better not see you in my yard again." She pointed to the gate, and Mr. Oscar rush out like the Devil hisself was on his tracks. Down the street he flew like lightnin.

Miz Williams turn and look at me. She grab me by my left ear and pull me back into the house. When she git me inside she lead me back to the kitchen still holdin on to my ear. Once we was in the kitchen she let go and push me toward the kitchen table. I fell on the floor. She stood over me and shook her finger in my face.

"You didn't know that I had been watchin you, did you? I better not ever see you talkin to anybody again ... you hear me...?" She bented close to my face and scream so loud I thought my ears would bust.

I laid there, lips tremblin, afraid to cry.

"You didn't even see me when I pulled back the curtains, did you? I heard everythin he said. He don't wanna take you home! You know what he wanna do? He'll take little dumb girls like you, rape and kill them. Nobody gonna care 'cause you jus a little niggard. Do you want that to happen to you ... Huh!"

"No ma'am." I said shudderin. Miz Williams stood up straight.and took a deep breath. She raise her arms up then let dem drop by her side.

"I don't know what's wrong wit you, Ruthie. I treat you good. Maybe I need to give you more work. Keep you busy all the time." She sounded calmer.

She left me on the kitchen floor and was gone for a few minutes. Tears started rollin down my cheeks. I laid there whimperin. Miz Williams came back into the kitchen. I felted her foot push me in the back. "Git up and stop your cryin. You got clothes to wash."

I wipe my eyes and look at her. She had a load of clothes in her arms. "Those is the same clothes I jus wash yesterday, Miz Williams. Those is clean."

"Wash them again."

"Yesum." I got off the floor and set my tubs up for washin. I had to scrub those clothes like I had never wash dem. Miz Williams watch me. From that day on, Miz Williams tried to keep me in her sight.

After a few days, Miz Williams sent me outside. I was jus a sweepin the porch when I hear Mr. Oscar. I drop the broom and ran in the house like I had seen a ghost. I was afraid of him because of what Miz Williams say.

CHAPTER THIRTEEN

It was October again. My birthday was comin up in a few weeks. It had been a year and one month since I left my home, and I thought I would ask Miz Williams about me goin home again. She was sittin in the sittin room one evenin listening to President Roosevelt fireside chat on the radio. She seem to be in a good mood. She was a smilin as she sat in one of the chairs wit her legs cross. She kept swingin one leg up and down as she listen to the President's speech.

The President's words was, "Some banks could not be saved, but the great majority of them, either through their own resouces or with government aid have been restored to complete public confidence."

The baby must have moved 'cause she rub her swollen stomach, and chuckle and spoke to it. "You like the speech too, don't you?"

I want to ask her again about leavin, so I sat on the floor outside the door until she was finish listenin to the radio. When the speech was over she got up and turn it off. I got up too and stood in the doorway. Her eye caught me watchin her.

"What you want, Ruthie?"

"I thought that I can go home now, seein that it been over a year now, ma'am."

I kept my head down lookin at the floor as I talk to her.

"I didn't hear you. Speak up girl."

"I wanna go home Miz Williams." I raise my voice a little higher. I wanted to cry, but I held back the tears. "After the baby comes, I'll let you go home."

"Well, can I write my mama? Its almost my birthday again. I ain't got no letter from her in a while." Just thinking bout it made my eyes fill wit tears. Miz Williams studied me for a moment, then sigh.

"All right. Let me git you some paper and a pencil. It seems to me that she don't want you there since she hasn't written you. Maybe 'cause you're not her own child."

Miz Williams push herself out the chair and left the room. My heart sank. Would Mama have come for me if I was her real child? Did Mama not want me to come back? Miz Williams came back in the room wit the items and gave dem to me. I went out to the porch to write. It was gettin dark, so Miz Williams turn the light on in the kitchen so I could see. "Ruthie, when you git through writin, you turn off this here light and close the door. You hear?" She raise one eye as she look at me.

"Yesum." I nodded.

When she left, I laid down by the door that separate the kitchen from the porch, and put the paper in front of me on the floor.

Dear Mama,

I know that I is not your child. But you raise me and I love you. Please Mama, can you and Papa come git me? I miss you so bad. Miz Williams don treat me so good now that I am here. I don git nothin to eat but beans all day long. Please Mama come git me.

Your loving daughter Ruthie

After I seal the letter up and put the address on it, I spread my blanket on the floor and put the letter by where I was gonna lay my head. I change into my gown wit the little white and blue flowers. It got a hole in it by the right arm, and I needed a needle and some thread to fix it. I wonder if Miz Williams would let me have some in the mornin. I git on my knees and say my prayer.

"Dear Lawd. Please make Mama write me. Lawd, I wanna go home. I don't wanna stay here no more. Please make Mama and Papa come git me. I will praise you forever Lawd. In Jesus name I pray. Amen.

I remember the kitchen light. I went over and turn it off, then I went back to the porch, laid down on the blanket, and wrap one side of it around me.

"I know my mama and papa gonna come for me," I kept thinkin until I fell to sleep. I was waken up by a hand shakin me.

"Ruthie, git up. It's mornin."

I blink and rub my eyes.

"Where is that letter you wrote?"

"Right here, ma'am."

I reach under my head and took the letter from under it.

"Give it here. I'll mail it for you today." Miz Williams took the letter and put it into her dress pocket. "Git on up. I need you to sweep the front porch."

When Miz Williams left, Susie came on the porch where I was. She sat on the the floor. I yawn and reach for my comb. I notice that it only had a few teeth in it. When I comb my hair, the last few teeth fell out.

"I guess I better start usin my fingers."

"You can use my comb, Ruthie."

"I don think I better. You Mama might git mad."

"Then what you gonna do? You can't comb you hair forever with you fingers."

"My mama and papa gonna come and git me. They gonna buy me a comb when they come."

"When you leavin?"

"As soon as my folks gits my letter, they gonna come a runnin."

Susie watch me struggle, tryin to comb my hair wit my fingers.

"You certainly got a lot of hair. It's really thick."

"I got hair like my mama. Hers is real long and thick." I stop tuggin at my hair and look at Susie. I hear the pride in my own voice.

"Naw, you don't. Your mama's hair is short."

"That ain't my real mama. That my aunt that raise me, that got the short hair."

"Why your real mama didn't raise you? She didn't want you or somethin?"

When Susie said that I thought about my real mama and the day I last saw her. I thought about how she didn't wanna look at me or talk to me. I thought about the hurt I felted inside. It had been years, but the pain was still there.

"I don't know why she didn't want to raise me, and I don't miss her." I tried to sound like I didn't care.

"I would feel bad if my real mama didn't want me. Real bad."

"Well I don't. I have my Aunt Flo. Maybe she jus might come git me before my birthday."

"How old you gonna be this time?"

"Thirteen."

"I know how you can git a new comb."

"How?"

"A birthday party." Susie's face lit up like a Christmas tree. "You git presents if you have a birthday party, jus like me. Somebody might give you a comb."

"Ain't nobody gonna give me a birthday party, Susie." I look away from her. I felted like a wounded animal layin on the side of a road wit people passin by not botherin to help.

I would be lucky if Miz Williams put some scraps of meat in my beans. I went back to tugging at my hair.

"My mama might, if you ask her."

I pick up a piece of string that I had laid beside me and tie up my hair wit it. "I hope you mama buy me a comb."

"I'll ask her for you, Ruthie, if you like."

"Naw. I is gonna ask her."

We heard Miz Williams stirrin in the kitchen. Susie got up from where she was sittin and went inside. I took off my gown and put on my dress and went in the kitchen too. They was Miz Williams dress in a light brown dress wit white stripes. The dress hung loose off of her to allow room for her growin stomach. I stare at the dress; this was the first time I ever seen her in any other color except white.

"Why you lookin at my stomach like that?"

"I was lookin at you purty dress, ma'am. Ain't never seen such a nice dress."

She jus look at me.

"Can I have a piece of soap for my hand washin, ma'am?"

Instead of answering, Miz Williams went over by the stove and got a broom. "First you take this here broom, go outside, and sweep the porch like I told you." she said.

When I was through sweeping the porch, I came back inside and put the broom back in a corner where Miz Williams had took it from. She hand me a bar of soap.

"Here. Wash your hands. I need you to help me slice this bacon when you are through."

I went to the front door wit the soap, walk around to where the faucet was and turn it on. I wash my hands and face, but I didn't have a towel to dry dem wit. So I use the front of my dress.

Susie was in the kitchen talkin to her mother when I return. She look at me and smile, then started talkin to her again. I went over to the table, pick up the long butcher knife that Miz Williams had put on it.

"Mama, I think Ruthie is gonna have a birthday soon. Ain't that right, Ruthie?"

"Yesum. Gonna be thirteen soon."

"I thought that you was gonna be twelve." Miz Williams said as she handed me the slab of bacon.

"No ma'am. I been here almost a year and a few months. I turn twelve that same year you move here in October. It almost October again, so I is gonna be thirteen."

I slice the meat in long even slices.

"Well, I have just got to do somethin different for you on your birthday." She pick up the long slices of sweet smellin meat and put dem in the fryin pan.

I stood in the kitchen smellin the bacon cookin wit my mouth waterin. I stared at the skillet.

"Ruthie, Ruthie!"

I didn't hear Miz Williams callin me.

"You gone deaf or somethin? I've been callin you, and you are just standin there with a stupid look on your face."

"I is jus thinkin bout my birthday."

"Well, you can stop thinkin about it right now. Go git your beans, so that I can warm them up."

I went to the icebox, got the navy beans, and handed dem to her. She took a cupful out, put dem in a pot, and started the fire under dem.

"Why are you jus standin there watchin me like that?"

"I was wonderin ma'am...if on my birthday, if you can buy me a new comb? The one I got has all the teeth broke out." I said hopefully.

"I'll do somethin better than that. Now come on and eat."

Susie and I look at each other and smile. Maybe Miz Williams was gonna give me a cake for my birthday and maybe even a new comb. Or maybe Miz Williams had change her mind and was gonna send me home for my birthday. I couldn't wait.

One week pass. Every day Miz Williams would go out and git the mail, and I would look at her hopin for a letter when she return. But no letter came for me. The next week came and still no letter. By the time my birthday arrive, I was sick at heart.

Miz Williams came on the porch that mornin to wake me up. But I is already woke and starin at the ceilin.

"Mornin Ruthie. Git on up so you can start your day."

"Yesum."

She left the porch and went in the kitchen. I put on my clothes and wash up as usual. I took my time about washin up. When I git back inside, the family was already eatin. They ate pancakes and sausages. Miz Williams had warm me up some more navy beans. I took my plate out to the porch, but I could hear Mr. Williams and Miz Williams talkin.

"Why do you have to leave so early again?" I heard her ask him.

"It's my job. You know that."

"But every day you have to leave earlier and earlier."

I didn't wanna hear what they were sayin. So I hurried and ate my beans then put my hands over my ears. I was about to go outside to wash the plate, when I seen Susie at the kitchen table lookin sad. Her mama and papa had left the kitchen and were standin by the front door talkin.

"You're a mean woman. I never realized that before."

Both of dem turn and saw me comin. Mr. Williams went on out the door, leavin Miz Williams standin there. I went out the door behind him. He went out to the front gate and down the road. When I git back in the house wit my clean plate, Miz Williams announce that she was goin to the store.

"You wash these here dishes, Ruthie. When I come back, I am gonna have somethin nice for your birthday."

My spirits started climbin when Miz Williams left. Susie and I started cleanin up the kitchen. I didn't ask Susie why she was looking sad.

"You think she is gonna git me a comb?"

"I hope she will. Maybe she'll buy you a birthday cake too with ice cream."

"I sho nuff would like me some cake and ice cream. I could jus taste it."

We finish the dishes, wipe down the table, and put everythang away. I went in Miz Williams room, and start makin up her bed wit Susie's help. I hear Miz Williams come in the house. Susie and I finish what we was doin and went to the sittin room. There she was with two small bags. Miz Williams smile at me while swingin the bags in her hand.

"These are for you, Ruthie. I'm gonna give them to you after you finish your work."

"Yes ma'am," I said, wit glee.

I had to wash clothes again. When I hung up the last few pieces, Miz Williams call me in the kitchen.

"Sit, Ruthie. I brought somethin that I know you need."

I jus knew that it was my comb. I started feelin excited inside.

"Thank you, Miz Williams. I know I really need this."

"Yes, you do. Now open it." Miz Williams stood there grinnin at me.

I open the bag. It was black wit yellow flowers on it. I pull out a scarf. My heart sunk.

"Like it? Now you got somethin to cover that nappy head of yours."

"Yesum, but I don't know how to tie it on."

"Didn't your mama show you anythin? Just wrap the thing around your head; make sure all that nappy hair is in it. Then tie it up."

"Yes ma'am."

I put the scarf on and tie it around my head.

"Now ain't that better? You don't have to worry about combing your hair anymore. I should have thought of it months ago."

There I was, lookin like one of those colored folks back in slavery times. It was a look that seem to please Miz Williams. She kepted grinnin at me. I went on back to washin the clothes. When they was dry, Susie came to the backyard wit a friend. The girl that was wit her looked at me wit that rag tied around my head and bust out laughin.

Susie look at me all puzzled. "Why you have that scarf on your head?"

"Your mama gave it to me for a birthday present."

"It's ugly."

"Come on, Susie, let's go." Susie's friend start runnin toward the front yard, and Susie follow.

I was glad when they left. Tears roll down my face. "Lawd, I ain't gonna cry. Help me to smile, Lawd, and give me strength," I kept prayin over and over.

Finally, it was time for supper. I wash my hands and went on in the kitchen to git my navy beans for Miz Williams to heat up. Miz Williams stop me.

"Don't git those beans out, Ruthie. I have somethin else for you to eat."

"Yesum?" I wonder what she could have for me. I hope that I would at least git a real dinner and maybe even a cupcake. My mouth start waterin. They was havin roast beef, mashed potatoes, peas, and rolls.

"Git your plate, Ruthie, so I can give you your surprise."

I hurried and got my plate. She was standin by the stove. She reach out for my plate and I handed it to her. She fill it. The white mess laid there curled in half moon shapes. My mouth gaped. It was butter beans, and I hated them. The look on my face amused Miz Williams. She laugh so hard that her stomach shooked.

"Happy birthday, Ruthie. I thought you needed a change."

I took my usual piece of cornbread and went on back to the porch wit my head down. Sittin down on the floor wit my spoon in hand, I pray again. "Lawd, help me to be thankful for what I given." I took a spoonful, and shove it in my mouth. I imagine the beans was ice cream and the cornbread was cake. I pretend that I was at home wit Mama and Papa. Mama would have made me somethin special like a real purty dress. Blue and white wit ruffles and lace. Mama would give me a hug. I smile at the thought, and sung to myself softly.

"Happy birthday to me, Happy birthday to me, Happy birthday...dear Ruthie...Happy birthday to me."

CHAPTER FOURTEEN

Miz Williams kept me busy everyday cleanin the house and washin clothes. She didn't give me no free time. When I was through washin dirty clothes she would go into her drawers and pull out clean ones to wash over again. The only time that Susie and I could have any time together is when I had to clean Susie's room.

Those times, Susie would tell me about places she and her other friends went. She told me about what they saw, heard, or tasted—like special ice creams. I never got a chance to play or talk to no other chillins except Susie.

Sometimes Miz Williams would come in to Susie room and stand around givin orders until I was through cleaning it. When she did that, Susie would leave. I hated bein left alone wit Miz Williams starin at me at every turn.

One day, I was outside hangin up some clothes, and I seen another colored girl in the yard next door doing the same thing. I drop what I doing and ran up to the fence. "Hi!" I shouted.

She look up and saw me standin here smilin from ear to ear. "My Lord, you is gonna wake the dead," she said. "I can hear you. You don't have to shout."

"I is sorry. It's jus that I don't see any color folk around these here parts. You is the first one I've seem in a long time."

The girl was taller than me and look older than me too. She was brown-skin wit short hair—she eye me like somethin was wrong wit me.

"How old is you?"

"I is thirteen."

"Girl, you is as thin as a rail pole. You must don't eat."

"Miz Williams feed me beans. That's all she give me."

"Don't you go home in the evenin to you folks? I know you eat there."

"Naw. I ain't seem my folks in more than a year."

"Why?"

"Miz Williams here ask my mama to let me come work for her for two weeks so that I could help her straighten out her house. She promise mama she would send me back home after two weeks wit a lot of money. Well, the house is straighten up; she ain't paid me and she ain't done send me home."

"Do you ever hear from your ma?"

"Naw. I wrote her a three letters askin her to come git me. She wrote back tellin me to have a good time; she miss me; and do what Miz Williams say. One time Miz Williams made me write her a letter askin her if I could stay a little longer."

I look over at the window of Miz Williams house to see if she was watchin me.

"What you lookin for?" The girl asked.

"I's lookin for Miz Williams; she always watch me like she has nothin else to do." I turn my head back to face the girl. "Well anyway, Mama send me back a letter sayin that I could stay for another two weeks. It seem like I is gonna be here forever." I drop my head. Tears fill my eyes. "I wanna go home. I Miss my mama and papa!"

"Maybe she' ll send you home if you ask her again?"

"I ask her agin and agin. This time, she says 'after the baby comes.' I hope she send me, 'cause I don't wanna stay here no more."

"Why don't you write you mama again? She'll come git you."

"She won't let me write no more."

"What you mean? She won't let you write a letter to you folks?"

"Miz Williams say I can't keep usin her stamps and paper. She say my mama should write me. But Mama don write me."

"Does you Miz Williams treat you poorly? The reason I is askin is 'cause you don't look too healthy. In fact, you look kind of bad."

"Well, she jus make me work and feed me beans and corn bread every day. Sometime I won't eat but a spoonful; I is so tired of beans. Miz Williams said niggards only suppose to eat beans. Now look at me; I's as skinny as a rattlesnake.

Jus then Susie came a runnin from the house.

"Ruthie, Mama gone to town and you know what that means."

"Yesum. We can eat now!" Susie and I started runnin toward the house, and I was almost to the front door when I remember my manners. I turned back around.

"Where you goin, Ruthie?" Susie asked.

"I jus remember my manners." I ran back to the fence and Susie follow. The girl was still standin there. "I is sorry. I forgit to tell you my name. My name Ruthie. What's yours?"

"Betty Ann."

"Please to meet you, Betty Ann. I's goin now; I hope I git a chance to talk to you again."

Susie and I dash into the house and went straight to the icebox. We pulls out the meat loaf, potatoes, and stringbeans that Miz Williams had made the night before. Susie wanted me to heat dem up, but I was starvin for something other than beans. I told her I was gonna eat dem cold. "Ain't got no time to warm dem up, Susie."

I slice a piece of the meatloaf and ate it fast, jus like a hungry dog, not even bothering to chew very well. Susie passed me a handful of cold potatoes, and I ate dem as fast as I did the meat. I took a spoonful of string beans and ate dem a little slower, savorin the taste, rememberin the string beans Aunt Flo use to make. When I was through eatin, Susie and I put the rest of the food back in the icebox. I start laughin.

"Why is you laughin?" Susie look at me real strange-like.

"'Cause I is so happy."

"Guess what, Ruthie? Mama gonna give me a birthday party. There will be lots of cake and ice cream, and I am gonna save some for you."

"I ain't had me no ice cream in a long time. I is gonna be glad when you birthday party comes." We both gits up and go back outside. When I git back to the fence, Betty Ann was gone, so I went back to hangin out clothes, and Susie went back to playin wit her friends.

When the day of Susie party came, Miz Williams brought plenty of ice cream and cake. The party was held outside in the front yard. I had help Miz Williams set up a table and decorate it for the party. When the chillins arrive, Miz Williams told me to go in the house. I sat on the sofa in the sittin room, but every once in a while I would git up and look out at the chillins laughin. I pray that Susie would remember and save me some ice cream and cake.

When the party was over and everyone had gone home, Miz Williams told me to come outside and help her clean up. When I gits out the door, I see Miz Williams and Susie talkin. Susie had a slice of cake on a plate in her hands.

"But I promise her, Mama. Why she can't have any?"

"Because I said so." Miz Williams snatch the cake out Susie hand.

Susie started whimperin, puttin her hands over her eyes when Miz Williams threw the cake in the garbage can. She start gatherin up the plates and throwin the scraps of food in the garbage can too. Miz Williams had told me to help her, but it seem like she was doin all the work. I look at Susie.

"Happy birthday, Susie."

"I am sorry, Ruthie," Susie cried. Tears was runnin down her face as she ran into the house.

Miz Williams didn't seem to care that Susie was cryin. She jus kepted doin what she was doin. She had me take the tablecloth off the table and clean up the scraps that was on the ground. When she left me in the yard and went in the house, I had hopes that she would come back wit a piece of cake. But she didn't.

The next day I was given a pile of clothes to wash again—the same clothes I had wash the day before. When Miz Williams went inside, Betty Ann came out the lady's house next door. She had somethin in her hand. I left what I was doing when I seen her comin.

"Hi Ruthie. Guess what I got?" She helded up her hand.

"It looks like cookies, Betty Ann."

I step closer to the fence, hopin she would give me one.

"It sure is. You can have all of these here cookies."

I grab the cookies from her hand, thankin her and thankin her.

"The lady I works for—Miz Brooks—she baked dem. She say I could have some and give you as many as you want, so I took a handful for you."

"That was really nice of you and Miz Brooks." I bit off a piece of the chocolate chip cookie, and begin to chew it. "Thank you for thinkin about me."

"You welcome. Miz Brooks said I could come over and talk to you sometimes."

"Git away from my fence!" Miz Williams scream at Betty Ann. Both our mouths gape open. Miz Williams hurried up to the fence and look at Betty Ann. "Git away from my fence I said, niggard!"

Betty Ann ran back to Miz Brook's house like a bolt of lightenin had hit her.

Miz Williams' eyes narrow at the cookies in my hand.

"Where did you git those cookies!"

I was shakin all over. My mouth tremblin. I didn't answer her.

"I know where. Give me the rest of them."

I hand dem to her, and she went straight to Miz Brook's house. She knock on the door and Miz Brooks open it. Miz Williams didn't give Miz Brooks a chance to say a word before she holler out "Don't you ever send my niggard nothin.... you hear me! I don't want your niggard talkin to my niggard ever again!"

Wit those words, Miz Williams threw the cookies on Miz Brook's porch, turned, and hurry back to her own house. Miz Brooks slam her door.

Then she told me to hurry up and hang up those clothes and come in the house when I is done. When I was done, I went into the house, scared of what she be doin next, but Miz Williams was actin like nothin happen. She jus a sittin in a chair rubbin her stomach and hummin.

After that day, Miz Williams never left me alone outside when she knew that Betty Ann was at work at Miz Brooks' house. And one day Susie told me that her mama had made it clear to all the neighbors that no one was to talk to me or ask me to do anythin for dem. Susie felted sorry for me and wonder why her mama said that. I jus hung my head down and hump my shoulders.

CHAPTER FIFTEEN

Months passed. Then early one morning, Mr. Williams came on the porch and woke me out of a sound sleep. "Ruthie, git up! Miz Williams is havin the baby! You got to take care of Susie while I go to the hospital with my wife. I'm goin to find somebody with a car."

I sat up, blinkin and rubbin my eyes. Mr. Williams hurried back inside, through the sittin room and out the front door. He start out the door in his white with blue stripe sleepers. He didn't have no shoes on. He came back through the door. By this time I was standin in the sittin room.

"Forgot my shoes." He smile sheepishly at me.

He ran back to his room and came out wearin one black shoe and one brown one. He still had on his sleepers. He left the house and hurried toward the gate. He open it. Then he turn around and came back to the house.

"Got to put on some pants."

I snicker under my breath at him. He went back to his room. In a minute, he came back out wearin a pair of blue pants, but he hadn't zip dem up.

"Mr. Williams, your..."

He was out the door before I could tell him.

Susie came out her room rubbin her eyes, and seen me standin in the sittin room. "What's the matter, Ruthie? Why you jus standin here?"

"I was watchin you papa."

"Why?"

"You mama havin her baby. He went to git help or somethin."

"Mama havin the baby!" Susie ran to her mama's room, and I follow her. Miz Williams was fully dressed and lyin on the bed. Beads of sweat was on her brow. She was moanin in pain. She on her side wit her legs fold up in front of her. Her hands was around her stomach and her hair was uncombed .

Susie peer at her. "Mama are you gonna be all right. Are you gonna have the baby right now? Do you want me to git you some asprin?"

"No Susie. I'm alright."

Miz Williams stopp moanin and unfold her legs. Wit one hand still on her stomach she moved to the side of the bed and ease off it. She stood up, took her hand off her stomach. She went over to the dresser.

"I got to finish gittin my things before the next one comes."

"What next one, Mama?"

"The next contraction. Git that suitcase for me, Ruthie. The one that's by the bed."

I gits the suitcase, but I didn't know what to do wit it.

"Put it on the bed and open it!"

"Yesum." It had one gown in it, a pair of house shoes, one comb and a few personal items.

Miz Williams reach in a drawer, pulls out another gown and hand it to Susie. "Put this in my suitcase, Susie."

Susie brought the gown over and laid it in the case. Miz Williams put both of her hands on top of the dresser, close her eyes and moan again, louder than before. She be tremblin. The next thing I seen, water was comin down her leg. It ran down in her shoes and onto the floor. Miz Williams body relaxed and she looked down at herself.

"Mama. You jus pee on yourself!"

"My water jus broke, silly. On my, what a mess. Ruthie, go git the mop and clean this mess up."

As soon as I ran into the kitchen, Mr. Williams and another white man bust into the house. Mr. Williams wasn't in the bedroom wit his wife but a second when he call out to me.

"Ruthie, bring me a towel."

I drop the mop and bucket and went around to the bathroom where I founded a pink towel to bring him. "Here you towel, sir."

Each one of the men had hold of one of Miz Williams arms, supportin her.

"Give it to Miz Williams."

"I ain't gonna carry that! You take it for me."

"Put the towel between your legs so if there's more water, you won't wet Jeff's car."

"I ain't gonna wet Jeff's car."

"Right now the bottom half of you is wet, and water is still a comin down," Jeff said.

"All right. I will put the towel under me when we git in the car. Benny Roy, you hold it for me until then."

I gave the towel to Mr. Williams.

"Git the suitcase, Ruthie, and bring it to...Oh they're comin again!" Miz Williams moan again, even louder. I picks up the suitcase. The men wait until the contraction was over before they help her out. Water was still tricklin down her legs. When they got her to the car, Mr. Williams spread out the towel on the seat, and Miz Williams sat on it. Mr. Williams sat down beside her in the back seat. I hand him the suitcase. He look at me. "Ruthie, make sure you feed Susie."

"I will sir."

Susie walked in front of me and peeped into the car at her Mama. While they was saying goodbye, Jeff got in behind the wheel and start the car. Susie and I watched as the car disappeared down the road. When they were out of sight, I went straight to the icebox and pulled out the bacon, eggs, bread jelly.

"What are you're doing?" Susie ask. "It's too early to eat breakfast."

I danced around the kitchen singin as I started cookin. When I was through, Susie and me sat down and ate. I ate like a pig. I put ten slices of bacon on my plate and almost all the scrambled eggs. I don know how many pieces of bread I ate. When I was through I felted sick in my stomach. I started talkin to my stomach, tellin it that if it didn't make me throw up, I promise that I would give it something else good on the next meal. I didn't throw up.

After breakfast, Susie and me wash the dishes and put dem back in the cabinet. We played with a few of Susie's games after that. Later, we went outside and play hide and seek in the backyard. We took turns swingin on the swing. When we were through swingin we went back inside, open the ice box and finish a whole carton of ice cream. I lick the cardboard.

For lunch we had fried chicken with mash potatoes and peas, and I ate without gettin sick. By supper time, we didn't wanna eat regular supper food. So we decide to polish off the apple pie that was left in the icebox. Mr. Williams didn't come home until later that evening. He founded us on the back porch where I slept.

"Hi Susie, Ruthie."

Susie went up to her papa. He look down at her.

"You mama had a boy."

"Yea!" Susie shout and jump around. "What he looks like, Papa?"

"Jus like you when you were born. Except his feet are bigger. I guess he's gonna be tall."

"I can't wait until Mama gits home so I can see him."

"Well she is gonna to be in the hospital for a couple of weeks."

A sad expression came over Susie's face, but a smile came over mine. "Good." I thought. Then I remember she say that when she git back she gonna send me home. My heart leaped for joy.

"Did you girls eat?"

"Yes sir," I sing out.

"Good. Ruthie, you use the bathroom in the house instead of my garage. I need to work in there, and I don't want you in there while I'm workin."

"Yes sir."

He didn't know how happy I was. I went to the bathroom and sat on the toilet even when I didn't have to use it. This was better than the garage and doing number two in paper bags. I even got to take a bath in the bathtub and wash my nappy hair, as Miz Williams call it, in the bathroom sink. I wonder what she would say if she knew I had done that. That night I didn't sleep too well; my stomach hurt from all the food.

The next day when Mr. Williams and Susie git up, I fix breakfast. I didn't eat as much as the previous day. Mr. Williams eat in a hurry. He told Susie and me that he had to leave even earlier because he had to stop by the hospital before he went to work.

"Ruthie, I want you to take care of Susie. She's only eight and might git into trouble if a grown up is not here."

"I will, sir."

"Ruthie ain't grown, Papa."

"I know, but she is in charge since she will be the oldest one left in the house. Ruthie, be sure to cook. I want you gals to eat food and not junk while Miz Williams I are away."

Since anything seem possible right then, I ask him if I could go outside and talk to the girl next door.

"Why you askin me somethin like that? You can talk to anyone you want." He looked at me real puzzle-like.

I wasn't about to tell him that Miz Williams didn't want me to talk to no one.

Mr. Williams kiss Susie on her jaw, put on a sweater, and went on his way. I began to think about my mama and wonder why she hadn't wrote me.

Well, in a few weeks I will be headed home, I said to myself. I couldn't wait to see my mama.

After Mr. Williams left I put on a old sweater that Miz Williams had given me, and Susie put on a purty pink one. It was a little chilly that February morning, but we both wanted to jump rope outside. While we was jumpin rope I spot Betty Ann comin out the next door neighbor's house wit a bag of trash. I stop jumpin rope and call out to her. "Hey Betty Ann, have Miz Brooks baked some more cookies?" I was grinnin from ear to ear.

Betty Ann drop the bag on the ground. "Hi Ruthie. Is you all right? You better not let your missus see you talkin to me. You is in the line of fire, babysittin her child out here and trying to talk to me."

"She ain't here, Betty Ann. Miz Williams in the hospital. She jus had a baby."

Susie heard me say her mama's name; she stop jumpin rope and join me at the fence. "I got a little brother now." Susie smile proud-like.

"Now you can't play as much. Now you got to share everythin. You got to change stinky diapers, and one day that baby is gonna spit up on you." Betty Ann stood there wit her hands on her hips peerin down on Susie.

"No, he won't. My mama is gonna have someone else change the baby's diapers and take care of him. I am going to be havin fun. So there." Susie licked out her tongue at Betty Ann.

Jus at that moment, a friend of Susie's came in the back yard and asked Susie if she could come over to her house and play. Susie said yes and promise she would be back for supper.

Betty Ann and me watch the two girls walk hand in hand out the back yard.

"How old is Susie, Ruthie?"

"This year she turned eight."

"Boy, I is glad she's gone to play. Now I can talk to you in private."

"What you wanna talk about, Betty Ann?"

"Well, since you Miz Williams is gone, you can leave and go back home where you belong."

"I can't do that. I ain't got no money and I can't leave Susie here by herself. She too young."

"She eight, Ruthie. Beside you can leave her wit these here white folks. They will take care of her."

"I don't know. Miz Williams has been gone for a few days now and nobody has shown up yet to even ask about her. Mr. Williams has to work all the time. He trusts me to take good care of his little girl. I can't disappoint him."

"I could bring her over to Miz Brook's house. She would take good care of Susie. Miz Brook is real nice."

"I don't wanna do that, Betty Ann."

"You know what? You missie has made a slave out of you, Ruthie. You even think like one."

"No, I don't. Miz Williams said she gonna pay me as soon as she gits home from the hospital wit her baby. She say she gonna send me home to my folks. I know she ain't tellin me no lie this time. Besides, Miz Williams said that if I ever run away she would hide all her jewery and then tell the police I stole it. I don't wanna go to jail. I is gonna wait until she comes back wit the baby. I hope she keep her promise this time."

Betty Ann sighed. "Have you heard from your folks yet?"

I hesitated. "Naw."

Betty Ann was quiet for a few moments. Her voice soften. "If you folks come git you, then she won't be a tellin the police dem lies. You know what, Ruthie, I believe that you Miz Williams must have written somethin that's a keepin you folks from writin you. Or somethin must have happen. I don't know what it could be. I jus can't put my finger on it, but somethin is wrong."

"I hope that Miz Williams didn't write anythin bad about me, Betty Ann. But if she did, Mama wouldn't believe her. Do you think that Miz Williams would really do a thing like that?"

"I don't know what you Miz Williams is capable of. After all, she told Miz Brooks off and Miz Brooks was jus tryin to give you a few of her cookies. Look at you. I know that you wasn't that skinny before you git here. It ain't like they ain't got no food. The nerve of dem, jus feedin you beans. You look like a walkin skeleton. Like desperation."

I rub one of my arms. "That what Mr. Oscar call me. I know I is skinny, but I eats now. Mr. Williams said for me to eat anythin I want."

"Not for long. Your missus will be comin home purty soon, and you gonna be back to eatin jus beans."

"But she promise that she gonna send me home." I felted a heaviness swellin inside me. Anyway, who gonna give me the money to go, beside Miz Williams?"

"I have a little, and I is sure that I can git some more from my folks if I tell dem that you need it to leave, Ruthie. I told dem about how you missus won't let you talk to nobody and how she won't feed you nothin but beans. You think about it, Ruthie. Right now, you can git free." I jus look at her.

"Well, let me git on back to my work." Betty Ann turn back toward the bag she had left on the ground. My mind kept goin back to what she had said. I wonder if Miz Williams had written somethin to my folks. I thought about it for a while. If she did, I couldn't figure out what she might have said that would stop dem from writin.

Maybe Mama lost the address. I knew how Mama sometime loses things. Anyway, I would be goin home soon. Mama and I could talk about it after I git there.

I walk over to the swing and sat on it. I had been out there lots of times, but I never got the chance to swing. Feeling the cool air rushin again my face, I felted free. I wished it was spring so I could smell the grass and flowers that usually grow in Miz Williams yard. But it was winter in Alabama. I had been among those flowers every day in the spring and summer, and never got the chance to enjoy they beauty or smell they sweetness.

CHAPTER SIXTEEN

T he sky was cast over that day in February of 1935, lettin us know that it was gonna rain. It had been two weeks since Miz Williams had the baby. When Mr. Williams came to wake me up, I was already woke. I was lying on my stomach wit my arms fold in front of me, my chin restin on top of dem. I stare at the floor in front of me. Mr. Williams knock on the door.

"Ruthie. Wake up."

"I is already woke, sir."

He open the door. I gits up off my folded arms and turn around to look at him standin there barefooted in his brown and white pajamas. "Miz Williams is comin home today. I want you to clean the bedroom up for her and the baby. It's gonna be a little while before I go git her. Right now it's only seven. I think the hospital is gonna let her go at twelve o'clock. You go ahead and fix breakfast first. I'm really hungry today."

"Yesum, Mr. Williams."

He left the porch and I got up.

"I is goin home soon now." I thought. "Maybe she let me go this here week." I felted happy inside thinkin about home, and started hummin a song about it as I cook. Susie sniff her way into the kitchen. "Sure smells good Ruthie. I is so happy. Did you know that my mama was comin home today?"

"Yeah, I know, Susie. Your papa told me." Susie took a seat. Mr. Williams came in the kitchen all dressed for the day. He took a seat at the table too.

We all sat down to a breakfast of grits and sausage. I toasted some bread and made Mr. Williams a small pot of coffee.

"I can't wait to git your Mama, Susie. You help Ruthie out wit the house cleanin."

"Yes, Papa. Ruthie and me is gonna clean real good. Right Ruthie?"

"Yesum. We sno nuff is."

When breakfast over, Mr. Williams say he gonna try to find somebody to take him to the hospital. "When I come back I am gonna have my family back together again."

Susie and me was washin the dishes when I spot Betty Ann from the window.

"Susie, You stay in the house. I wanna talk to Betty Ann for a minute."

Betty Ann saw me outside and came over to the fence.

"Hi Ruthie. Where is the little girl?"

"Susie in the house washin dishes."

"When is you missus a comin home?"

"Today."

"You should go now before she gits back home. I have some money for you to leave wit."

"Susie would know I is leavin. She still in the house. Besides Miz Williams promise me that she gonna send me home when she gits back wit the baby."

"She ain't gonna send you nowhere, Ruthie! Miz Williams gonna keep you here. You is her slave and that's the way she gonna keep it. Now git you things."

I felted confused. "I don't know, Betty Ann. What if she send the police after me?"

"She ain't gonna send no police after you. She jus bluffin. Git your things."

"I is scared." I said, droppin my head.

When I look up, Betty Ann had both hands on her hips and she frownin at me. "What wrong, Betty Ann? Why you lookin so mean at me?"

"Every time I find a way for you to leave, you give me an excuse. I have this here money for you to leave wit, but you still givin me excuses. But one day desperation is gonna cry, then you's gonna leave."

"But I cry almost every day, Betty Ann."

"I didn't say you. I said desperation. Is you gonna leave, Ruthie?"

"Naw. Not until Miz Williams send me. I jus know that she is gonna send me home this time. She promise."

"Fine. You keep on believin her. I is gonna give the money back to my folks."

At that moment, I heard footsteps comin in the yard. It was Mr. Williams. "Ruthie, can you do somethin for me?"

"Yesum. What is it sir?"

"I forgot to git the baby's clothes together to take to the hospital. Can you git them together for me?"

"Yesum."

I said goodbye to Betty Ann, and went in the house wit Mr. Williams. While I was getting the baby's clothes ready, I thought about what Betty Ann said. I hoped she was wrong.

About one o'clock, Mr. And Miz Williams come home wit the new baby. Susie ran out to greet her mama, but I stay in the house. I didn't know if Miz Williams would want me to touch her baby. Mr. Williams help his wife in the house. She sat in a chair in the sittin room, and look at me.

"Ruthie you have another job now. You gotta have to wash little Johnnie's diapers and take care of him."

"Oh no," I scream in my mind, "Please God, don't let Betty Ann be right."

"I won't be here for long, ma'am. You promise you gonna send me home when the baby came. I sure would like to see my mama."

"I can't send you home now. I need you to help me with little Johnny," Miz Williams rock the baby in her arms.

"I really wanna go home. When you gonna send me ma'am?"

Mr. Williams hear us talkin and he came and stood over by his wife. "If she wants to go home, send her home. I'll get your mother to stay with you for a few weeks or until you're strong again."

"You will do nothin of the sort. Ruthie will stay wit me until I'm strong. My mother is not well herself. I will not have her here when I have Ruthie." The baby start cryin and Miz Williams git up and start walking, tryin to console him.

"Bear with us, Ruthie, for a while longer," Mr. Williams said. "As soon as Miz Williams gets better you'll be on your way home." He smile at me.

"Why are you tellin her that?"

"She wants to see her folks. I don't see nothin wrong with me tellin her that she'll be able to go home soon."

"She will go home when I send her. Not before."

"You told her that you was gonna send her home after you got out of the hospital. I am just lettin her know that we need her help for a little while before we can let her go." He sounded frustrated.

Miz Williams pick up the baby and say that she was takin him to her room. Mr. Williams follow her.

I wanted to cry, but I held back my tears like so many times before. I pray, "Oh God please help me git home. I know that I should have left when Betty Ann told me to, but I was tryin to do what Mr. Williams told me to do, take care of Susie. Now Miz Williams won't let me go."

Susie pull on my arm. "What's the matter Ruthie? You look like you is gonna cry."

"No I ain't.I jus wanna sit by myself for a little while."

"Okay. I is goin to see if Mama will let me hold the baby."

I went to the porch and eye my blanket on the floor. Pickin up the blanket, I balled it up like a pillow and place it back on the floor. Then I laid down on the floor starin up at the ceiling. I had no thoughts. Mr. Williams came out a few minutes later and ask me to git up and fix supper for Miz Williams and Susie. When we gits to the kitchen, I ask him what to cook.

"Anything. I don't care."

He gather his hat and walk on out the kitchen to the front door. I thought it was too early for him to be leavin for work. They must have been fussin again. I made the dinner, and carried Miz Williams' supper to her on a tray. Susie was standin beside her mother's bed wit her arms folded lookin down. I set Miz Williams food next to her on the bed.

"I is gonna put Susie's food on the table if you want her to eat now, ma'am."

Miz Williams look over at Susie "Go on and eat now, darling."

"I ain't hungry."

"Come on Susie I made your favorites." I was trying to sound cheerful. Susie jus cut her eyes up at me and ran out the room. I hear the front door slam.

"You want me to go after her, Miz Williams?"

"No. She'll be back. You can leave now, but come a runnin when I call you."

"Yesum, Miz Williams."

I went on back in the kitchen and wait for Susie. She came back after a little while lookin like she had been cryin. "Susie, what the matter."

I took hold of her arm. She pull away from me and ran to her room. Miz Williams call me to come git her dishes. When I git in the room I told her about Susie bein upset.

"Jus take the dishes."

"But Susie, ma'am. Do you want me to try and git her to come and talk to you?" I pick up the tray.

"Whatever is wrong with Susie is not your business. Just go and clean up the kitchen."

"Yes ma'am."

I went and clean up the kitchen, and I never tried to ask Susie what was wrong wit her. I jus wanted to go home.

CHAPTER SEVENTEEN

The sound of the baby wailin filled the house. I could hear footsteps come in the kitchen but the baby cryin almost drown out Susie and her mama voice.

"Why do I always have to wake her? She is so lazy. Doesn't she hear the baby cryin?"

"I can warm the bottle Mama. While you was gone Ruthie even let me help her cook."

"She did what?"

"She let me help her cook and clean."

"Where was your papa?"

"He was here. He said that it was alright Mama."

"I guess while I was away he let Ruthie do whatever she wanted."

I sat up on the floor of the porch and listen to Susie and her mama talkin. They came closer to the door. Miz Williams open the door wit one hand while holdin the screamin baby in the other.

"Ruthie, didn't you hear me callin you?"

"No ma'am. I was sleep. It ain't mornin yet."

"I don't care if it's not mornin yet. The baby needs a bottle. He's been screamin his head off. Now git up and warm him a bottle!"

"Yesum."

"Mama. Can I hold him now?" Susie was lookin at her mama, pleadin.

"When he gits older, Susie. Ruthie, hurry up."

I got up and walk pass her to git a pot of water. Miz Williams and Susie started walkin toward the hallway, but Miz Williams tell Susie go back to bed.

"Can I stay up with you a little while and watch you feed the baby?"

"No Susie. You'll have plenty time for that. Right now you need your rest. Now git on back to bed."

Susie went to her room and I took a bottle from the icebox and warm it. I look out the window as the bottle was warmin and seen it was still dark. Mr. Williams usually come home at the crack of dawn. He wasn't home yet so I know that it real early in the mornin. When I thought the bottle warm enough I took it out the water and test the milk by shakin some of it on my wrist. The milk was jus right so I took the bottle to Miz Williams. She place the nipple of it in the baby's mouth and he started suckin on it. Miz Williams give me a mean look.

"I hear that while I was gone Mr. Williams let you do whatever you wanted. He even let you use my bathroom. Well, now you git to clean it. Take the bucket and scrub it down, now."

"Can I do it when it gits morning? I is mighty tired and sleepy."

"You will do it now."

"Yesum."

I went to the bathroom and got the bucket that she always kepted by the sink. I gits a rag along wit some scrubbin powder and scrubs down the bathtub, sink, toilet, and the floor. When I was through cleanin the bathroom I went back to her room to tell her.

"Now you can wash all of my dishes Ruthie 'cause I don't know which ones you ate out of."

"Yesum."

I went in the kitchen and wash all of the dishes that was in there. The sun started coming up when I was jus about through. Mr. Williams open the front door and walk through the sittin room to the kitchen to find me still up.

"What are you doing Ruthie? You supposed to be in bed asleep."

"Miz Williams told me to clean up these here dishes."

"Didn't you wash the supper dishes before you went to bed?"

"Yesum. But Miz Williams said that she want me to wash all the dishes in the kitchen 'cause she don't know which ones I ate out of."

"You put the last dishes up and git on back to bed."

"Yesum."

Mr. Williams went to his bedroom and I finish puttin up the dishes and went back to bed. I laid down on my blanket and fell to sleep, but the next thing I knew Miz Williams was wakin me up tellin me to fix breakfast. Only after I fix breakfast and wash the dishes again did she allow me to git another hour of sleep.

Miz Williams stay in bed for about a week after she had the baby; I was the one that had to cook all the meals, but at least I could eat some of the food as soon as it git done. After the week was over, Miz Williams was strong enough to cook the meals and it was back to beans and cornbread for me. Only this time she didn't put any kind of seasonin or meat in the beans. I tried to git use to the nothin-taste but it was real hard.

Miz Williams couldn't watch me as much as she had before—the baby kept her busy. It had been bout two weeks since I seen Betty Ann. Finally, I seen her one day outside of Miz Brook's house hangin up the clothes. I came out the house and went to the fence while Miz Williams was bathin little Johnny.

"Nice day for winter, ain't it Betty Ann?"

"Yes, it sho nuff is. So how she treatin you now Ruthie?"

"Worse."

"She never gonna change. I told you that. You should have left when I told you to."

"Betty Ann, does you still have the money?"

"I gave my mama and papa back they money. I still have a little of mines."

"Do you think your can git enough money for me to go back home?"

"Maybe. But if I git it, you better take it and run."

"Betty Ann will you do a favor for me?"

"What is it?" She glance at Miz Williams' house.

"Before I git money from you and run, will you mail a letter for me to my mama?"

"Okay Ruthie. But I think you misses is watchin us again; I seen dem curtains go back."

"I hope not. She suppose to be givin the baby a bath. I is gonna write the letter soon and give it to you. Do you got a envelope I can use?"

"Yes, jus give me the letter."

"Does you have a stamp?"

"I'll git one. Jus give me the letter and you address."

"I git it for you tomorra."

"I gots to finish my work now Ruthie. I'll come out here again tomorra."

I went back in Miz Williams' house and found her rockin the baby in the sittin room. She never said nothin about me talkin to Betty Ann so I thought maybe she didn't see me, or maybe she didn't care." I went in the kitchen and got a piece of an old paper bag. She hear me tear it and ask why I needed it.

"To put my number two in ma'am. I ain't got no slop jar."

"For goodness sake, take the whole bag."

"Yes ma'am."

I went on out to the garage jus like I was gonna to use the bathroom. I puts the paper in a safe place until I git a pencil from Susie. First chance I git I went outside to the garage and git the paper and wrote my letter:

Dear Mama,

Please, please come git me. If you don't soon I feel like I is gonna die. Miz Williams treat me like a slave. I hate being here. I don't look like your Ruthie no more. I is real skinny since I don't git nothin to eat but beans. Please Mama, come git me.

Ruthie

I put my address on the front of the letter and put it in a safe place in the garage. A few days later I sees Betty Ann comin outside. I told Miz Williams that I had to use the bathroom, and I went to the garage and git the letter. I put the letter in my dress pocket, until I gits to the fence and hands it to Betty Ann over to the fence.

"How is I gonna know Mama send a letter?"

"When I come outside and you sees me drop a clothespin, that means that I ain't got no letter for you. If I looks up in the sky, that means I got one."

I went back in the house where Miz Williams is changin the baby. She told me to feed him and rock him to sleep. I did like she told me as she went back to her room. I was rocking the baby, sittin on the sofa, when Susie come home from school. That door open and Susie walk in, came right over to me, and look down at little Johnny.

"See, I told you that I wasn't gonna take care of no baby. But I wish that Mama would let me hold him even for jus a little while."

Susie reached out her hands and took one of the baby's and rub its tiny fingers. She put his hand down. "Where is my mama?"

"I think that she in her room."

Susie git up and head to Miz Williams' room. I kepted rockin little Johnny until he fall asleep. I carry him to Miz Williams' bedroom. When I gits there I seen that Susie gone. Miz Williams was alone on her bed readin a book. I whisper real soft, "The baby asleep."

She took the baby out my arms and put him in his bed.

"Now git on out of here."

"Yesum."

I was glad to go 'cause this time she wasn't tellin me somethin else to do. I went on back to the kitchen.

A few days later as I was cleanin the top of the stove, I seen Betty Ann from the kitchen window. I wave to her and she drop a clothespin. My heart sank.

This kept happenin everytime I seen Betty Ann. I felted better when I started thinkin that maybe Mama wouldn't write me a letter. Maybe she'll jus come. After a while I gives up. I started feelin that Mama might not have receive my letter or maybe she was sick and couldn't write. Papa gonna come, I know he is. But Papa didn't show up and a million more thoughts went through my head. The weeks run into months. I check wit Betty Ann every chance I git to see if I had a letter but every time she would drop a clothespin.

Finally one day I came up wit the worse thought of all. "Maybe they don't want me." After all, she wasn't my real mama, she was jus my aunt. Miz Williams had said before that they didn't want me 'cause I wasn't theirs. I was a motherless child who was left in this world alone and nobody cared. I felt like cryin my eyes out but I held it in and pray for strength. I didn't want Miz Williams askin me any question about me cryin.

One day when school was out, Miz Williams announce to me that she and Susie was going to town and I was suppose to keep the baby. I was happy for dem to leave and as soon as they was out of sight I took the baby and went outside. I stood by the fence until Betty Ann came out. I told her that Miz Williams was gone to town and we could talk.

"How long you think that she be gone Ruthie?"

"I don't know. But it sure feels good she gone." I took in a deep breath and let it out real slow.

"I gonna be leavin soon Ruthie, my family is gonna move up north. They say they is better opportunities for us colored folks."

"I don't want you to go Betty Ann. You is the only colored person I has seen in a long time. Please Betty Ann, can you ask you folks to stay jus a little while?"

Tears begin to swell up in my eyes.

"Don cry Ruthie. I can't stop my folks from wantin to leave. I wish I could for you sake. I feel so sorry for you. If I was older and had my own house I would take you home wit me. But I can't. I is only sixteen. My folks is takin care of me."

I wiped my eyes.

"You know what Ruthie? They is other colored folk around here.

Plenty."

"Where they is?"

"Right down there on 29th street."

"How do you git to 29th street Betty Ann?"

"Jus go out the gate and make a left turn. Walk down the street pass Mr. Grays' store until you come to a big street, bigger than this one, and make a right turn."

"What the name of that big street."

"I don't know but you can't miss it. Keep walkin about a country mile until you see a sign called 29th. You should see colored folk all up and down that street.

Betty Ann looked at the baby.

"Sho is a purty baby; looks like an angel." She eyed the baby in my arms. "Too bad you has the Devil for a mama."

"Betty Ann, I've been thinkin that my mama don't want me." Tears started swellin up in my eyes and rolled down my cheeks.

"Don't think that Ruthie. You mama love you."

"I is not her real child, she really my aunt."

"Still, she raised you."

"She was the one that wanted me to go wit Miz Williams. I wanted to stay at home and go to school, but she say no. I've been here ever since I was eleven. I turn twelve in October, the same year I came here. Now I done turn thirteen. Miz Williams ain't gave me one dime and I is still wearin the same clothes that I had when I first git here. The only reason why I can still wear dem is 'cause I is so skinny. I know at first that Miz Williams made me write Mama tellin her that I is doing fine and that I wanted to stay a little longer. Too much time have gone by—my mama should wanna see me by now. I tell you Betty Ann, she don't want me." My body shook as I balled my eyes out. The baby started cryin. I tried to comfort him but he cried louder, and Betty Ann jus stood there looking at me.

"He must be hungry," Betty Ann finally said. "I guess you best take him on in the house and feed him."

"I guess I better."

I started toward the house, promisin myself that one day I was gonna git back home. I would see Mama and I would tell her how awful this woman done treated me. me. Mama would have to tell me why she never came for me.

When I gits in the house I gave little Johnny a bottle and rocks him to sleep. Miz Williams and Susie didn't come back from the store until it was late.

CHAPTER EIGHTEEN

M iz Williams begin a habit of goin to town every day. She would leave as soon as her husband left the house. Sometime she would take Susie, and I would be left all day wit little Johnny. Sometimes she would leave Susie wit me, and Susie would stay in the house and help me wit little Johnny. Only after he asleep would she leave to play wit her friends.

Miz Williams always brought somethin back from town. Sometime it were a new dress for Susie or herself. Sometime it was somethin for the house. One day she went to town wit Susie. I waited for an hour before I left 'cause I wanted to make sure they was on the bus goin to town.

Wit the baby in my arms, I set off to 29th street, the street that the colored folks lived on. I walked so long wit the baby that my arms git tired from holdin him. It the last day of May and it was warm but I still took a light blanket for the baby. When we git to 29th street, sho nuff, they was colored folk all over the place. I walk down that street holding little Johnny and lookin around jus like it was Christmas. I ain't never in my life seen so many colored folk at one time.

The street had a lot of stores; I peeked in the some of the windows. In every one of dem they was colored folk behind the counters runnin dem. After awhile, I realiz that people was stoppin what they was doing and starin at me. I kepted on walkin down the street. Two diddy-lookin colored women moved to the side, away from me, like I was some sort of strange bein. Other people pointed at me and whispered. Still, I kept walkin.

Finally somebody say, "Hey little girl, where you come from wit that white baby?"

I turned to the voice and seen a tall colored man standin in front of a beauty shop.

"I come from 33th street. It a long walk from here, maybe a mile or so. Tis here is my misses baby. Can I go in your shop, sir?"

I shift little Johnny from one of my arms to the other.

"You shore can." He open the door for me.

I walk in a shop what smelled of burned hair and sweet-smellin shampoo. They was two ladies gittin they hair straighten. One look about Mama's age. They was three ladies waitin wit rags tied around they heads. The lady that worked on the older woman hair was a hefty woman wit kind brown eyes. As busy as they was, everythin stopped when they seen me. They stared like they had never seen a colored girl before. The older lady spoke first.

"My my, look what the cat drag in."

"No cat ma'am, jus me." I shift Johnny again.

I walked right up to the hefty lady that was doin the older woman hair.

"You do hair ma'am?"

"Of course I do," she said smilin.

I knew that. She was doing that woman hair right in front of my face. I jus didn't know what else to say.

"You want your hair done?"

"No ma'am, don't got no money." I shook my head.

"Where you come from wit that white baby?" The older lady learned forward to git a closer look at me. "I ain't seen you around here."

"I live about an hour walk from here ma'am wit the Williams family. This here is their baby." I turned little Johnny around so the lady could see his face better.

"Cute little fat baby. He sure gittin enough to eat, but you look like you ain't been eatin."

"I eat ma'am but they feed me nothin but beans all the time." I rocked little Johnny in my arms 'cause he was beginin to cry.

"Jus beans?" One of the ladies that was waitin said. "I thought that only us colored were havin it hard wit tis Depression."

"Girl, no. I heard that some of those rich white folk were jumpin out windows 'cause they done lost all of they money. They don't wanna be poor so they kill theyselves," another lady said.

"They eats all right ma'am, they jus feed *me* beans. I turned around and face her. Miz Williams said that I should be graceful to git dem. I eat beans for breakfast, lunch and supper."

"Why you there?" Another lady said.

"I there to clean and take care of the baby. Johnny started cryin louder and I knew that he must be hungry. "I take care of they little girl named Susie too."

"Where is you folks?" I didn't answer, Johnny was fussin too much.

"I got to go and take the baby home, he hungry." I rush out the shop.

I walked some and ran some down that street, going back the way that I had come wit Johnny screamin all the way.

When I gits back to the house I fed him. Johnny finish his bottle and went to sleep, so I put him in his crib. I had gotten hungry from all that walkin, but I was too scared to go into the icebox and git the beans. It was late when Miz Williams and Susie git home—about eight o'clock. Miz Williams came in the house lookin around.

"Ruthie, did you feed Johnny?"

"Yes ma'am, changed him too."

"Good."

Miz Williams started toward her room.

"I ain't eat yet, ma'am."

She turn around and look at me. "I'll feed you when I come back."

"Yes ma'am."

I went back to the porch and sat and wait for her to come back down. I wait for so long that I thought that she forgot about me. Finally when she came back I had fall asleep.

She woke me up wit a hot plate of navy beans and the usual cornbread on the side.

When I reach for the plate she say, "Make sure you wash this plate when you're through."

She turned and walk in the kitchen. She stay in the kitchen for a little while, then I hear her leave. I ate my beans, scrapin the plate clean. After I done, I went outside to the faucet and wash the plate and spoon. I brought dem back in the house and dried dem. I put dem back on the shelf away from the rest of the dishes, and went on back to the porch and laid down on the blanket. I thought about the colored people that I seen on 29th street. I couldn't help the excitement and contentment that whelmed up inside me, as I thought about going back. I was smiling to myself as I started taking off my clothes to put on my gown when the thought hit me about Miz Williams' neighbors. Somebody might have seen me. Suppose one of her neighbors tell her. I git on my knees and prayed to God.

"Dear Lawd, I thank you for lettin me find some people of my own kind. Lawd, please let me see dem again. Please Lawd, if someone saw me goin to town, don't let dem tell Miz Williams. And above all Lawd, help me to leave Miz Williams' house so that I can be free again. Amen."

I git up off my knees and lay down. I fell fast to sleep, but I was woke up the next day by the sound of Miz Williams and her husband screamin at each other.

"She shouldn't be takin care of little Johnny! You're his mama. You have Ruthie doing everythin around here. Why can't you take care of our baby instead of going shoppin every day and spending money we don't have?"

"You're always defendin her. You like that niggard or somethin?"

Mr. Williams came down the hall, grabbed his coat, and stormed out the house, slamming the door behind him. After a few minutes Miz Williams came down the hallway into the kitchen and made herself a pot of coffee. I smell it brewing so I gits up and went in the kitchen and watched her pour the coffee in a cup. She started sippin it while starin blankly at the wall. She didn't even seem to notice that I was in the room until I spoke.

"Mornin Miz Williams."

"How long have you been standin there?"

"I jus got here, ma'am."

"I am taking Susie to town with me today. I'll be back by supper. You take care of little Johnny."

"Yes ma'am."

"While the baby's asleep you clean my house and dust everythin." Miz Williams started starin straight ahead again.

I went back on the porch and start gittin myself ready for the day when I hear Miz Williams git up from the chair and leave the room. A few hours pass and Miz Williams comes in the sittin room where I was dustin and hands me little Johnny. I waited for about an hour after her and Susie left before I git ready to leave for 29th street. I fed little Johnny, put a white bonnet on his head, took a diaper, and headed off. I pass Mr. Gray's store on my way and hear someone yell, "Where are you gonin wit the Williams' baby?"

I turn around to Mr. Gray smilin face.

"I is jus takin him for a walk so that he can sleep good tonight sir."

Mr. Gray walk up to me and look at little Johnny. "Make sure that you keep his head covered. Don't want too much sun on the little fellow's head."

"Yes sir." I hoped that he wouldn't tell Miz Williams that he had seen me. A man call him from the store.

"Enjoy your walk Ruthie." He turne and went back in the store.

Little Johnny and me went on down the road to 29th street. This time it didn't seem to take me as long to git there.

I walk again down the store-lined street. I git the same stares I git the first day. I didn't care though as I made my way to the beauty shop. When I git to the door the same man that I see the first day was there. He was walkin out the store. He see me and stopped

"You back again?"

"Yes sir. Can I go in again, sir?"

"You shore can." He opened the door for me. "If you have to keep comin back you should tell me you name."

"My name Ruthie. This here little fellow name Johnny."

"Pleased to meet you Ruthie."

I went in and the same older lady that was gittin her hair done the first day was there. This time she was jus sittin in a chair watchin the other women git they hair done.

"Jus had to come back?" The older woman said.

"Yes ma'am."

I went over to the books that they had lying around and was about to sit down and take a look at some of dem when someone spoke to me.

"Why, hello again." It was the hefty woman. She was curlin a young woman hair. My name is Ms. Mable. What's yours?"

"Ruthie ma'am. This here Johnny."

"Why you got that old rag on your head?"

"Cause my head ain't been comb in a long time ma'am."

With one arm I helded little Johnny tighter to my chest, with the other I pull off the scarf. "See ma'am, it real nappy."

"Why you ain't comb you hair?" She said, as she examine my hair.

"Don't have no comb." She stopped touchin my hair.

"You need to git your hair done real bad."

"Amen." The older woman said, while raisin up one hand in the air.

"How much you charge to do hair, Ms. Mable?"

"Three dollars."

"I ain't got no money Ms. Mable. I can't git my hair done."

" I can do you for free if you can wait until I finish my last customer, Ruthie."

"Thank you ma'am but I can't stay today. Can you do it another day?"

"I don't see no problem wit that." Ms. Mable said, as she tied the scarf back on my head.

I eye two girls comin out a room. One look like she my age but the other look a little older. I watched dem walk up to me. The older girl was overweight, wit large hips. She had a round face, dark brown skin, and wore a frown. The younger girl was thin, brown-skinned, and had a real pleasant smile.

The older one look at me, wrinkle up her nose and said, "Mama, is tis the girl you was talkin about? She is about the size of a twig."

Ms. Mable walk over to the two girls and told me, "These two are my daughters. This one is Beulah. She the oldest and the other one is Fanny Mae."

"Fanny Mae smile and say hi. Beulah jus stood there lookin me up and down. She put one hand on her hip and reach over and touch my scarf. "You look bad, real bad."

I drop my head, feelin ashamed.

"Leave her alone Beulah." Ms. Mable grab Beulah hand and took it off my scarf. "Jus say hi."

"Hi, I is very please to meet you." Fanny Mae said to me.

"I is very glad to meet you both." I said, as I eyed the two girls. Beulah look up in the ceiling and said hi.

The older woman that was sittin in the shop, came over to where we was standin. She look at me."My name is Miz Ester."

"Please to meet you ma'am."

The woman who hair Ms. Mable was curlin said, "And my name is Ms. Late if you don't hurry up and finish my hair. Mable I told you that I don't have all day to be here. I got to git to work tis afternoon."

"All right, all right, I is a comin."

Ms. Mable went back to the woman, pick up the curlin iron and test it on some tissue.

"I want the same style as Billy Holiday," the woman inform Ms. Mable.

Ms. Mable started curlin Ms. Late's hair.

Fanny Mae looked at little Johnny. "He sure is cute, ain't he Beulah?"

"Look like a baldheaded white monkey to me."

With those words, she turn and walk to a room in the back; her hips swayin from side to side lookin like two big over ripe watermelons.

"He a cute baby to me." I look at little Johnny little sweet face.

"Don pay her no mind. Beulah don't know what she talkin about. He sure is a cute baby Ruthie," Fanny Mae said again.

Fanny Mae ask me if she could hold him. I gave little Johnny to her and he snuggle right up in her arms. He look at her for a little while as she talked baby talk to him, then he went to sleep.

"How long you stayin this time Ruthie? Mama said that you left in a hurry the other day."

"Little Johnny was hungry. I didn't know what time Miz Williams was gonna git back so I had to leave."

"I guess I better give the baby back to you, I got to git back to washin hair."

"Where does you wash those ladies hair at?"

"In the back where Beulah went."

"Can I go back there wit you Fanny Mae?"

"You shore can."

Fanny Mae hand Little Johnny back to me and we both walk to the back room wit two sinks. They was some bottles of shampoo that was by the sinks, and a chair that the ladies sat in while they was gittin they hair washed. A large pitcher was standin by the sink, and a few different colored towels was fold up on a shelf not far away. Beulah was washin one woman head. She had a towel over one shoulder and was leanin over as she massage the woman head. The shampoo foam on the woman head like a white cloud.

"Ain't it bout time for the truck to be a comin down the street?" Fanny Mae inform Beulah.

Beaulah stop washin the woman's hair.

"Take over for me please, Fanny Mae," Bealuh begged.

"Okay. Hurry up."

Beulah hurry and walk on out the room. Fanny Mae started washin the lady's hair. She told me to take a seat so I sat in one of the three chairs and laid little Johnny on his stomach across my lap. When Fanny Mae was through washin the lady hair she wrap her head wit a towel and told her to go in the room wit her mama. The lady handed Fanny a coin and went in the other room. Beulah came back in the room after the lady left, lookin all starry eyes.

"Thank you Fanny Mae. I almost didn't see him pass by today. One day, I swear he gonna be my husband," Beulah sighed.

"He don't even know you is alive, less be your husband." Fanny Mae threw off her hands at her.

"You jus wait and see he's mine." Beulah walked back out the room again.

"She know she too young. He grown. Somebody said that he was twenty-one. Beulah only fifteen."

"I thought Beulah was older than that," I said.

"No, she is only fifteen—are you hungry?"

"I sure is."

"If you can wait for a minutes, I'll go tell Mama and she'll send Papa to git us somethin."

"OK, Fanny Mae."

Fanny Mae left the room. When she came back, Ms. Mable was wit her.

"I is sorry Ruthie. I should have asked you if you was hungry as soon as you came in. I is gonna send Lester to git you somethin. What would you like?"

"Anythang ma'am, I will eat anythang." I started feeling excited about gittin a meal.

"Well I is gonna to tell him to go to the store and git you a big old ham sandwich and a soda. Would you like that?" Ms Mable asked.

"Yes ma'am!"

Ms. Mable went on out the room. Fanny and I talked for a while. I told her about why I was in Birmingham and about Miz Williams. When Ms. Mable git back she had two sandwiches wrapped up in paper and two red sodas. The sandwich smell filled the room and made my mouth water. She hand one of the sandwiches to me. I go to reach out for it but remember I didn't have no money. I drops my hands and look at Ms. Mable. "I ain't got no money to pay you for tis here food."

"I didn't tell you that you had to pay for it, I is givin it to you. Eat, child." She look over at Fanny Mae. "Fanny Mae, take the baby so Ruthie can eat. When she get done eatin then give her back the baby so you can eat."

"Okay, Mama."

I took the sandwich and soda, and Ms.Mable put Fanny Mae's soda and sandwich on one of the chairs and left the room. Fanny Mae took little Johnny and sat down in one of the empty chairs and watch me, smilin. I bit into my sandwhich like there was no tomorra. Without even sayin thank you to the Lawd, I ate until it there was nothin left but the wrapper. I drunk my red soda and loved the taste of the cool strawberry-favor drink as it ran down my throat. When I was through, I felt happy and ashamed. I hadn't said thank you to God nor Ms. Mable. I quickly said thank you

Lawd and look at Fanny Mae. "I forgit to thank you mama. I git up and went in the other room where Ms. Mable was pressin a lady hair. I walk up to her.

"Ms. Mable I is so sorry for not thankin you for the food. I truly thank you ma'am." She jus smile. "Its all right honey, I know you was hungry. You still want your hair done?"

"Yesum."

"Well I can do it for you and I ain't gonna charge you nothin, but tell the lady that your work for that I is chargin you three dollars."

"Yesum."

I went back into the washroom and look at little Johnny in Fanny Mae lap. He was asleep so I took him from Fanny Mae so she could eat. I stayed wit dem in the shop until little Johnny woke up. He had sleep about a hour.

I left the shop and started back to Miz Williams' house. On the way back I thought about how I was gonna ask Miz Williams about gittin my hair done. I hoped that Mr. Williams would be at home wit his wife when I ask. I was hope that he would jus stay at home for a few minutes instead of runnin out the house every mornin. I hoped that he would say yes and give me the money.

CHAPTER NINETEEN

Miz Williams came home late. I was sittin on the sofa holdin little Johnny when they came in. Susie was so tired that she went straight to bed. I had enough time before they came to clean the house and wash all of little Johnny's diapers. Miz Williams came over to the sofa and took little Johnny, but never said a word to me—like I wasn't there. I didn't ask her for anythin to eat 'cause I was still full.

Miz Williams went to bed, leavin me. I stay up a little while wonderin how I was gonna ask her about gittin my hair done. Finally I git tired and went to the porch. I git down on my knees and pray that the Williams' be in a good mood in the mornin so that I could ask dem about gittin my hair done. "Lawd, please let dem say yes. Amen." I git off my knees and roll up in my blanket and went to sleep.

God answer my prayers. The next morning Mr. and Miz Williams was at the kitchen table laughin and talkin to each other. I git up and went in the kitchen. I looked at both of dem drinkin coffee. I jus stood there, too scared to ask about gittin my hair done. Miz Williams notice me and put down her cup.

"Why are you standin there Ruthie?"

"I wanna git my hair done ma'am." I braced myself jus in case the answer was no.

"How much does it cost?" Mr. Williams reached in his pocket.

"Three dollars, sir." I secretly thanked God under my breath.

"Wait a minute." Miz Williams sounded suspicious. "Where did you go to find someone that would do a niggard's hair? You aren't supposed to leave this house."

I stood there with my mind racin, and my mouth open but nothin came out of it. My eyes dart between dem both, my body frozen.

"For heaven sake Martha, let her git her hair done. I'm tired of seein her with that rag on her head. She looks like an ad for slave trade," he laughed.

"I personally don't see nothin wrong with the scarf. I git tired of seein nappy niggard's hair." Miz Williams looked at me and narrowed her eyes. I had the feelin that she didn't like what was goin on.

"Well, she looks bad to me." Mr. Williams handed me the money.

"Thank you, sir."

I put the money in my pocket and walked on out the room back to the porch. They went on back to talkin. Later on that day Mr. Williams left for work. When he left, Miz Williams call me into the sittin room. She grab me in the back of my neck and wit a low tone she bent down and spoke between her teeth.

"I am gonna let you git your hair done today. But you know what I told you about my jewelry. You'll go to jail. You know what they do to little niggard girls in jail?"

"No ma'am." I trembled.

"If you don't come back, you'll find out." She turn my neck loose and look me straight in the eye. "Remember what I told you."

She left the room, and I went on to my work. Around five o'clock, I had finish the work so I went to her.

"Miz Williams, I done finish. Can I go now?"

"You ain't finish girl. You got clothes to wash."

She went into her room and gits all the clean clothes out her dresser draws and drop dem down in front of me.

"When you git through washin these here clothes, you can go."

I wash clothes until it was eight o'clock. I went to her again.

"Miz Williams, dem clothes is wash and dried. I done took dem off the line and fold dem up. Can I go now?"

"Git on outta here. You better be back here by ten o'clock or I ain't gonna let you in. You'll be sleepin outside for the night, you hear?"

"Yes ma'am."

I hurried on out the door and half ran and walked to 29th street. When I git there Mr. Lester Brown was lockin the door to the shop. Ms. Mable was beside him. I ran up to Ms. Mable .

"I is here to git my hair done ma'am."

Mr. Lester and Ms. Mable both look at me like they couldn't believe what they was a seein.

"I jus close the shop honey, what took you so long?"

Miz Williams wouldn't let me go Ms. Mable."

"Well, come on in."

Ms. Mable took the key from Mr. Lester and open the door.

"I guess this won't take long."

Mr. Lester was grumblin as he follow Ms. Mable in the shop. "I is tired Mable. Can't you do her hair tomorrow?"

"We can stay another hour Lester. Fanny Mae and Beulah is probably jus gittin home and haven't finish cookin yet. You can wait."

Mr. Lester went on in behin Ms. Mable and took a seat. Ms. Mable took off my scarf and told me to follow her into the shampoo room. We pass a small closet on the way to the room that I didn't notice before.

"What does you keep in there ma'am?"

"Jus supplies. When Fanny Mae was little she used to hide in there all the time." Ms. Mable chuckle. She told me to sit down in the chair by the sink. When I did she wet my hair and shampoo it. When she gits through, she start to comb my hair but had a hard time gittin the comb through 'cause it was so tangled. She stop for a moment and shook her head.

"I forgit that you hair ain't been comb in a year. It already past nine o'clock. This might take me half the night to comb."

"I hope it won't ma'am because Miz Williams said if I come home after ten she won't let me in the house."

"She what? Lester come in here. I want you to hear this." Mr. Lester came in the shampoo room, puffin on a pipe.

"What you want now Mable? You know I ain't helpin you do no hair. I jus cuts the men hair. That's all. I don't know nothin about fixin women hair."

"I don't want you to help me, I jus want you to hear what Ruthie jus told me."

He asked about what I had said to Ms. Mable, and I told him. He was silent for a minute.

"Why don't you stay wit us for the night? Mable can fix you hair in the mornin."

"I can't Mr. Lester. Miz Williams said that if I didn't come back tonight, she gonna hide her jewelry and tell the police that I stole dem. I don't wanna sleep outside or go to jail sir."

"That don't make no sense. She won't let you come early. But you can't stay late or you gonna have to sleep outside. If you don't come back, she gonna send the police after you. Jus don't make no sense." Mr. Lester shook his head.

"That woman is jus plain evil, Lester." Miz Mable looked at me.

"You need to git away from her. We got to help her Lester, somehow."

Mr. Lester looked up in the ceilin like his thoughts was comin from there. He was bitin on his pipe. He finally look back at Ms. Mable.

"You know, if I was to go over to you Miz Williams and tell her that you grandma died, she would have to let you go for the funeral, seein that I was there to git you."

"She would wanna know who you is sir."

"Tell her that I is you uncle."

"Yes sir. But where will I stay if I left her house?"

"You can stay wit us."

I felt happy inside. For the first time I felt that I finally was gonna to be free from Miz Williams.

Ms. Mable couldn't finish my hair because it was so long and nappy. She did the best she could wit the time she had. When she git through, it was at least softer, combed out, but still wet. She tie it wit a ribbon and promise me that she would give me a really nice curl as soon as I gits away from Miz Williams and live wit her.

I left the shop that night feelin hopeful. I ran and skipped along not thinkin about the time; I didn't know that it was almost eleven o'clock. When I was almost back to Miz Williams' street, I heard a noise by a vacant lot. I look around and see three white boys. They look at me and yell, "Catch that nigger!"

I started runnin. The faster I ran, the faster they ran. I jump a fence and land in someone's back yard. A dog started barkin and ran after me but I ran away and jump the fence again. But the boys were on the other side waitin for me. Fear grip my heart as they grab for me. I duck and slip by dem, runnin until I felted as if my heart was gonna bust. I didn't stop until I git to Miz Williams' house. I bolted through the gate and ran up on the porch and pounded on the door, yellin.

"Help Miz Williams! Let me in, some white boys is after me!"

Miz Williams turned on the lights in the sittin room and came to the door. She took a look at me through the glass and said, " I told you to be back here before ten o'clock. It's eleven. I'm not lettin you in."

"Please Miz Williams," I begged. "They gonna git me!"

"Why should I care?" She left the door and turned off the lights.

I stood by the door hopin that she would come back and open it. After a while I realize that she wasn't. I look around but didn't see the boys. But in my mind I knew that they were gonna git me.

"Oh Lawd, please help me. Please!" I screamed.

I sat down on the front porch and held myself, rocking back and forth. I felted alone and helpless. A hooting owl cry fill the air and I jumped, the hairs risin up on my neck. I sat down on the porch and helded my arms around me and listen to other scary noises in the night air. I tremble as tears fell down from my eyes, and I was scared of every sound. I thought that it might be the boys comin back. I stay awake all the night. Only when daybreak came is when I finally fell asleep. I was woke up by a hand shakin me. It was Mr. Williams, he had came home from work.

"What are you doin out here on the front porch Ruthie?"

"Miz Williams wouldn't let me in." I wiped the sleep out my eyes.

"Git on up Ruthie and come in the house." He open up the front door.

I walk back to my blanket and laid down. I fell back to sleep and didn't hear Miz Williams come on the porch.

"Git up you lazy niggard!" She yelled.

I jumped up from the blanket, shakin. "Mr. Williams let me in ma'am, please don't make me go back outside."

Mr. Williams came on the porch.

"Let her go back to sleep, I don know what has gotten in you," Mr. Williams told his wife.

"You like that niggard?" Her eyes flashed and her lips tremble.

"What in the world are you talkin about?"

"You are always takin up for her. Things must have ran amuck while I was in the hospital havin the baby. I jus knew you were carryin on with her!"

"What kind of man do you take me to be? Carryin on with a child!"

I could hear little Johnny cryin. Miz Williams didn't pay him no mind, she jus stood there eyein her husband. Susie came on the porch cryin.

"Mama , Papa, please don't fight," she begged dem.

Miz Williams looked at Susie and left the porch. Mr. Williams went wit his wife. Susie was left standin on the porch cryin, facin the kitchen door. I went to touch her shoulders but she jerk away from me and left the porch. I heard Mr. Williams call her. I went on back and laid down on floor of the porch. I pray that Mr. Lester would come soon and save me but he didn't come, at least not right away.

After a while Miz Williams came on the porch again. I guess that Mr. Williams was asleep.

"Go take a bath. You been around those niggards all last evenin and you smell like them. Make sure you wash your hair."

I git up and did like she said.; I was too afraid not to.

Miz Williams went to town again when Mr. Williams left. Miz Williams didn't take Susie wit her so I knew I couldn't go back to 29th street. Susie stay in the house wit me most of the day but she didn't talk to me at all. Later that afternoon Susie left the house and went to her friend house. I was doin my regular chores while little Johnny was asleep, when I heard someone in the neighbor yard next door. I thought it was Betty Ann and I went outside to talk to her, but it was Miz Brook in the yard, hangin out clothes.

She look at me. "She's not here, her family moved up north."

My heart fell. Betty Ann was gone and I didn't git a chance to see her before she left.

"When did she leave, ma'am?" Tears start rollin down my cheeks.

"About a week ago. Don't cry little girl." Miz Brook came on up to the fence. "I know that you're gonna miss her." Her kind face smiled at me wit pity.

"I sure will ma'am. I hadn't realize that it had been that long since I talk to her." I said, barely gittin the word out 'cause of me cryin.

"I am sorry. Is Miz Williams at home?"

"No ma'am, she ain't. She went to town and left me wit Susie and the baby."

"Where is Susie?"

"Somewhere wit her friends."

Miz brooks looked around like she was lookin for somethin then she smile at me. "Miz Williams don't want me to give you no cookies. I don't know the reason but I jus baked some. If you want, I'll give you some."

"I would sure like some, Miz Brooks."

"Okay."

She left me and went back in her house. She return wit a small bag of cookies and handed dem to me.

"Thank you ma'am."

I open the bag and take one out. Before I could git it in my mouth I saw Miz Williams comin in the gate. She saw me in the backyard wit one cookie in my hand and the bag in the other. She eye Miz Brooks and hurry around to both of us. She snatch the bag of cookies out my hands.

She turn to Miz Brooks, her eyes on fire. "I told you not to feed my niggard!"

"I do't see anythang wrong with givin her a few cookies," Miz Brooks said.

Before Miz Brooks could say anythang else, Miz Williams grab me by the collar of my dress and storm in the house. When we was in, she slammed the door.

"Haven't I told you not to eat anything but what I give you? You continue to disobey me. Since my food is not good enough for you, then you won't eat until you learn!"

I stood there in disbelief as Miz Williams left.

When evenin came, she fed Susie and herself. But she didn't warm up a plate of beans for me. I went to bed hungry that night, but I said to myself that I could take it. The next day she didn't feed me either, but she made me do my same amount of work. When the evenin came, my guts was hittin against theyself. The pains of hunger was worse than I could've imagin. When I went to bed I couldn't sleep because it hurt so bad. I roll and helded my stomach, moanin in pain. I heard someone come in the kitchen. I pray that it would be Susie. I git up and walks in the kitchen to see Susie gitting herself a glass of water. I approach her by the sink.

"Susie," I whisper, "could you please give me somethin to eat? I is so hungry."

I was holdin my stomach.

Susie look at me. "I ain't gonna give you nothin 'cause I don' like you anymore. You makes my mama and papa fight all the time. I wish that you would jus go away," Susie said, her face was all frowned up. One of her hands was clinched in a tight little fist. Wit the other she held the glass of water.

"I wanna go away but your mama won't let me. My mama won't come and git me. I don't know why. I don't have no money and you mama won't send me home. She is the one that is keepin me here. Even now, she promises to hide all of her jewelry and tell the police that I stole it, if I go away from her. I wanna go home Susie. I don wanna stay here. Please Susie. Please give me somethin to eat; you is my only hope now. If you don't, I is afraid I gonna die."

"You're lyin on my mama," Susie said, wit tears tumblin down her eyes.

"Please, Susie."

Susie stopped cryin and wiped her eyes with one hand, dranked her water and put the glass in the sink, and walked away from me. I watched her sadly, knowin that she was goin back to her room for the night. As much as the pain hurted in my stomach, it hurt more in my heart. I felted that Susie didn't care about me anymore. I went back on the porch. Tears fell down from my eyes, and I git down on my knees and pray.

"Oh Lawd, why Lawd, do I have to suffer like this? What did I do wrong? Please tell me. I feel so bad inside. My mama and papa ain't came for me and it been almost two years, and I don't know why. Sometimes I feel like they don't care about me. Mr. Lester ain't came here either and I is so hungry. Lawd, I jus wanna die. I don't have nobody. Please Lawd let me die."

I laid on the floor wit my tears runnin down like water. I thought about how it would be to be at home wit my sweet Lawd. I close my eyes and imagine that I would never be hungry for food or love again, if I was to die. I didn't hear Susie come in the kitchen wit two pieces of bread wit a slice of roast beef in between dem. She also brung a glass of water.

"Here, I made you a sandwich. Eat it quick jus in case Mama heard me."

I git up and took it out her hand.

"Thank you, Susie."

"I still like you Ruthie. You still my friend," she whisper. "I don't want you to be hungry and die."

I smile at Susie, and she smile back as she left the porch, goin back to her room.

"Thank you Lawd," I said, and gulped down the sandwich and drank the water. After I ate, my stomach was full but my heart was still hurtin. I laid down on the floor and stared into the darkness until I felled to sleep.

CHAPTER TWENTY

It was at the crack of day when Miz Williams woke me up and gave me a plate of beans.

"I hope you learned your lesson. Don't ever disobey me again."

"Yes ma'am."

I ate the beans like I was real hungry while she stand in front of me. When she left the porch I pour the rest of the tasteless mess into one of my dresses. I folded the dress up over the beans. I intentions to git rid of the meal as soon as I could git my dress out the house. I came out to the kitchen and walk over to Miz Williams.

"Can I go out and wash the plate?"

"Go ahead Ruthie."

I went outside and wash my plate. When I came back in the house I dry it and put it away. Miz Williams left the kitchen. I went back to the porch, closed the door, laid back down on the blanket and went back to sleep. I was woke up by the sound of someone movin around in the kitchen. I gits up and open the door and look out and saw Mr. Williams. Soon Miz Williams came in the kitchen and started makin a pot of coffee. I close the door and took off my gown and put on a dress and shoes. I walk out the door to the kitchen where Susie was, jus as she went up to her papa. He pick her up in his arms, huggin her, and gave her a kiss on her jaw. I stood there watchin wit a feelin of sadness and loneliness coverin my mind as I thought about my own papa and mama. Miz Williams interrupted my thought.

"Ruthie, you go outside and dig up a little plot of dirt in the front yard next to the fence."

I look at her but didn't say nothin. A new feelin was growin inside of me for Miz Williams—it was hate.

"Don't jus stand there girl, go git the flowerbed ready for planting. I want another fowerbed *today*, not tomorrow. So, go dig up that yard."

I left the house and went to the front yard by the fence. I eye the shovel what was lying on the ground by the bathroom wall. I looked at the sweet-smellin flowers with their bell-shaped heads gently swayin. I pick one from its little patch of dirt, that kepted it alive, and crush it in my hand. I threw it and watched its crumbled body fall to the ground. I took the shovel, walk over to where Miz Williams want me to dig, and jam it in the ground as hard as I could. When I was liftin the dirt I heard a voice saying, "Don't hurt youself." I look up and there was Mr. Lester Brown.

I scream for joy, drop the shovel, and ran to the gate and threw it open. I ran up to Mr. Lester Brown and hug him and he hug me back. Mr. and Miz Williams heard me and came a runnin out the house wit Susie runnin behind dem. Mr. Brown and I stopped huggin each other when he saw dem. I turn around and look at dem, and proudly say, "Tis here is my Uncle Lester."

"Hi you," Mr. Lester politely said, but kept his eyes down.

"Hi Lester," Mr. Williams said. Please to make your acquaintance. This is the first time I ever met any of Ruthie's family. I was beginnin to think that she had none."

"She has plenty of family, sir. I is here 'cause my poor old mama died. The family like Ruthie to come home for her grandma funeral."

"Grandma dead?" I cried, tryin to look upset.

"Yes honey, she died of a heart attack a few days ago," Mr. Lester said, lookin real sad. I hate for you to come home on such a sad note but you gotta, to be wit the family."

I started cryin like I was real upset and I bury my head in Mr. Lester's chest.

"There there, child. Try to be strong." He pat me on my back.

"I am sorry that you lost your grandma Ruthie, I guess that you should be packin to go now." I took my head from Mr. Lester's chest and turned around to face Mr. Williams.

"Yes sir," I said, tryin to hide the joy in my heart.

"Go on and git you things Ruthie so we can leave."

"Yes sir."

As I was walkin to the house I hear Miz Williams askin Mr. Lester a lot of questions.

"How did you git here Lester?"

"I came by bus ma'am."

"When did you git here?"

"Jus git here today ma'am."

"How is Ruthie's mama? Land sake, I forgit her name. What is her name, Lester?"

"Honey please. Why you givin this poor man the third-degree? He just lost his mama."

I came back to the yard wit my clothes all tied up in a rag, including the dress wit the beans. I was still cryin. I was about to leave, when Mr. Williams remember that I hadn't been paid for my work.

Mr. Williams told Mr. Lester Brown to leave and come back around three. Mr. Williams was gonna go to the bank and git the money to pay me for workin the past years.

"I'll make sure that Ruthie is ready to go with you at that time," Mr. Williams promised.

"Okay sir. I'll be comin back for Ruthie at 3:00."

Mr. Lester Brown looked at me and said, "Don you keep on cryin like that, you gonna make yourself sick. I'll be back around three, for sure, to git you. Be ready, you hear?"

"Okay Uncle Lester." I was sniffin and wipin tears from my eyes.

Mr. Lester said goodbye to the Williams' and took off walkin down the street. Mr. and Miz Williams went back in the house along wit Susie, leavin me outside to watch Mr. Lester disappear down the road. When I came in the house Mr. Williams told me that he was gonna pay me good for the time I had been wit dem.

Mr. Williams left for the bank and I went to the porch, where I had slept for more than a year and nine months. I was there for about five minutes when Miz Williams came on the porch. I was feelin very good inside when I noticed her.

"Where do you think you are goin?"

"Home, ma'am."

"You're not goin nowhere."

"But I got to go to my grandma funeral." I swallowed hard.

"The niggard's dead, why you wanna see a dead niggard?"

"She my grandma." Susie came on to the porch and stood beside her mama.

"When Mr. Williams gits home, you tell him that you don't wanna go—you hear?!"

Susie looked at her mama like she couldn't understand what she was saying.

"My uncle is here to git me." I felted my stomach tighten up.I hung my head down.

"You tell him the same, that's *if* that niggard comes back. I don't believe that he's your uncle anyway."

Suddenly a strength came over me that I never realize. I answer Miz Williams, but it weren't the answer she wanted. I straighten up my head and look her straight in the face and say, "I is leavin ma'am, and I ain't tellin Mr. Williams nothing but thank you for my money."

"You filthy niggard! We'll see about that. You know what I told you the last time!"

She scream and ball up her hands into fists and I thought she gonna hit me. "I am gonna hide all of my jewelry and tell the police that you stole it." She stormed out the room, pushin Susie aside.

Susie and I both ran out the room and watched her go down the hall to her room. My head start to feel like a horrible weight was on it and I shook all over. I open my mouth and howl, "No!" Tears stream down my face and wettin the front of my dress. I felted weak and helpless. I let out another cry and my knees felted like they couldn't hold me anymore. I felled to the floor and my heart heart felted like it was gonna bust wide open. I held my little sag of clothes to my chest and looked up into the ceilin and let out another cry. I looked over at the front door. With no thought at all, I git up and stopped cryin. I look over at Susie and the tears runnin down her face. Her eyes was filled with pity as she look at me. Witout a word, I bolt for the door.

I ran, flyin down the steps like a bolt of lightin, wit all the power I had in me. I ran like the colored slave people. The streets was my swamp and the houses was my forest. The overseers was the fright that controlled me for a year and nine months. I ran from fright, I ran from despair, I ran from hunger, and I ran to freedom that was once mine and embraced her.

In the distance I could hear Miz Williams screamin over and over again. "HAS ANYBODY SEEM MY NIGGARD?"

CHAPTER TWENTY-ONE

I was exhausted when I git to 29th street. I made my way to the beauty shop where there was women waitin to git their hair done. I ran pass dem to the back room where the supplies was kept. I open the supplies' door and ran inside. I closed the door and sat on the floor, all balled up against one wall until Beulah open the closet door. She took one look at me and holler, "Mama, they is a skeleton in our closet!" Then she laugh.

"You don have to holler Beulah, I is here."

Ms. Mable came over to where I was and pulled me off the closet floor. Beulah left the room.

"What happen Ruthie?"

"I is gonna go to jail."

"Why you is goin to jail?"

"Cause I ran ma'am," I cried.

"Did Lester make it there?"

"Yeh, I made it there."

Mr. Lester was standin in the doorway behind Ms. Mable.

"You pass right by me girl, didn't you see me? You was runnin like the Devil was after you!"

"Miz Williams said for me not to go wit you, Mr. Lester. She said if I did she was gonna hide her jewelry and tell the police that I stole dem. I git scared that I might have to stay wit her, so I ran. I don wanna go to jail. I didn't do nothin. I is tired of being her slave. I jus couldn't stand it anymore."

"Did you git your money?" Mr. Lester was rubbin his hands together.

"No sir."

"Damn!" He shook his head and hit one of his hands against his leg. He then turn and went on out the door.

I look at Ms. Mable.

"I don't know what gonna happen to me now."

Ms. Mable look at me and smile.

"Don't you worry about nothin. The police ain't comin down here. You is free." Ms. Mable hug me. Wit tears runnin down my eyes I look up at her.

"I don't know where I is gonna stay now. I guess, in the streets."

"Like I told you before.You is stayin wit us. Right now I got to go finish the lady's hair I was workin on. You hungry?"

"No ma'am."

"Go sit in the shampoo room for the rest of the day. Fanny Mae will be right in there in a few minutes." Ms. Mable went back in the room where she did hair. I look in the direction of the shampoo room, walk in, and took a seat. Beulah was in the room readin a magazine and she look up when she saw me.

"Why you is so scared, Ruthie, that you has to hide in that closet?"

"I is scared 'cause the police might git me and put me in jail."

"No wonder I seen dem lookin in here."

I ran back to the closet. I purty much stay in there for the rest of that day. Ms. Mable tried to git me to come out but I was too scared. I only came out to use the bathroom—I even ate in the closet.

When it was time for dem to go home, Ms. Mable told her family that I was gonna be living wit dem.

"That wonderful Mama," Fanny Mae sound very happy about the idea.

"It's barely enough room for me and Fanny Mae in that bed. Where you gonna put Ruthie? She can't sleep wit us."

"Beulah, shut you mouth." Beulah frowned, but she wasn't about to protest anymore wit her mama.

I was too scared to go on the street without a disguise. Ms. Mable thought it was silly but she put an old wig on my head and threw a trench coat over my shoulders. It was hot but I kept that coat on all the way to her house.

Ms. Mable family live in Madison Heights. That where colored folk that was better-off, live. The house was much bigger than Miz Williams; the front porch stretched the whole length of the house. The first room we enter was the sittin room. A large brown sofa was in the room along wit a chair, and a lamp that sat on a end table. A black chair sat in one corner wit a footrest in front of it. Along side the chair was another end table wit a ashtray on it. The room had a tall radio sittin in another corner. A long table sat in front of the sofa wit some figurines of animals on it. Right off from the sittin room was two bedrooms and a kitchen. The bedroom on the left was the room where Mr. Lester and Ms. Mable slept. The one on the right was the girls' room. The kitchen sat in the middle of those two rooms, and the bathroom was jus off from the kitchen. The house had wooden floors in every room cept the kitchen. It had a real bright linoleum floor.

Ms. Mable made me take the coat and wig off before I follow her over to the girls' room. It had one large bed, one dresser, and a small chair sat in the corner. The room was so large that another bed could have been put in it and it still would have room to move around wit ease. A closet was in the room, and a window look over the backyard. Fanny Mae came in after us and open the window, letting a warm breeze fill the room. The curtains flapped in the air.

Ms. Mable left me in the room for a few minutes while Fanny Mae talked to me. Beulah came in the room, sat on the bed, and jus look at me, rollin her eyes. When Ms. Mable came back she brought a rollaway bed. Fanny Mae ask her where she git the bed, and Ms Mable say that she borrow it from one of her neighbors. Ms. Mable spreaded two sheets on the bed then put a pillow on it.

When I git ready for bed that night, I slid in between the cool sheets and laid my head on the soft pillow. I looked at Fanny Mae.

"I ain't slept in a real bed in over a year, Fanny Mae. This feel like heaven."

I smell the sheets and close my eyes, enjoyin the softness of the bed. Beulah start talkin about the police.

"You know Ruthie, I hear stories about dem draggin poor colored people out they beds and hangin dem. They even kill chillin. Have you ever seen a person that was hung? Their eyes bulge out and their tongues comes out of they mouths. The person would shake real bad jus before they died. Yep that's what they do to people that steals from white folks."

When she git through wit the story I was too scared to sleep in the bed. I waited until Beulah and Fanny Mae was asleep. I git up and went in the bedroom closet and stay there for the rest of the night.

The next day Ms. Mable found me balled up in the closet, asleep. She came over and took me by the hand wakin me. She pulled me up.

"Child come on out of that closet. I made that bed up for you, and here you is sleepin in the closet."

"I was scared, Ms. Mable. That's why I git in the closet." I stood up.

"You can't stay in the closet for the rest of you life. I told you, ain't no white policemen comin here."

"Yes ma'am."

"Now go git ready for breakfast."

I went in the bathroom and washed up. When I was through I went back in the room to put on one of my dresses. Fanny Mae was in the room watchin me.

"Girl, you look so bad in that outfit, let me give you one of my dresses."

Fanny Mae was a little bigger than I was, and the dress she gave me hung off a little bit, but I was happy to be wearin it.

"Oh thank you Fanny Mae. I promise that I won't mess it up."

"Girl, don't worry bout that."

Ms. Mable came in the room.

"Don't you look purty." Ms. Mable smile at me. "Now give me all the rest of those clothes you brought wit you."

I git my little sag of clothes and gave dem to her. She took the clothes to the back yard and put dem in a large can and set dem on fire.

"I don't want anythang around to remind you of the time that you spent wit your Miz Williams.

She even burn the panties that I had on. I had to wear Fanny Mae panties until Ms. Mable took me to the store that day. They fell off me twice before Ms. Mable could pin dem up to fit me.

When we went to the shop, Ms. Mable didn't give me nothin to hide my face wit. I tried to keep my head down so nobody see me. Ms. Mable kept encouragin me to pick my head up. We all sauntered down the street that day like a family of ducks. Mr. Lester Brown in the lead wit Ms. Mable behind him. Then it was me and Fanny Mae. Beulah was last. Ms. Mable had a hard time tryin to keep up wit Mr. Lester 'cause she kept lookin back at me.

Beulah was lingerin in the back tryin to git attention from the few boys that was walkin down the street. She would bat her eyes and say hi to every boy who pass by.

When we git to the shop, Ms. Ester was there waitin at the door.

"Mornin. How's you little package?"

"She is a doin jus find Ester," Ms. Mable said.

Miz Ester was a nosey busy-body. She came to the shop every day jus to gossip. I guess she didn't have nothin else to do. She would talk about everybody in a way that was funny to me. I would laugh every time.

As soon as the door open, Ester march right on in. She took a seat by the window so she could to see what was goin on outside as well as what was goin in the shop.

Ms. Mable told me to jus sit down in the shampoo room and look at some magazines 'cause she was gonna take me shoppin later that day. Ms. Ester kind of look at Ms. Mable in a sly way.

"You gonna have her stay at you house and not work? Huh, I should have it so good."

"The girl is still scared Ester."

"You need to stay out our business Ester." Mr. Lester sounded irritated.

"I ain't in your business. God know I mind my own business. But, if she was livin wit me, I would have her work somewhere." Ester turned her head and look out the front window.

"I don' feel right if I don't work Ms. Mable."

"Ms. Mable look at me like she wasn't sure if she should put me to work.

"Let me think. Do you know how to shampoo heads?"

"Don't look hard ma'am. I believe I can do it."

"You can help Fanny Mae and Beulah wash heads after we git back from the store. You all can divide up the customers. For now, jus sit back there in the shampoo room."

"Yes ma'am." I went back to the shampoo room and sat in a chair and waited.

When Ms. Mable git a break from her customers she took me shoppin. She brought me three dresses, seven pair of panties, two slips, two pairs of shoes, and a lightweight coat for cool nights. As we shopped, excitement bubbles over in me, as I run around in the store like a little child in a toyshop. When Ms. Mable brought an item for me, my thoughts rang out in my head. "This is my very own." Before the ladies at the counters bagged anythin I hug each item and smell the newness. As we walked back to the beauty shop I kept laughin.

"What's the matter child?"

Ms. Mable stop and look at me. I held each bag close to my body like someone might come and take it away. Wit a voice between cryin and laughin I replied, "It's Christmas Ms. Mable. It's Christmas."

As we walk back to the shop, Ms. Mable told me that when she git back that she was gonna do my hair. When we git back to the shop, she told Fanny Mae to wash my hair. Afterwards, Ms. Mable dried, press, and curled it, letting the curls fall on my shoulders. Ms. Ester said that I look like a little chocolate doll. Ms. Mable and Fanny Mae smiled. Beulah jus look at me.

"You ready to start shampooin hair now?"

"Yesum Ms. Mable. Oh, yes." I was feelin very happy at that moment.

"She's gonna put shampoo in they eyes, you mark my word." Beulah came over to her mama and me. Fanny Mae was sittin in a chair not far from the three of us. She look over at Beulah and me.

"Don pay her any attention Ruthie. She jus mad because she gits a dime for every head she washes. Now she can't git as many dimes since it's gonna be the three of us washin heads."

"Oh shut up Fanny Mae, you make me sick." Beulah turn and went back to the shampoo room. Fanny Mae git up from the chair and follow behind Beulah. Ms. Mable jus shakes her head at dem as she watch dem walk back toward the room. Ms. Mable then look at me.

"Ruthie go on back there and tell dem to give you the smallest apron."

"Yesum." I went back to the shampoo room. Fanny Mae and Beulah was still bickerin as they divided up the towels. I interrupted dem.

"Beulah, you mama said for you to give me the smallest apron."

"I know Mama don't really mean that. You don't know how to shampoo a head."

"What to learn, Beulah? You jus put some water on they hair, then the shampoo."

"Girl, you still nervous about dem police, you jus might git shampoo in the ladies' eyes."

"She is gonna do jus fine." Fanny Mae handed me a bottle of shampoo and a towel.

Beulah went into the closet and git the apron for me. I put it on and waited for the customers to arrive.

"Let me give you some advice to make you relax," Fanny Mae advise me. "When you are shampooin the ladies' hair, talk to dem."

"What could I say to a grown woman they wanna hear?"

"Ask dem about their chillins and if they have a girl around you age. Grown women like to talk about their chillins."

"Okay, I'll try it Fanny Mae. Is that really true that Ms Mable is gonna give me a dime for shampooin each head?"

"Yeah, thats right," Fanny Mae said.

"That's real nice of her." I tied my apron tighter on my waist.

"That's *if* you wash a head," Beulah said, lookin at me wit her arms folded.

We all sat down and waited. I was nervous but I trys not to show it. I was still thinkin about Miz Williams' threats. As Fanny Mae and I talk, I couldn't stop my legs from bouncin. About a half hour later a lady came to the shampoo room and stood in the doorway lookin at Beulah.

"Where you want me to sit Beulah?"

"Right here, Miss Bertha."

The lady sat down in a chair by the first sink. Beulah git out a a bottle of shampoo as the lady relaxes her head back toward the sink. Beulah comes over to her and put the shampoo on the sink and turn on the water. She reaches down under the sink and picks up the large pitcher. She filled it with water and put it on the sink. Beulah then walk over by Fanny Mae and me to pick up the towel the she had left on the chair that she was sittin in.

"Beulah. Why don't you let Ruthie shampoo Miss Bertha hair?" Fanny Mae ask .

Beulah look at me, then in the direction of Miss Bertha, and wit a smirk on her face she said, "Go right ahead." Beulah walk back over to the sink where Miss Bertha was wit her eyes closed.

"Beulah, massage my head real good while you shampooin it."

"I ain't gonna be shampooin you hair today Miss Bertha. A new girl is gonna be doing it."

"A new girl?" Miss Bertha open her eyes.

"Me ma'am." I walk over to the sink.

Miss Bertha look at me and kind of chuckled to herself.

"I guess your little bony fingers can massage my head good."

"Yes ma'am, they can."

Miss Bertha was tall wit medium-length nappy hair. She wasn't a purty lady. She had a meanness about her that show on her face. I started askin her questions about her chillins.

"I ain't got none." Miss Bertha's voice sounded uncarin.

I was stunned. I didn't know what to ask her. I decided to jus wash her hair. I took the pitcher wit the water and started pourin it on her head. Beulah walked out the shampoo room as I was pourin the water. She came back jumpin up and down, shakin her hands like she scared.

"I think the police jus came in the shop!"

I jumped. The water I was pourin on Miss Bertha head now all over her, coverin her from head to foot.

"Miss Bertha scream. I dropp the pitcher and run into the supply room closet slammin the door behind me. Through the door, I could hear Beulah laughin her head off. Miss Bertha started cussin, and I heard her scream that she wanted to kill me. She came over to the door and jerk it open, and I jus knew I was gonna die. Fanny Mae scream for her mama, and Ms. Mable came into the room jus as Miss Bertha grab me by my hair pullin me out the closet.

"You turn her loose right now, Bertha!" Ms. Mable shouted. "Shame on you wanting to beat up a child."

"Look at what that child did to me!" Miss Bertha was breathin heavy but she turn my hair loose.

"Beulah told her the police was a comin," Fanny Mae said, as she came over and put her arms around me.

"What the Police git to do wit her wettin me up like this?"

"It's not her fault. The poor thing is scared to death and Beulah keeps teasin her. Where is Beulah?" Ms. Mable turn around lookin for Beulah. "Where is that girl?"

"She left jus a second ago Mama, runnin."

"I is gonna git her later. Let me find somethin for you to wear Bertha. I'll hang you dress out back to dry. Fanny Mae will wash your hair, and I do you hair today, free of charge.

"Well, that the least you can do," Miss Bertha sounded calmer.

"Okay then. I is gonna go and git you a dress."

Ms. Mable was about to leave the room when she look at me. She grab me by the hand.

"You comin wit me."

She took me in the room where she did hair and sat me down by Ms. Ester.

"Ester, Ruthie gonna be wit you for a little while. Seem she had a little accident and pour water all over Bertha."

Ester turned around in her chair and look at me. I sat there feelin stupid wit my arms folde around me. I hated myself for spilling the water on Miss Bertha but I hated Beulah even more.

Ms. Ester, at first, jus kept laughin under her breath. Her body kind of shooked. When she finally stopped, she smile at me .

"I been wantin to do that to Bertha for years. Old evil heifer." She cover her face wit her hands and start laughin all over again.

Ms. Mable found a dress and gave it to Miss Bertha. Then she took the wet dress outside and hung it out to dry.

Fanny Mae shampoo Miss Bertha's hair and dry it out wit a towel. Mr. Lester came in the room wit Ms. Mable.

"I hear some commotion while I was cuttin a man hair upstairs. What happen in here?"

"Beulah. That's all I got to say Lester."

Mr. Lester left the shop. Later he came back wit Beulah, and march her up to Ms. Mable.

"Where you find her, Lester?"

"In the sandwich shop wit some of her friends."

Ms. Mable was doing Miss Bertha's hair, but she stop and look at Beulah.

"So you the one that 'cause all of this?"

"I is sorry Miss Bertha." Beulah kept her head down. She seem to be embarrass.

"Now come over here and say you sorry to Ruthie." Mr. Lester pushed her in her back toward me.

Beulah look at me and then up at the ceilin. "Sorry Ruthie."

"Okay Beulah."

Soon as Mr. Lester turned his head, Beulah stuck her tongue out at me.

When we gits home that night Ms. Mable made supper and pecan pie—Beulah favorite dessert. Beulah kept teasin me about Miss Bertha and the police. Ms. Mable told her since she couldn't obey her and not tease me, she wasn't gonna git any pie. Beulah sat at the table and watch us eat the pie until it was almost gone. Finally, before the last slice, she beg her mama for it. Ms. Mable said no. Beulah made a big fuss about it, and Ms. Mable git mad and send her to bed. When Fanny Mae and I went to bed, Beulah was already asleep.

"Thank God," I whispered, as I crawled into bed.

CHAPTER TWENTY-TWO

I kept tryin to do heads at the shop, but I jus wasn't good at it. Either I put too much shampoo in the ladies' heads or not enough. Ms. Mable thought that I might do better at pressin hair, but that was a disaster. I burn so many ladies' heads that Ms. Ester would warn everybody about me that came in. She say things like, "Sit at your own risk." Or, "If you value you hair don't go to the chair."

One lady came in the shop with short nappy hair. Ms. Ester hadn't yet arrive at the shop. I took out the straightenin comb and put it on the hot plate. I part a section of her hair to straighten when Ms. Ester step in the shop. She scream jus before I put the hot comb in the lady's hair.

"Lord have mercy. It took old bald-headed Rita fifteen years to grow some hair, now Lord, in a matter of minutes it gonna be gone."

Rita git up from the chair and put her hands on her hips. She look at me and said, "You're not touchin my hair, girl."

She look at Ms. Ester. "So that is what you call me, huh?"

"I ain't call you nothin." Ms. Ester put her pocketbook down in a chair and put her hands on her hips too.

"You makin fun of me."

"Who could help it? I bet you git more hair on you butt than you head. You even git the nerve to want curls."

"Old woman, don't you know I'll knock you into tomorra?" Ms. Rita ball up her fist.

"You and who army?" Ms Ester ball up her fist too.

Ms. Mable rush over to dem.

"Ladies please. I ain't gonna have tis in my shop. Rita come on over here, I is gonna do you hair. Ester, you sit over there by that window in your usual seat and keep your mouth shut."

Ms. Rita went on over and sat down in the chair where Ms. Mable pointed. Ms. Ester went over and sat by the window. Ms. Ester kept mumblin somethang but I couldn't hear what she said. Ms. Mable told me not to do any more heads for that day, so I ask her if I could go outside for a little while. She shook her head yes, and I went on out, draggin a chair wit me. I sat in the chair in front of the shop wit my head in my hands. "What is I gonna do?" I thought. I didn't know if Ms. Mable would let me live in her house if I didn't have a job. I thought about home, and wonder if it even worth it tryin to go back. After all, Mama never answer my letters. In my mind, she didn't want me. I was about to cry, when Ms. Ester came outside wit me.

"Too hot in there." She fan herself wit a piece of paper. "Mine if I sit down?"

"No ma'am." I git up and Ms. Ester sat down in my seat. She look back at the shop window. "Is she lookin out here?"

"Who, Ms. Ester?"

"That old crazy woman."

I look in the window at Ms. Rita. "No ma'am, Ms. Mable got Ms. Rita chair turn away from the window."

"Good. Old cow."

As soon as Ms. Ester was about to say somethang else, a man that was across the street from us caught her attention.

"Oh boy, here come ugly." The man started walkin across the street towards us. "Somebody should beat the hell out his mama for bringin somethin *that* ugly into this world," Ms. Ester said, under her breath.

I almost laugh but I held it in so Ms. Ester wouldn't git into trouble again.

"Hello Ms. Ester."

"Hello Lee Roy. You sure look handsome today. What have you done to yourself?" Ms. Ester smile at him.

"Jus me, Ms. Ester. I ain't done nothing special to make me look tis good. Its jus natural." He smile through a mouth of missin teeth.

The man, name Lee Roy, look like he about twenty-seven or so. He was tall, thin, and bowlegged. He was brown-skinned wit a big flat nose and large eyes that look like they was about to pop out. His face had a lot of bumps on it.

"Boy, if I wasn't so old, you would be mines. You need to git married boy. I know that you must be beatin dem girls off wit a stick. That mus be the only reason why you not married yet."

"Nah, Ms. Ester."

"They jus don't know what they missin."

Lee Roy look at me. "Who is tis purty young girl?"

"Her name is Ruthie and she is too young for you. Jus thirteen, she is."

"She is gonna git older, Ms. Ester." Lee Roy smile at me and wink. I took one step back.

"Now Lee Roy. You gonna make Ms. Rita jealous talkin to tis girl." Ms. Ester threw off her hands at him.

"Who is Ms. Rita?" Lee Roy asked.

"Look in the window. The lady that Ms. Mable is workin on is Rita. She told me she jus crazy about you."

"I think that I should jus go in there and talk to her. Maybe I can take her to the picture show tonight." Lee Roy lift one of his hands and rub it across the top of his head.

"She jus love that. Go on in there." Ms. Ester motion wit her hands toward the door, and Lee Roy went in. Ms. Ester chuckled . "He ain't git enough sense to fill a gnat butt to make it fly straight. Look in the window. What Rita doin Ruthie?"

I look in. Ms. Rita look like she was happy to have Lee Roy talk to her.

"What happenin Ruthie?"

"Ms. Rita jus talkin to Lee Roy and smilin."

"Oh well, they deserves each other." Ms. Ester sound kind of downhearted

I think Ms. Ester wanted Ms. Rita to be mad. Her voice sound disappointed that she wasn't.

Ms. Ester and I sat out there and talkin for a spell. Everybody that pass us knew Ms. Ester and she knew dem. As soon as they say hi and pass by, Ms. Ester would tell me somethin about they business. I wonder if they knew Ms. Ester knew that much about dem.

When Ms. Rita and Lee Roy came out the shop they was all smiles and holdin hands. Ms. Ester looked at dem both and said, "Well, I'll be." They didn't pay Ms. Ester no mind, they jus walk down the street.

I went back in the shop and Ms. Ester came in behind me, draggin the chair. She place the chair by the window and sat down.

"Lee Roy and Rita. Now, that a match made in hell."

Everyone in the shop laugh except Ms. Mable.

Beulah came out the shampoo room and ran on out the front door of the shop. I knew she goin to see that boy she like; he pass by at the same time every day. Ms. Mable start cleanin a straightenin-comb. She ask me to go to the shampoo room and git Beulah.

"She jus went outside, Ms. Mable. She jus pass you." I points to the front door of the shop.

"Go git her please, Ruthie."

"Yes ma'am." I went out the door and found Beulah leanin agin a pole not far from the shop.

"Your mama said for you to come here."

Beulah act like she didn't hear me. She jus sighed and said, "He sho nuff is easy to look at."

I look around, and sure enough, there was that boy comin down the street. I don't know what made Beulah do this but she bent down wit her butt facin the street. She kind of look back to see if that boy was watchin her. She never seen Mr. Lester a comin behind her. Mr. Lester stop and look at his her and he look at the boy a comin down the street, and slapped Beulah on her butt .

"Gal, your ain't gonna catch nothin all bent over like that, cept mosquitoes and flies. Git on in that shop!"

Beulah seem embarrass. She stuck out her lips and hurry back in the shop wit me right behind her. Ms. Mable seen Beulah and open her mouth to say somethin but Beulah ran pass her, back to the shampoo room. Mr. Lester came in the shop after me and Ms. Mable look at him.

"What done happen now, Lester?"

"Nothing done happen Mable."

Ms. Mable went on back to cleanin her comb.

When we git home that night I ask Ms. Mable if I could do another job at the shop. Ms. Mable looked thoughtful then she answer me. "I have a better idea. I know a place where you could work."

"Where, Ms. Mable?"

"Miz Johnson's."

I knew Miz Johnson must be white, and I wasn't too happy bout workin at another white woman house. After workin for Miz Williams I didn't want anythang to do wit any one of dem. Ms. Mable look at me—I guess my face must have warn her of what I was thinkin.

"Everybody is not the same, Ruthie. Miz Johnson is the nicest woman, white or black, I ever meet."

Well, Miz Williams was nice too til she git me away from my family. Then she turn and start actin like the Devil to me. I didn't know what to say to Ms. Mable cept yes ma'am, being that she took me in. I hope and pray that Ms. Mable wasn't about to tell me to live wit that Miz Johnson.

If she did, I wouldn't know where to go. I only knew that I wasn't gonna live in no white person house again and be treated like a slave. That night when I went to sleep, I kept havin nightmares about Miz Williams and that last day at her house. When I came in the kitchen for breakfast the next day Mr. Lester look at me.

"Ruthie you look terrible. Did you sleep at all last night?" Mr. Lester was eyein me as he sat down in a chair. "Is you feelin nervous about workin for Miz Johnson?"

Ms. Mable was lookin at me too, as she fill Mr. Lester plate wit grits.

"You gonna be jus fine Ruthie. After you done work there for a week I is gonna give Fanny Mae, you, and Beulah some money to go to the picture show for a celebration of you new job."

"Thank you Mr. Lester."

I knew after what Mr. Lester said that they meant for me to continue livin at their house. I smiled.

CHAPTER TWENTY-THREE

"Why those little niggards. What possessed them to tie cans on that poor cat's tail? They scared it almost to death."

The white lady was standin in front of a tree lookin at an old gray cat that was up in it lying on a limb wit about seven cans tied on it tail. Every time the cat move, the cans bang together, startlin it, and the cat run higher up the tree.

The lady was of average height. Small built wit gray hair that was comb back and put in a bun. She look old but she act like she had a lot of fire in her.

I was hopin that tis wasn't Miz Johnson 'cause she had jus call some white boys niggards. I knew they had to be white 'cause no colored boy, wit half a brain, would have the nerves to come to a white person town, tie cans on a cat tail, and live to tell about it. If tis was Miz Johnson and she call those boys niggards, what she gonna call me?

Ms. Mable walk straight up to the woman and said hello.

The woman turn around. "Why Mable, how are you? I thought you had forgot about me!"

She grab ahold of both of Ms. Mable hands like she was real glad to see her. She was a smilin. Ms. Mable was too. "Oh no." I thought. "Tis is Miz Johnson. I is in for it now."

"I ain't never gonna forget you Miz Johnson. If it wasn't for you, we wouldn't have our shop. I can't help but think about you night and day, and I thank God for a woman like you."

"I been meanin to ask you. What did you name the shop?"

"Ms. Mable's and Lester's Beauty and Barber Shop."

"Good Name. How is the shop doin? You must be makin some decent money by now."

"We is holdin up well. Especially in these times."

"Good. Is this one of your daughters? I haven't seen them in a long time."

"No, I wish she was. Ms. Mable put one of her arms around my shoulder, hugging me close. She is really a nice young girl. Her name Ruthie; she live wit us."

"Why, hello Ruthie."

"Hello ma'am."

The cat ran higher up the tree, takin Miz Johnson attention away from us for the moment.

"I feel so sorry for that cat, I am gonna git some food to try to coax it down. I feel if I don't git it down and git those darn cans off its tail, it might have a heart attack and die."

Miz Johnson started walkin toward her house. "Follow me in the house Mable, we can talk there."

Ms. Mable and me follow Miz Johnson inside her big house. It was filled wit a lot of nice stuff. Some of her furniture needed dustin and her front room floor needed a good washin, otherwise, the house look very nice.

"You and Ruthie can have a seat in the parlor while I go to the kitchen."

Ms. Johnson left the room and Ms. Mable and me sat down in a room wit furniture seem like it was made for a queen. They wasn't a lot of it but it all was made very rich and purty. The chair I sat in had arms made of carved wood. They was groves and twists in dem that seem like it took some one a long time to carve out. When I look real hard I could see little circles of tiny angels carved in the wood. All the arms of the chairs was painted gold. The seats was padded in a soft, gold and white, cloth.

"You know Ruthie, Miz Johnson gave me my first job. I work in tis house, cleanin. She treat me very good. You know that shop we have?"

"Yes ma'am."

"Well, if it wasn't for Miz Johnson, we wouldn't have it. You see, Miz Johnson loan us the money. We pay it back but when we was late she never worry us. She jus wait until we could pay her. She a wonderful lady and you is gonna like her."

"Yes ma'am." I didn't know if I would like her or not after hearin her say the niggard word. Ms. Johnson returned wit a can of tuna in her hand. Ms. Mable and I git up from our seats.

"You don't have to git up Mable, sit there a spell."

"I didn't come to stay long, I jus came to ask you a favor."

"What is it? Wait, let me guess. You want me to give this young girl a job."

"Will you Miz Johnson? She a good worker and jus as sweet as she can be. You won't be sorry."

"You can start tomorrow Ruthie."

"Thank you ma'am." I was tryin to sound happy, but inside I wasn't happy at all.

"I jus got a idea." Miz Johnson face lit up. I thought that she was gonna say somethin about me workin there.

"What Miz Johnson?" Ms. Mable eye Miz Johnson for an answer.

"I need a pair of scissors. Mable git my scissors for me. I am gonna go down the street to see if Loretta will let me borrow Sam. Be back in a minute."

Miz Johnson hurry on out the house. Ms. Mable went in another room of Miz Johnson's house and returned wit a pair of scissors in her hand.

"I wonder what she gonna do wit these? Come on Ruthie, let's go outside and wait for her."

When we git outside we seen Miz Johnson a comin up the street follow by a big muscular, colored man. Both of dem was walkin like they was in a hurry.

Miz Johnson came up to Ms. Mable. "You get the scissors, Mable?"

"Here they is."

Miz Johnson hand dem to the colored man.

"Which tree it in?"

"That one over there." Miz Johnson pointed.

"I gonna git me a cat. Be right down I reckon, in a minute."

The man walk over to the tree and put the scissors in between his teeth. He rubs his hands together, grab hold of a branch that was a hangin from the tree, and pulled hisself up. He climb the tree until he reach the the cat.

I looks around to find white folks was all over the place. It seem that the whole neighborhood came out to watch the man git the old cat out the tree. The man sat on a large branch wit the cat. He lean up again the trunk of the tree and took the scissors from between his teeth. It look like he was a talkin to the cat, and the cat move in closer to him. The man reach out one hand and rub the cat head, calmin it. Wit the other hand he reach around the cat and cut the cans from its tail. The cans come crashin down the tree to the ground, and the cat jump but it don't run. The man put the scissors in his pocket and took a hold of the cat wit one hand, puttin it close to his chest, and climb down the tree. The people on the ground cheer like he a hero. When his feet touch the ground , he was smilin from ear to ear. He hand the cat to Miz Johnson.

"Here you cat, ma'am."

"It ain't my cat."

"Well ma'am, since you was so concern bout it to git me to climb this here tree, you should be concern bout his welfare from now on." The man left, walkin back down the street.

Miz Johnson hug the cat, and it purr in her arms and close its eyes as she rub it head. The people start thinnin out, goin back to what they was doin, and Ms. Mable told Miz Johnson that we better be goin too. Miz Johnson said goodbye and told me to be at her house around nine the next day.

I return at Miz Johnson house the next day at nine like she told me. I work there all day and return to Ms. Mable and Mr. Lester house in the evenin. Miz Johnson had me to do the dustin and waxin of her furniture and wash her floors. When it was time for lunch Miz Johnson told me to go in the icebox and git somethin to eat. She was still in the house and I was scared to go in her icebox. I told Miz Johnson that I wasn't hungry but I really could had eaten a whole raw chicken.

The next couple of days when she told me to go and fix myself somethin I told her the same thing. One day she left the house for a minute and I ran in her kitchen, grab some meat out the icebox and shove it in my mouth. The next day I did the same thang. Miz Johnson must have seen me cause when she came back in the house, she look me straight in the eye and told me to sit down.

"Ruthie, what is wrong with you?"

"What you means, Miz Johnson?"

"I told you to go and fix yourself something to eat. Every time you say that you aren't hungry. When I leave, you go in the icebox and grab something. I watched you eat several times like you were a thief and had to eat the evidence before you get caught. In fact, one day when you left here I notice that you had grabbed the cat food and eaten it instead of tuna. Now, are you gonna tell me what is wrong?"

I wait a minute before I answer. I felted like a fool and I put my head down. "I was afraid ma'am."

"Afraid of what?"

"That you might git mad at me goin in your icebox and takin you food."

"That doesn't make any sense. I told you to go in there."

"Well, Miz Williams didn't allow me to take anythang but beans out her icebox.

Beans is all she allow me to eat. You is white like her, and I be thinkin that you be wantin me to eat the same thang. But I couldn't find any beans in you icebox, so I took you other food. I is awful sorry ma'am."

Miz Johnson seem like she was taken back at those words. At first she jus stare at me, then it seem she gather her thoughts.

"Ruthie, I am not Miz Williams. Be she white or not, I don't think like her. You better be getting that in your head if you're gonna be working for me. My word! What kind of woman is she to make you eat just beans?" Miz Johnson shook her head.

"I don't know what kind she was. The only thang I know is that she treated me real nice when we both live in Demopolis."

Miz Johnson left the room and I went back to doin my work. When I was done workin for that week Miz Johnson paid me and I thanked her and walked back to the beauty shop. When I git there, Mr. Lester hand me a quarter.

Mr. Lester had kepted his promise and sent us girls to the picture show. Beulah walk in front of me and Fanny Mae on our way to the show. Before we gits there Beulah stop walkin, turn around and look at me and Fanny Mae, and headed in another way, opposite the picture show.

"Where you goin Beulah?" Fanny Mae shout.

"To my friend house."

"If you gonna go to you friend house, we be goin wit you."

"I don't care."

Fanny Mae and I follow Beulah to a house that wasn't far from the picture show. When we gits there, a light-skin girl about Beulah age met us at the door.

"Hi. You all come on in."

"Annabelle, I didn't come for a visit . I come here to ask you if you wanna go to the picture show wit us."

"Well come on in, still," Annabelle said. "I got to ask my folks, Beulah."

We went in and stood by the door where they was five other chillins in the room. They look over at us and say hi. Annabelle went over to a woman that was in a chair in the sittin room. She was dark-skin and had her head down as she sew on a pair of pants. I looked over at the sofa—

that when I saw him. He was tall and light-skin, and his hair was brown—every strand of it stood straight up. He was talkin to a man that was lyin on the sofa, whose face I couldn't see. I jus look at his white hands. I wonder why a white man be lyin on a colored woman sofa. I kepted lookin over at dem until the boy caught my eye. He stop talkin to the man and went over to the woman that was sewin. The woman look up at the boy and Beulah friend. The woman face look familiar to me. The man that was lyin on the sofa, gits up in a sittin position and look over at us. He stare at me, then smile and look over at the woman.

"Honey, that the girl I try to git to come home wit me." He git up and came over to me. "Why you didn't come wit me, little girl? That woman you live wit was treatin you real bad."

"I thought you was white. Miz Williams scared me about going home wit some white man."

"Well I show you a picture of my family. I thought that you know I wasn't white by dem pictures. Well, I is glad that you all right. I thought you would die if you kept stayin wit her. You look terrible back then."

He look over at his woman. "That my wife Nellie. All these youngin is my mines." The chillins came over to where we was standin and walk to their papa side, all cept the boy and Annabelle.

His wife Nellie put her sewin down and came over to me. She hug me and look me in the eyes. "God bless you child. Are you back at home now?"

"No ma'am, I is stayin wit Ms. Mable. She took me in after I ran away from Miz Williams."

"Well then, God bless Mable. You know you can come and stay wit us anytime you like. I have eight chillins and we all would be glad to have you. The more the merrier."

"There use to be fourteen of us," Annabelle said, as she walk over to me. "Jus imagine all those sisters and brothers."

"What happen to the rest of dem?" I asked.

"They all went to heaven." The boy walked over to us.

Annabelle look at him. "This here is my brother Oscar junior. He the oldest."

Oscar turn his head to the side away from our faces and said hi. That when I notice he eyes. Even though he turn his head, I see his eyes jump.

"You girls better git goin before it git late," Miz Nellie motion for us to leave. "Oh, here you quarter Annabelle."

Oscar look at me shyly. "Bye now."

"Bye Oscar." I look at the rest of the family. "I is really glad to meet you all."

Mr. Oscar look at me and say, "Come back and visit us sometimes, you hear?"

"I will, sir."

We left going to the picture show, and when we gits there, the boy that Beulah liked was there. He was by himself, givin Beulah the opportunity to say somethin to him. He talk to Beulah for a while after we had bought our tickets, then he ask her to sit by him. Beulah was in seventh-heaven, and never came over to us.

"Youw best go find youw a seat far away from me 'cause I want this here man all to myself."

"We don't wanna sit by you anyway, does we, Annabelle and Ruthie?"

"Girl, I rather be by myself then to be sittin in a show watchin dem two kissin," Annabelle said, and turn around to find herself a seat. Fanny Mae and me follow her.

The boy walk us home that night after the show. First we stop at Annabelle's house and wait until she git in, then we walk home. Beulah and the boy walk in back of us all the way. Fanny Mae kept turnin around lookin dem, and finally asked the boy his name.

"His name Jeremiah Buford," Beulah said. "Now stop turnin around lookin at us." Fanny Mae and I made fun of the couple as we walk home. We whispers about dem so Beulah and Jeremiah wouldn't hear. Beulah hear us laughin and promise to beat me and Fanny Mae up if she found out that we was makin fun of dem. When we finally git home, Beulah talk about Jeremiah most of the night. She even plan their weddin that night. Fanny Mae and me thought Beulah was goin too far to even talk about marriage, 'cause she didn't know him. Turn out we was wrong 'cause Beulah became Miz Jeremiah Buford not many years later.

CHAPTER TWENTY-FOUR

F anny Mae, Annabelle, and me become good friends. Fanny Mae and me would go to Annabelle house almost every day after we git off from work. I try to talk to her brother Oscar, but he seem like he shy or somethin. He wouldn't say nothin but two words to me most of the time, and they was hi or bye.

Miz Johnson turn out to be a very nice lady. She was funny, yet serious, and she spoke her mind about most everythang. She had a daughter who live in Europe, and Miz Johnson spoke about her a lot. She wanted to see her daughter, but it seem that the girl too busy to come home, although she wrote her mama often.

Miz Johnson was a person that like to always be doin somethin. She love to take long walks in the afternoon, taking long strides as she walk. She always had me walk along wit her but I had to run most of the time to keep up. Some days she would be tired for no good reason.

Miz Johnson was well-liked in her neighborhood, but at times she curse too much. One day she call a white man a niggard. He had said somethin to her, makin her mad, and I was in the house watchin dem from the open door. He left with his face all red and lookin around like he hope nobody hear what she call him. After he left I went up to Miz Johnson in the front yard.

"Why you call that white man a niggard?"

"If you act like one, then you are one."

"I thought only colored folk are called niggards."

"Hell naw! Anybody could be a niggard no matter if they are black, white, purple or green, they just have to act like one."

One day Miz Johnson ask me to go to the fruit market wit her. When we git there I notice they was some white people that seem not to want me there. They didn't say nothing, they jus took one look at me and sneer; some even left the store. Miz Johnson seem not to notice and kept shoppin. She had me to pick up some oranges for her. I picks up one orange then drop it to pick a better one. I put that one down and reach for another one. I hears a little white boy beside me say, "Don't git that one Grandma, that niggard done had her hands on it."

The white lady drop the orange like it was on fire, and Miz Johnson saw her do it. She came over to me, pick up an apple that was on a bin and toss it at me. I caught it.

"Nice catch. Does that apple feel ripe?

"Yes ma'am."

"You sure know your fruit. Help me find some more."

I put the apple back in the bin. We went to another fruit counter jus when the other woman git there. Miz Johnson told me to touch the fruit jus when the other woman was about to touch it. Soon as I did, the other woman left for another bin wit her grandson. Miz Johnson left, followin her and draggin me along. It seem like Miz Johnson and the woman was in a race to git to the fruit. Every time we made it to the fruit first, Miz Johnson would tell me to feel the fruit. I touch it and the lady head for another counter. Miz Johnson would race behind the woman and jump in front, makin sure we git to each bin first. Finally, the lady give up and left empty-handed.

When the lady left, Miz Johnson look through her things.

"Ruthie. I think we done enough shoppin for today."

She paid for her fruit and vegetables and went home. Miz Johnson chuckle and talk about the lady.

"Old fool. She is the same age as me and hasn't learned anything yet. Used to be a loose woman in her young days; did more tricks than the people in the circus. Now she thinks she's better than everybody."

I jus look at Miz Johnson as we made our way back to her house. I listen to her make fun of white folk that didn't like colored and colored people that didn't like whites, all the way home.

Miz Johnson had a car but she would walk most everywhere she went. Sometime I wish she git the car and drive where she had to go 'cause I git tired of walkin. I ask her about takin her car one time, and she jus laugh at me.

"Ruthie, I need to keep my girlish figure. Nothing like walkin to help you keep your curves. Besides, it's good for the heart. There is nothing like a good walk to strengthen the heart and oil the old joints. I only take the car for emergency. Otherwise I just start it up once a week to make sure it's still runnin."

I worked for Miz Johnson for almost three years. She was always so nice to me that I look forward to goin to work.

It was gittin close to my sixteenth birthday, and Miz Johnson told me that we were going to walk to the big town to buy me somethin nice. We walk, for what seem like hours, to the big city stores. Finally we gits there, and I ain't never seen such tall buildins. I stretches my neck, lookin up, to see where the tops of the buildins end. They was more stores on one street than I every seen in my life.

Miz Johnson and me went in one store called Loveman and Joseph that sold women clothes. It was on 19street and 3rd I never seen a store so large, wit so much to buy. They was even stairs leadin up to other floors where you could buy men clothes. They was perfume and makeup layin on the counters. Shoes, pocketbooks, stockings, and dresses—you name it, it was in that store. I eyes the items, turnin around, tryin too see everythang while standing in one spot.

"Don't just stand there Ruthie. Go pick out something for yourself."

"Yesum."

I left Miz Johnson and went over to a rack of dresses and began lookin through dem for somethin perfect for me, when I saw *her*. Miz Williams was a standin by another rack of dresses in the store, but she wasn't lookin at any of dem. She was staring at me, sendin a cold shiver up my spine. I was frozen in the spot as I eye her back. Her chillins were wit her. Susie smile and raise up one hand to say hi to me. Miz Williams grab her hand and pull it down. Jus then, Miz Johnson came up to me.

"Ruthie, ain't these dresses just plain lovely?"

I couldn't answer her 'cause I kept starin at Miz Williams. Miz Johnson stop talkin and look at her. Miz Williams raise her eyebrows, took a hold Susie and little Johnny and disappear in the store.

Miz Johnson look at me. "Who in the Devil's name is she?"

A store clerk, standin in back of us, answered, "That's Miz Williams. She comes to the store mostly every day. She has the cutest little boy."

"Ruthie. Do you wanna shop anymore?" Miz Johnson said.

"No ma'am. I jus wants to git out of here as fast as I can."

As we was a walkin back to Miz Johnson house, she talk to me, tryin to make me feel better. "I don't like that Miz Williams. She seems like she is full of hate. You don't have to be afraid of her Ruthie. You shouldn't fear anyone but God."

"But I is still afraid of her, Miz Johnson. You don't know what she done to me and how she treated me."

"Of course not, you never told me."

As we walked home, I told Miz Johnson about Miz Williams and how she treat me so bad. I told her about me not gittin a letter from my aunt that raised me.

"I don't feel that my aunt love me Miz Johnson. I wrote her and wrote her but she never answer. I beg her to come and git me on one of my letters. Miz Williams said that my aunt didn't want me. At first I didn't believe her but now I does."

"Have you ever thought that Miz Williams might not have mailed the letters? Or, maybe Miz Williams might have taken the letters that you wrote and wrote somethin else on them that made your mama not write."

"But still, she should have came and git me after awhile. If I had a child, I would have come for it after a while. Miz Johnson, wouldn't you do the same?"

"Wild horses couldn't keep me from mine. That's why I think that something else was done. Try writin her again."

"But I did. I even wrote her witout Miz Williams knowin. She never wrote me back."

We reach Miz Johnson's house and she open her door so we could walk to her kitchen. She stood by the brown wooden table and kept tappin on it like it help her think. Miz Johnson didn't say a word. Her face look like she thinkin about somethin. She went to the sink and put both her hands in it and lean down into it. Finally she turn around and spoke.

"Ruthie, do you know someone else that knows your mama, who you can write?"

I thought for a minute. "Mary Ann. Mary Ann knows my mama."

"You have her address?"

"Yesum."

"Then write her. Tell her that you haven't heard from your mama. I have a gut feelin that your Miz Williams done somethin that was very low down and dirty. I don't know what it was, but it was very wrong."

"I guess I could write her tomorra. I ain't got no pencil and paper."

"You write her, now. I keep pencil and paper. Sit down at this here table, and I'll be right back."

I sat down and Miz Johnson left out the kitchen. She was only gone for a minute when she came back wit a stamp and stuff for me to write wit.

"Here. Now write."

I started writin the letter while Miz Johnson made us some tea.

Dear Mary Ann,

How is you? I miss you somthin awful. I wish I could see you all. Can you do me a favor? Please tell my Mama Flo, that I want her to write me. I haven't hear from her for so long. I don't live wit the Williams no more. I live wit somebody else. Please tell her I miss her. My address is on the front of tis here envelope. Please tell my mama to write me back soon. I kindly thank you.

Ruthie

"You finish writin already?"

"I ain't got too much to say. What I has here says it all."

"Give them my address Ruthie. You will be most likely be at my house when the letter comes."

I address the envelope, and me and Miz Johnson walk to the mailbox, and mail it.

"It's time for you to go on back to Ms. Mable's now. I guess that I'll be seein you tomorrow."

I chuckled. "Its Friday Miz Johnson, tomorra is Saturday."

"Well then, I'll be seein you, come Monday. Maybe we can get you somethin for your birthday on Monday."

"Yesum. We try again Monday."

I walk to the beauty shop, but nobody was there so I walk to the house.

When I arrive there, Ms. Mable meet me at the door.

"Hello sweet-sixteen. Come on in."

"Hi ma'am." I walk inside, thinking it was strange for Ms. Mable to greet me like that.

"Surprise!"

They had give me a party wit jus her family and Annabelle. I was so happy I finally had a birthday party. They was cake, ice cream, and decoration in the shape of flowers made of different color paper. I started to cry.

"Don't cry Ruthie." Ms. Mable hug me. "This is you special day. Be happy."

I held back the tears as Ms. Mable gave me a present. I open it to find the most prettiest dress I ever had. It was sky-blue wit little white buttons goin down the front. It was short sleeves wit a white collar and a blue belt.

"Oh thank you, ma'am."

"Try it on Ruthie."

I look at her, smile, then I took off to the bedroom. The dress fit perfect. I was smiling when I came out the room.

"You look so purty Ruthie." Ms. Mable eyed me.

"Thank you Ms. Mable and Mr. Lester." I hug dem both.

"I have a present for you too Ruthie." Fanny Mae hand me a comb for my hair.

I hug Fanny Mae. "Thank you kindly, Fanny Mae. I will keep it forever. Even if all the teeth falls out, I will keep the remains."

Fanny Mae laugh. "Don't do that. Jus buy another comb if that happen."

Annabelle came up to me and gave me a pair of white socks. "A girl could always use socks. I thought you might like these."

"I does like dem Annabelle. Thank you." I hug Annabelle.

Beulah was lookin out the window, and we all look at her. She turn around and look at me. "Happy birthday and all that stuff. I is gonna git you a present tomorra." She turn back around and look back out the window.

"Well, since the presents are given out, let's go eat some ice cream and cake," Mr. Lester said, as he head to the kitchen.

We all follow him, except Beulah who stay lookin out the window. Everybody sang happy birthday to me, and I blew out the candles, and we ate cake and ice cream.

"Papa why don't you take out the phonograph so we could dance," Fanny Mae said.

"Sound like a good idea to me."

Mr. Lester went to his bedroom and brought back the phonograph. It play records and look like a box with a horn on top. The records spin on top and the sound come out the horn. The phonograph only plays 33 -1/3 records, and you have to crank it up to play.

Mr. Lester crank up the phonograph. "I ain't got no new records, but this one is jus as good."

He put on a record by Mr. Louis Armstrong called, The Harlem Strut. It crackled as it spun around. Finally, a man raspy voice started to sing. The music had a up-beat tone. Everybody but me and Beulah started to dance. They moved their hips and arms to the music, and Mr. Lester pop his fingers as he dance, his shoulders movin up and down.

"Come on and dance Ruthie!"

"I don't know how to dance sir."

Beulah, who was still standin by the window lookin out, spoke,

"Anybody can dance. Jus move to the music."

"I'll teach you Ruthie." Fanny Mae came over to me and told me to first swing my hips.

Beulah ran to the door 'cause Jeremiah jus arrive. Beulah open the door, and Jeremiah stood there smilin. He heard the music and look at the family all dancing, and me havin my first lesson.

"Havin a party?"

"It Jus a little somethin for Ruthie, Jeremiah, lets go," Beulah say, as she started toward the door.

"Hi Jeremiah. Want some cake and ice cream before you go?" Ms. Mable stop dancin and motion for him to come in.

Mr. Lester stop dancin. "Come on in boy for a spell. Show ain't gonna start for another hour yet."

Jeremiah walked past Beulah. "I sure would like some cake and ice cream."

Beulah stood there all huff up. Jeremiah walk over to where Fanny Mae and me was dancin.

"You lookin mighty purty, Ruthie."

I stop dancin. "Thank you Jeremiah."

"What dance you tryin to do?"

"What this called, Fanny Mae?"

Fanny Mae stop dancin. The record had stop playin. "The Jitter Bug."

"Well you doin it wrong. Let me show you how. Come on Ruthie, let's dance."

Mr. Lester started up the record again.

"I don't know how to dance, Jeremiah."

"Jus do as I do."

Jeremiah started kickin his legs and movin his shoulders. I did the same. He swung his hips. I swung mines. He took a hold of my hand, and Fanny Mae and Annabelle clap their hands to the music as they watch us. He took me by the waist.

"Hold it right there! Jeremiah, come on here!" Beulah voice sounded agitated.

Jeremiah stopped dancin. "I is jus tryin to show Ruthie how to dance, Beulah."

"Come on, Jeremiah!"

"Come on, Beulah. I jus wanna show her a few more steps."

"Oh no you won't!"

Beulah grab one of Jeremiah hands and led him to the door.

Jeremiah look back at us jus before he went out the door. "I guess we better go. I'll be seeing you all."

He and Beulah left the house and I could hear her arguin. Mr. Lester went to the door and look at dem going down the street. He came back in the sittin room, took off the record, and sat in his favorite chair. He pulled out a cigar and started smokin it.

I walks over to him.

"I is so sorry that Beulah and Jeremiah is arguin. I feel it is 'cause Jeremiah said I looked purty. I don't want Beulah to be upset."

"Don worry about it." He crossed his legs, still holdin his cigar between his teeth. "Beulah shouldn't be so jealous. She is mean sometimes. She wants to marry that boy even if she has to hog-tie him to the altar. If she keep a treatin him like that, that the only way she git him there." He laugh and then started back puffin on his cigar.

Ms. Mable looks at her husband. "Shame on you Lester for talkin about your daughter like that."

Mr. Lester didn't even look at her. He jus kept puffin on his cigar and chucklin.

CHAPTER TWENTY-FIVE

"Ruthie. Here's you letter! It finally came!"

Miz Johnson ran in the house wit the letter in her hand, wavin it in the air. I was moppin the kitchen floor. When she said *letter,* my heart leaped.

"Ain't no time to mop nothin now, read this here letter."

I drop the mop on the floor as Miz Johnson hand me the letter. It been two weeks since I mailed mines. On the return address was Flo Mitchel, but I didn't know the address of the house. I grab on to a chair and sat down.

"Well hurry up and open it Ruthie. What you waitin for?"

I didn't realize, but I was starin at the front of the letter. I open it and begin to read. Miz Johnson pull up a chair beside me.

Ruthie, my baby,

Please come home. You don't know how much I have cried from missin you. Even now I is havin a hard time writin this here letter from stoppin and cryin, thankin God for you being alive. I was told that you was dead by you Miz Williams. She said that you been struck down by a car on you way to the school that she had you to. She told me not to come and pick up your body, for she was gonna send it home. What we got was an urn filled wit ashes. I never cried so much in my life. Not only did we not git a chance to see you sweet face but she had burn you body, so we thought.

I pause and look up at Miz Johnson, tears formin up in my eyes. "Why would she do somethin like that, Miz Johnson?"

"I don't know why Ruthie, but I do know that she's a dirty heifer!"

I started readin more of the letter.

Papa was broken-hearted. He never was the same after the ashes came. He would stay up most of the night. Sometimes he wouldn't eat. He said that he wasn't hungry. One day Papa had a heart attack. Ruthie you papa is—

I felted like a ton of brick had jus hit me. I couldn't say the word, I felted like it was stuck in my throat. I starting cryin and shakin, and put my head on Miz Johnson table. I felted hurt, and like I was the cause of my papa's death. He might would have still been alive if I had gone home after I left Miz. Williams. Miz Johnson took the letter out my hand and finish readin it.

"I am so sorry Ruthie."

Miz Johnson pull her chair close to mines and hug me. I lifted my head off the table and lean into her arms, a sobbin, my tears wettin the front of her dress. She kept sayin over and over, "I am sorry. I am so sorry."

"How could I be so stupid?" I said in between tears. "Why didn't I go home? Maybe if I had, Papa would still be alive."

"You ain't stupid Ruthie. Maybe it was your papa's time to go. You goin home or not, couldn't stop his time."

"But I believe Miz Williams when she said that my folks didn't want me. That why I feel so stupid."

"You were just a child. You are grown up now and you know that some people will lie. Miz Williams is just a lying, hateful person. One day she is gonna pay for what she done."

" I hate her."

"Don't hate her Ruthie. In fact, you should feel sorry for her. She can't be a happy person with so much hate inside. You stay as sweet as you are, and God will take care of her for lyin and doing mean things like that."

Finally when I stop cryin Miz Johnson hand me the letter agin. "Read on Ruthie. You gonna find out why she never got the other letters that you wrote." I took the letter out her hand and start back readin where I left off.

Papa is dead. After he die I couldn't pay the rent for the house we was livin in. I move in wit my sister, your real mama. She needed my help real bad. Please Ruthie, come home. Write me to let me know when you a comin. I will find somebody to pick you up at the bus station.
                    I Love you Always,
                    Mama

I put the letter down. Miz Johnson look me in the face.

"Now Ruthie what are you gonna do? Are you gonna go home now since you know the truth?"

I pause for a little while. "I don't have enough money to buy my fare to git home right now Miz Johnson. I gave some of my money to Ms.

Mable and I can't ask her for it back. I spent the rest. I got to work and save money for my ticket now, but it gonna take me at lease a month to save for it."

"I didn't ask you about your fare. What did I tell you before? Now answer me. What are you gonna to do? Are you going to continue to be dead or are you going to be alive and go home?"

"I ain't dead Miz Johnson, I is alive." I look at her bewildered of what she was tellin me.

"Good girl. There is no more work for you today. First we got to write a letter to let your mama know that you're comin. I am gonna buy your bus ticket as soon as we get an answer from your mama."

"Miz Johnson, you don't have to buy my ticket. I can save for it."

"I want to Ruthie. That will be my present to you."

Miz Johnson git up from the chair.

Now let me get you some paper and a pencil so you can write this letter." Miz Johnson left the roon and returned wit the items. I wrote my mama, and we mail the letter.

After I left Miz Johnson that day and made my way back to the shop, I told Ms. Mable that I was goin home. Ms. Mable was happy for me, and Fanny Mae say she sad to see me go but she understand. The next day when I git to Miz Johnson house, she tell me some of her best friends would be comin over. I thought they was comin over for tea. Around noon, some ladies show up at her house and Miz Johnson open the door for dem.

"Ruthie, come in here," Miz Johnson called to me from the sittin room.

I was in the kitchen washin dishes, so I dries my hands on a cloth and went in the sittin room. When I gits there, I found about five ladies all standin there smilin at me wit clothes in they arms.

"Hi Ruthie," one of the ladies said. The others jus smile at me.

"They all have presents for you Ruthie." Miz Johnson motion to me to come over to her.

I went over to Miz Johnson, and one lady hand me a arm full of dresses.

"I thought you might like these."

I was speechless.

The next lady walk over and hand me some money." A gal could always use some money."

I nod my head for yes.

All of dem gave money or some articles of clothin, everythang new. When they was through, Miz Johnson give me two suitcases. I was so happy, I starts crying.

"You don't know when to stop do you?" Miz Johnson was tryin to sound irritated.

"What do you mean ma'am?" I wipe my eyes.

"Ruthie, you're goin home in style. Now stop cryin and smile."

I stop cryin and smile for Miz Johnson.

When the ladies left, Miz Johnson told me to pack the suitcases. I pack dem both full. Miz Johnson went to her garage and start up her car, and I put the suitcases in it. She droved me to the beauty shop where Ms. Mable, Mr. Lester, and the girls was waitin for me. When Miz Johnson let me out the car, she git out it too and hug me. "Ruthie I am going to buy your ticket just before you leave, but would you do me a big favor?"

"What is it, Miz Johnson?"

"If you ever git married and have a baby girl, would you name her after me?"

"I sure will Miz Johnson, but I don't know you first name."

"My first name is Erin."

"Then Erin will be the name of my first girl child, if I every git married and have one."

She tap the top of the car wit her hand. "See, I do fire up this old car on special occasions."

Miz Johnson git back in her car, said goodbye to Ms. Mable family and me, then disappear down the road.

"Oh looka here. What in the world did she buy you that took two suitcases?" Miz Mable eye the suitcases.

"I can't wait to show you."

Mr. Lester took a look at the suitcases and reach down to pick dem up. He drop dem. "She should have given you a ride all the way to our house. These suitcases is sho nuff heavy."

We all laughed, all except Beulah.

As we walk home that evenin I saw Annabelle comin out a store wit a bag in her arms. I call to her and she came over to us. She look at the suitcases.

"Hi, everybody."

"Hi, Annabelle," everybody greet her.

"Who leavin town?" She asked.

"I is leavin, Annabelle. I is going back home to my mama."

"When you leavin?" She ask.

"As soon as my mama send me a return letter to let me know somebody gonna pick me up at the bus station."

"Is you comin back?"

"I don't know."

"I sure is gonna miss you."

"I'm gonna miss my *arms* if somebody don't help me wit these here suitcases," Mr. Lester said.

"I'll carry dem." I reach for the suitcases.

Fanny Mae reach her hand out . "I'll carry one too." She carry one and I carry one. We continue on down the road, and when Ms. Mable hear Annabelle and me talking, she turn around.

"Ruthie, I do hope you comes back and see us. You are such a sweet girl and we all gonna miss you."

"I is gonna try to come back Ms. Mable. I would miss you terrible if I never seen you again."

"Oscar gonna miss you too," Annabelle said.

"Your brother don't like me, he jus might be happy I is leavin."

"No he won't, Ruthie."

"He never said nothin but two words to me all the time I visit you. They was hi and bye."

"He likes you, I can tell," Annabelle insist. "Ruthie, don't leave witout lettin me know. Okay?"

"I'll make sure that I tell you, Annabelle."

"Well, I got to be going now. I got to git these groceries home to my mama." Annabelle left.

When we git to the house, I took the suitcases to the bedroom, and Ms. Mabel, Beulah, and Fanny Mae follow me. I open the suitcases and pull out each item as Ms.Mable and Fanny Mae ooh and aah over the clothes and shoes. Beulah jus sat in a chair in the room, lookin the other way from us. Sometime she would look over at the clothes.

Finally, I puts everythang back in the suitcases, and Ms. Mable and Fanny Mae left the room. When Beulah see her mama and sister had left, she close the bedroom door and start talkin to me about Miz Williams.

"She really did you wrong, Ruthie. I wouldn't take that from nobody if I was you. I don't care if she was white or not."

I jus look at her.

"You ain't nothin Ruthie. You like a rabbit, always scared."

"I ain't no rabbit. You ain't never been in my shoes and been been treated like I been. 'Course you ain't scared. You always had you mama and papa. I had nobody—jus Miz Williams, to do whatever she want to me. Yes, she made me afraid when she threaten me. I don't know even now if she will carry out her threat. When Miz Johnson and I saw her at the store—"

"What you mean, you saw her at the store?" Beulah interrupt me.

"Miz Johnson and I saw her at the clothin store. The store clerk say she come to that store everyday. Well, jus lookin at her made me freeze up. I git so scared that she gonna call the police and have me arrested for something I didn't do."

"Wait a minute. You mean to tell me that you see that woman that made you life miserable and you didn't hit her? You jus git scared. Girl, I would have been whippin her draws off. She would have been scared of me instead of me being scared of her. You even had Miz Johnson wit you. No police is gonna touch you wit Miz Johnson around."

"What you mean?"

"Haven't you ever notice how people treat Miz Johnson? Her husband used to be the chief of police afore he died. She well respected. Nobody would even mess wit you knowin that Miz Johnson is your boss-lady. She has money too and she like you."

"I didn't know that. I ain't seen nobody treat her special."

"But they do. If I was you I would go to that store tomorra and beat that woman behind. Your papa wouldn't be dead and your mama wouldn't have to move if it wasn't for that woman tellin lies. She a devil. Everybody be on you side if you whip her good."

Fanny Mae came in the room and Beulah stop talkin.

"I hear you two talkin before I come in here. Was you talkin bout me, Beulah?" Fanny Mae ask.

"What make you think we talkin about you? You ain't that important." Beulah hop in the bed.

"Whatever she said, don listen to her Ruthie. She name after the Devil's daughter and she act jus like her too."

"Oh shut up Fanny Mae, the Devil ain't got no daughter." Beulah turn her back to us.

I thought about what Beulah say. The thoughts kept goin over and over in my mind. "Should I confronts Miz Williams? After all, she *did* do me wrong. Would Miz Johnson help me, like Beulah say? I knew she like me.

CHAPTER TWENTY-SIX

"If you hit that woman, there isn't anything I can do for you but cry. Ruthie, you know better. I am sorry for what she did to you but I can't change that. You can't change the past but you have a future now—you are going home. We have the letter. Your mama is gonna have someone meet you at the bus station tonight, and you are gonna be leaving this afternoon."

"But you told me not to be afraid."

"Yes, but I didn't tell you to be a damn fool!"

I was startled. Miz Johnson never spoke to me like that. "But I thought, you dead husb being the police chief and all that—"

"That what, Ruthie? That I could stop them from putting you in jail. Believe me, they would do worse to you than jus put you in jail if you hit that old crazy woman."

Miz Johnson voice git softer. She put her hand on my chin and lift my face so she could look me in the eye. "Ruthie, I really care for you. I thought you were a smart girl but right now you are talking like a fool."

"I is sorry, Miz Johnson."

She let go my chin, and I really felted bad. How could I let Beulah talk me into thinkin somethin so foolish.

"Ruthie, I'm taking you back to the shop, and we are gonna get Mable, then we are gonna go get your things. I am gonna take you to the bus station myself and make sure you git on the bus."

"Yesum."

Wit the letter in my hand, Miz Johnson and I left her house and went to the garage where the car was. I start feelin anxious again. I was finally going home. We git in the car and took off to the beauty and barber shop. When we got there, Miz Johnson git out the car and went in the shop; I follow her. When Miz Johnson git in the shop, two of the women spoke to her.

One say, " Hi Miz Johnson. I know you didn't come to git you hair done."

Miz Johnson jus smiled. "Naw, I jus came to git Mable."

"It sure nice to see you Miz Johnson," the other woman say.

"It nice to see you again too. Where's Mable?"

Right then, Ms. Mable came out the shampoo room. "Miz Johnson. How nice to see you. They ain't nothin wrong, is they?" Ms. Mable look at me.

"Naw, there isn't anything wrong. Ruthie just got her letter and I want to take her to the bus station. I came by here so you can go to your house, and Ruthie can get her clothes."

Ms.Ester was in the store. "So you finally goin home?"

"Yesum."

"Come give me some sugar."

I went over to her and she kiss me on my cheek. "I is sure gonna miss you, child."

"I is gonna miss you too, Ms. Ester."

Fanny Mae came out the shampoo room and was dryin her hands on a towel. She hear what we sayin and she look sad-eyed at me. She came over and hug me. "Ruthie, I is gonna miss you too. Annabelle is down the street wit Beulah gittin somethang to eat. I is goin right now to tell her you is leavin."

Fanny Mae left the shop.

Ms. Mable look at the ladies "Ladies, does you mind if I run home for a few minutes?"

One of the ladies say she don't mind. The other one said it okay if Ms. Mable go for a few minutes 'cause she had nothin but time. Ms. Mable look at Ms. Ester.

"Ester, could you mind the shop while I run home?"

Miz Ester nodd her head for yes. I ran up the stairs to where Mr. Lester cut hair.

I enter the room what smelled of musty old men. I ain't never been upstairs to the barber shop until now. There was a ball of cut nappy hair around a chair, and I figure it must be the chairmen sat in to git they haircut. Mr. Lester was sittin in the chair readin a newspaper. They was two other colored men in the room playin checkers, both of dem had gray hair.

"King me!" One of the men said.

I walk pass dem, over to Mr. Lester, and he look up from his paper at me.

"Mr. Lester, I is going home now."

Mr. Lester git up from his chair and give me a quick hug.

"Sure is gonna miss you Ruthie. You make sure you write now."

"I will, sir."I left him and went back down the stair. As I was goin down the stair I hear a man say, "I won again, you fish." Then he let out a hearty laugh.

Ms. Mable, Miz Johnson, and me, left the shop before Fanny Mae come back. We went to Miz Mable house and git my things and then we left. When we arrive at the bus station I began to feel a little sad to be leavin Miz Johnson and my new founded family. Tears of joy and sadness fill my eyes as I watch Miz Johnson buy my ticket. I kept wipin the tears from my eyes wit a piece of tissue I had taken from Ms. Mable house.

Miz Johnson watch as Ms. Mable and me gave my suitcases to the bus driver. He load dem under the bus.

Miz Johnson held out her arms to me and I went over to her and hug. "Ruthie, I am gonna miss you."

Ms. Mable was standin along side us. Miz Johnson and I stop huggin, and it was Ms. Mable turn. After I hug Ms. Mable, I told her I was gonna write her. Suddenly I hear someone callin my name, and I stop and look around. There he was, Oscar, runnin like a madman toward me. When he finally reach me he stop and say, "Little girl, little girl, you so fine. Little girl, little girl I wish you was mine."

I look at him, smile, and walk on the bus witout sayin nothin to him. The bus took off, and I sat by a window and wave at the three. Oscar look sad-eyed as he, along wit Ms. Mable and Miz Johnson, wave back at me. Finally, when I couldn't see dem any more I settle back in the chair.

CHAPTER TWENTY-SEVEN

I left Briminghan around twelve that afternoon, and the bus ride seem long. When we arrive in Demopolis, it was about eight hours later. I was met by my aunt who scream for joy when she seen me step off the bus.

"Ruthie, Ruthie, come on baby, it Mama."

"Mama!" My heart leap for joy.

I ran to her, cryin wit my arms outstretched. She was shorter than me now, wit hair as white as snow. But I still recognize my mamma face. We helded each other and cried. "Mama miss you so much. I thought you was dead. My heart was so broken. I never thought I would see my baby again, but you is alive." My Aunt Flo was cryin and kissin me all over my face.

"Mama, I was afraid you wouldn't know me."

"I could know my baby anywhere. Look at you. You is so tall and purty."

My mama was holdin my hands and leanin back lookin at me.

"I sho ain't as small as I use to be," I said, as I look down at my aunt.

"Come on honey, let's git home. Mr. James is waitin for us wit his car."

I git my suitcases and walk wit my aunt to a light-blue car wit a man sittin in it. When he saw us, he hurry and git out, grabbin my suitcases.

"Hi young girl, I is Mr. James, Flo friend."

"I jus told her that, James."

"Hi, Mr.James."

Mr. James was a short man in his forty, wit a toothie grin. He loaded the suitcases in the trunk of the car and open the door for us. Mama sat in the front seat and I sit in the back. The man took off and we we head to my real mama house. I start thinkin about my real mama and how she gonna treat me. I remember the time when I was six. Now I was sixteen.Would she accept me now?

Mr. James look back at me. "You visitin?"

"No sir. I is gonna live here."

"She's gonna be livin wit me and her real mama," Mama said, soundin real proud. Durin the ride, Mama would turn around, look at me and smile.

When we finally git to the house, Mr. James stop the car.

"End of the line, let me git your suitcase."

He went to the back of the car while Aunt Flo and me git out the car. I look toward the porch of the house that I travel to ten years ago. I eye a woman sittin in a chair on the porch—she was lookin at me too. She was thin, wit mix gray and brown hair. She look like she about fifty years old. The woman held tightly to a shawl around her shoulders. She look as if she been very ill, and I wonder if she was my real mama. I walk to the fence that surround the house. As I reach the gate, my aunt walk up to me.

"Ruthie. You see you mama sittin on the porch? She been waitin for you."

"She don't look the same."

"None of us do, child. None of us do."

I walk to the porch wit Mr. James and my aunt. My real mama watch me as I walk toward her. She said, "Mama, it me, Ruthie."

Her face had no expression.

"Mattie, tis here is you oldest child, Ruthie," my aunt told her, as she stepped on the porch. My real mama look at me again.

"You Ruthie? Flo, you told me Ruthie dead."

"Then, I told you Ruthie alive. Remember when Mary Anne came over here wit the letter?"

Mr. James brought in my suitcases in the house and set dem by the door.

"I thank you James." What do I owe you?"

"Nothin Flo, and you is welcome."

"Flo, is tis really Ruthie?"

"Yes Mattie. This here is you baby. Both of us baby."

I went over and hug my real mama. I hope she would hug me back but she kept holdin on to the shawl. I release her, and Mr. James left.

"Lets go in the house Ruthie."

I follow my aunt in the house. The house was small but held four rooms. The first room I walk in, like so many in the south, was the sittin room. It had an old blue sofa and one chair in it. Two windows, both facin the front porch, had grayish white lace curtains on dem. A small table sat in front of the sofa covered wit a white cloth. A jar wit wild flowers sat on top of it. Right across from the sittin room was the kitchen wit a long brown table wit four chairs. On that table sat another jar filled wit different color wild flowers. A wood-burnin stove jus like Mama and Papa had, sat in a corner wit a metal teapot on top of it. The kitchen shelves helded different color dishes, cups, and saucers. The rooms was neat and tidy like nothin been cooked that day, or somethin was cooked, and the kitchen scrub down. My mama lead me down to a bedroom wit a large bed in it. The cover on it was homemade and it remind me of the one my aunt made. It was made of different pieces of material left over from some article of clothes she had finish wit. My mama pointed to a dresser in the room that stood tall and brown, wit a bronze urn on top.

"Those are the ashes the lady sent me. Now, take dem and throw dem away. My baby was dead, now she alive—my baby is home."

I when over to the dresser and pick up the jar that held so many lies. I cradle it in my arms and walk toward the door, outside pass my real mama, still sittin on the porch.

"Baby, take those damn ashes from tis house and let dem blow away in the wind."

My heart leap for joy once more. My real mama call me baby.

"Yes ma'am!"

I ran down to the gate. Upon openin it, I took a deep breath and let the feelin of joy seep through my most inner being. I ran out the gate to the road. Down the road I went yellin, "I is alive, I is alive."

I pass a old man as I ran down that road, almost knockin him down. He must thought I was crazy. He yell back to me, "Fool you is alive and tryin to *kill* me." I laugh and kept runnin.

A wind came up that day, stronger than I ever felted that time of year. To me, it was God tellin me to let the ashes go. I open the urn and pour dem so the wind blow dem away. I watch as the particles scatter in the wind.

CHAPTER TWENTY-EIGHT

My real mama had had another child, her name Alice. She was six years old, and was in the house when I first arrive. She hadn't seen me 'cause she had been asleep in one of the rooms. I peep in at her after I came back from thowin the ashes away. She was a light-skinned child wit long hair jus like mine. I close the door carefully, not to wake her.

"Does she go to sleep every day at tis time?"

"Naw, Ruthie. Today she was jus tired from school. It seem that the kids tease her about her mama. When she came home, the poor child couldn't eat. She asked to go to bed. She been sleepin every since."

"Why would they tease her about mama?"

"Cause you mama never git married. You have another sister and had two brothers, but Mattie never git married." Mama whispered so my real mama wouldn't hear her.

"Where are they?"

"You other aunts is raisin you sister and brothers. One of you brothers is dead."

The word *dead* hit me real hard. I never seen my brother, but a feelin of loss came over me.

"How did he die and what age was he?" We were still standin by the room my sister sleepin in.

"I tell you later. For now, let's see about you mama."

My real mama was in the kitchen drinkin a cup of tea, and still holdin on to the shawl like she was cold. I walk over to her and put one hand on her shoulder.

"Mama, you cold?" My real mama look up at me and put her cup down.

"You throw the ashes away?"

"Yesum."

"Good."

I look over at my aunt, and she say, "She stays cold all the time. It November but she act like she cold even in the summer time. I don't know what wrong wit her Ruthie."

My aunt walk over to my real mama and spoke to her. "You know, Mattie, you needs to see a doctor."

"I don't need no doctor." My real mama took her tea and went outside on the porch to drink it. I sat down in the chair she jus git up from.

My aunt came over to me and put her arms around my shoulders, and I smile at her. She look at me real thoughtful like. "Ruthie, I wanna asked you somethin."

"What Mama?"

"How long you say that you was away from Miz Williams?"

"Three years."

"How come you wait so long to write me a letter after you left her house?"

I hung my head. "Cause I thought that you didn't want me."

"Why you think that?" My mama took her arms from around me and lift my head so that I could face her.

I hear you talkin to Papa, sayin that the reason why you was lettin me go to Miz Williams was 'cause I wasn't yourn. Miz Williams said you didn't want me. At first I didn't believed her, but when I didn't git a letter from you I felted she right." Mama dropped her hands from my face, and tears swell up in her eyes.

"Oh Ruthie, you misunderstood what Mama was sayin. I know I say that, but it wasn't 'cause I didn't love you. It was 'cause people kept tellin me I wasn't gonna raise you right 'cause you wasn't mine. I thought if I kepted you workin for what you wanted, that you wouldn't be actin like you mama. You see, I refuse to believe that somethin was wrong wit you mama. I believe that she was jus doin that things she done to git back at my mama. You see, your mama want to be a teacher too, but my mama told her that girls don't need no money spented on dem 'cause they was jus gonna be at home, makin babies. Your mama seem like she was all right to me, jus broken-hearted after my mama told her that. Mama knew better. You see, Mattie mind ain't good. Whether she went to school or not, she keep forgittin things. And sometimes she seem like she don't understand. Your mama ain't a loose woman either, but since her mind ain't good, people take advantage of her, specially men. I know for a fact that she wanted to git marry to your papa, but if she marry him or not, her mind would still not be strong. Ruthie, at that time, I thought that you might git discouraged. I didn't want you to start dealin wit boys. I thought you should work. I was wrong, Ruthie, wit part of my decision 'cause in life you has to work for what you want. The part that I was wrong in is when I judge you and Mattie. Roy said I was wrong but I didn't believe him. Now look what I has done. If it wasn't for me you wouldn't been wit Miz Williams and been treated bad all those years." Aunt Flo's eyes was in tears and searchin mines.

"Mama, I hear what Mr. Verney say about Mama."

Aunt Flo rub her hand across her forehead. "Mr. Verney was sweet on your mama once. But someone else git to her—that made him mad at her. He should have gotten mad at the man."

"Who the man Mama?"

"You real papa is Mr. Verney's stepbrother, Sweetchild."

I jump up from my seat. I felted like a ton of bricks jus hit me. "Naw Mama, naw. Your don't mean me and Mr. Verney is family. I don't want him to be any kin to me.

"Verney won't own up to that 'cause he didn't like his stepbrother after he found out.

"I is glad," I said wit relief. Jus to think that he even wanna act like he was some kin to me made me feel sick.

"Where is Sweetchild now?"

"Dead. He buried not far from your Uncle Roy."

"How he die?"

"A woman kilt him. Not his wife, but another woman."

Before I could ask my aunt anythang else, my sister Alice had woke up and was walkin in the kitchen. Mama wipe the tears from her eyes, git up from the chair, and walk over to the stove. Alice walk over to me and said, "Is you my sister?"

"Yesum, I am."

"Sure is tall. Is I gonna be tall as you when I grow up?"

"Maybe."

"Is you gonna stay wit us forever and not die no more?"

"Maybe I is gonna stay forever until I git married or somethang. Now, can I ask you a question?"

"What?"

"Can I have a hug?"

I git on my knees and helded out my arms and Alice fell into dem. I hug my little sister real tight.

"I is so glad I have a another big sister that finally live wit me."

I release my hug and look at her face.

"I is glad too that I have a little sister. Wanna help me hang up my clothes?"

"Yesum." I took Alice by the hand and went in my aunt's room. Aunt Flo follow behind us. I took my clothes out the suitcases and started puttin dem on hangers. "Ruthie you got some migthy fine clothes here."

"Mostly all of dem was give to me by Miz Johnson and her friends, Mama."

Aunt Flo continue to look through my things for a few more moments admirin dem. Finally she stop.

"Ruthie, I am about to fix dinner."

"What we havin Mama?"

"We a havin potatoes and bread. I thank the Lawd that we got somethin to eat. You know that a lot of folks don have nothin. Remember those white folks that I use to wash and iron for?"

"Yesum."

"Well they husbands lost they jobs and they havin a hard time findin other ones. They couldn't afford to hire me to wash for dem anymore. It git so bad for me that I couldn't afford to pay that seven dollars for rent after papa died. People stop worryin about clean clothes if they don't have food for they table. I tell you Ruthie, it is gittin so bad that almost every day somebody comes by here, black or white, asking for food. Sometimes we can spare dem somethin, sometimes we can't. I pray to God that somethin happen so people can at lease have food on they tables again."

"Mama, I have some money to buy food wit."

"What you got child?"

"Twenty dollar that Miz Johnson and her friends gave me. I can buy some food wit it."

My mama felled to her knees and cried out. "Oh Lawd, thank you! Thank you, Lawd Jesus!"

My real mama came runnin in the room. "What the matter Flo?"

"Tis here gal of yourn has brought some money home. We can eat somethang else beside potatoes. Ain't God good?"

"All the time." My real mama was smilin.

I hadn't seen her smile and it made me happy to see it now.

"Come on child. Lets run on up to James' house. Maybe he there and can run us to the store in his car."

"Can I go too?" Alice eyes was beggin.

"Can she, Mama?" I look at my aunt.

Both of dem said she could.

Aunt Flo, Alice, and me, took off for Mr. James house. He was at home and say he be happy to take us to the store. It was the same store that I used to stop in after school and buy the "Damn If I know" candy bar. Alice looked around as Aunt Flo brought enough food to last for at lease two months.

"Ruthie, can I git a candy bar?"Alice asked, while tuggin at my dress.

"Yes you can."

I bought the candy bar for Alice and she smile as I hand it to her. She ate it in the store while my aunt shopped. It cost me ten dollars to buy the food. I pay Mr. James an extra dollar and he seem happy to git it.

On our way back, Mr. James ask mama if he could stay for dinner.

"You sure gonna have a spread. What you gonna cook today?"

"Fried chicken, mashed potatoes wit gravy, corn, buttermilk biscuits, and soda to wash it down."

Mr. James stay for dinner. We said the blessin, sat down and ate good. After dinner, Mr. James patted his stomach. "Well ladies, I guess I be goin now."

We all bid him a good night, and my real mama told Alice to go to bed. Alice git up from her chair and kiss me goodnight, then she kiss my real mama and Aunt Flo. She went to the room where she and my real mama slepted.

After Alice went to bed I started talking to my aunt and my real mama about the time I spented wit Miz Williams. I told dem about Miz Johnson, Ms. Mable, and her family. I told dem about the good times and the bad times I had wit Beulah.

"I is so sorry, baby. I wish I known, I would have come a runnin if I know the truth." My aunt hug me again as I sat in the chair dryin the tears fallin from my eyes as I told dem what happen to me. My real mama cry too.

My aunt looked over at my real mama as she git up from her chair and pick up a dish.

"Mattie you don have to help wash the dishes. Ruthie and I gonna wash dem."

"I got a good girl. Don't you think she a good girl Flo?"

"Yes, she is a good girl Mattie."

My real mama came over and kiss me on my cheek.

"You a good girl Ruthie. I didn't raise you. Mama is sorry for not raisin you. Mama loves you and I hope you loves me. I don't blame you if you don't."

I git up from my chair and went over to her.

"I love you Mama. I always will, 'cause you is my mama."

My mama eyes was lookin up at me kind of sorrowful-like. I hugged my real mama and she hug me back.

"I is so sorry Ruthie. I is so sorry."

My mama was ballin her eyes out, but I felted happy that my real mama said that she love me.

"Mattie, you go on to bed. You gonna make yourself sick carryin on like that," Aunt Flo told her.

Alice came out the room, draggin a doll. I notice that the doll was Patty.

"Mama, what wrong?"

"Nothin Alice. You gone on back to bed, I is a comin in there soon."

"Go on now Mattie," Aunt Flo said. "Ruthie and I is gonna take care of these here dishes."

"Okay Flo."

My mama went in the room huggin on to her shawl again like it was cold. She took Alice by her hand. "Come on here Alice, you go to bed now."

I watch dem both as they went into their bedroom. My aunt and I gather the dishes. When I had put the last one in the sink I ask my aunt about my other sisters and brothers.

"Can you take me to see dem one day Mama?"

"Yesum, I will."

"And, Papa grave?"

"We can go visit Papa grave soon."

We wash the dishes and put dem away. All the while I kept thinkin about the other sister and brother I had. I felted like I belonged to a family—a scattered one, but still a family.

CHAPTER TWENTY- EIGHT

I slept in the bed wit my mama. I woke up early the next morning and I ask my mama about jobs workin in people houses.

"You lucky if you can find one. Like I say Ruthie, most of the people around here ain't got nothin, includin the white folks. There is a farm not far from here that grows cotton. Pickin-time is almost over, being that it's winter fall now. Maybe they let you pick cotton. They be a lot of folk there for the job."

My mama wash up and start breakfast. It was potatoes and onion, along wit a large pan of biscuits, and coffee.

"Why so many biscuits Mama?"

"Cause like I said, its not a day goes by that somebody don't comes a knockin askin for food."

Alice and my real mama woke up and came in the kitchen.

"Mornin Aunt Flo. Mornin Ruthie," Alice said.

My mama and I both spoke to Alice while my real mama sat at the table.

"Mornin Mattie. You sleep well?"

"Yesum Flo. But I kept dreamin about Ruthie, you know, you child. I dream that she was alive."

"I is alive, Mama."

My real mama look at me, bewilderd.

"Who is you?"

"I is Ruthie."

I look at my aunt but she jus shook her head and turn away from me toward the stove. A knock came on the door, so I git up to answer it. I see a white man standin there. He was tall and thin, dressed in dirty overalls and shirt. Even his hat was dirty. He look at me wit tired eyes . He helded his hat in his hand.

"Please ma'am. Can you spare some food? I ain't eaten in two days."

My aunt came to the door beside me.

"I got some potatoes and onion and a biscuit or two I can gives you. Maybe I even have a cup of hot coffee."

"Thank you ma'am."

The man sat on the front porch. My aunt fix him a plate, along wit a cup of coffee, and give it to him.

"Thank you Lawd, and thank you ma'am."

"You is welcome."

I went back to the kitchen and sat down to eat. Before we could finish our meal, the man called to us. He had finish his meal and hand my aunt the plate and cup. He thank my aunt one more time and went on his way.

After we finish eatin, my real mama help Alice git ready for school. When she was dressed, a girl about the age of twelve came by to walk wit Alice.

"I hope that we can git you mama to the doctor soon," Aunt Flo said. "I is worried about her."

I look at my Aunt Flo and remember about the money I save in the jar under my bed. "Mama," I said, "what happen to the money that I had save for college?"

"I had to use it to bury your papa." Aunt Flo hung her head. Her face had a saddness about it so I decid not to say anythang else about the money.

My real mama sat down at the table and started drinkin coffee. Sometimes she would rub the cup across her forehead as if to warm herself. I thought about my dead brother again and ask my aunt how he die.

"He die of the fits. He was so young, jus seven. We laid him to rest in the same graveyard your papa and Sweetchild is in. I didn't wanna say anythang about it while Alice was here. She still cry when we talk about him. She love her brother very much."

"What was his name?"

" Jed."

After we git through eatin I told mama that I was goin to go to the cotton farm to see if I could git me a job. "Maybe I can make enough money so I could git Mama to the doctor," I told my aunt. My aunt bid me good luck and I was on my way.

When I git there, sho nuff, they was a lot of people there for the jobs. A boy about my age stood in line, hopin to git picked. He was dark brown-skinned and had a small mole growin on the side of his face by his nose. I look over at him, and he smile at me. A short, burly white man came and pick out people to work pickin cotton for that day. It was about twenty people that was given the chance to work, including me and the boy. We was given sacks to put the cotton in, each one could hold about a hundred pounds of cotton.

I took mines and went on out in the fields. I work the fields pickin until it was about noon, that when everybody stop to rest. Since I had a biscuit in my pocket for lunch, I sat down on the ground and pull it out. I had forgot about the boy that I had seen earlier. He found me in the fields sittin down, enjoyin my biscuit. He came over and sat down beside me wit a sandwich in his hand.

"Would you like some of my sandwich? It got meat in it." The boy held out the sandwich so that I could see the salt pork.

"No thank you. I got a biscuit."

The boy took a bite out of his sandwich. He chew and shallow it. "It sure taste good, sure you don't want any?" The boy held out his sandwich, offerin it to me again.

"I is sure." I kepted eatin my biscuit.

"I ain't seen you in these parts. You new?"

"Naw I ain't new, I use to live here but I went away. Now I is back."

That boy stare at me. "What is you name?"

"My name Ruthie."

"You sure is purty, Ruthie. The rest of the girls around these parts ain't as purty as you is."

"Thank you. What is you name?"

"My name is Wilson."

"Please to meet you, Wilson."

We finish eatin in silence. The burley white man shouted that the break was over. I rubbed my hands together to git the remainin crumbs of the biscuit off. I then pick up my sack and Wilson pick up his. For the rest of that afternoon until the day was over, Wilson be by my side pickin cotton. When our sacks was fill, Wilson offer to help me carry mines, as well as his sack, to the weightin station. I said okay, and Wilson drugged both sacks to the station. I follow behind him, watchin him tryin to prove his manhood. I seen the muscles strain in his back and the sweat pop out his forehead as he handle the almost two-hundred pound bags. When he finially made it to the weightin station, he handed the man his bag. The man weight it and give him thirty-five cent. The man weights mine and gave me only thirty cent, since I didn't have one hundred pounds of cotton in the sack.

We put our money in our pockets, and Wilson ask me if he could walk me home. I said no, maybe another day, so he left. When I git home that evenin I didn't tell Mama about Wilson. That next day I returned back to the fields and was picked again. So was Wison.

Wilson came over to me wit his sack. "How old is you Ruthie?"

"I is sixteen. How old is you?"

Wilson hesitate then he answer, "I is seventeen."

"You look younger."

"Some people jus look young for they age. I guess that I is jus one of those people."

We started pickin cotton, and Wilson stay close to where I was pickin. He look at me like he want to say something, but then turn his head away. After a while it look like he git his nerves up. He look at me again and say, "Ruthie would you like to go to the show wit me some day?"

"I don't know Wilson, maybe when I knows you better."

Wilson smiled. "Then, that a yes, huh?"

I smile at him and went on back to pickin cotton.

That evenin when I git home I told my Aunt Flo about the boy, and she ask his name.

"His name Wilson, Mama."

My Aunt Flo didn't say anythang for a few seconds, then she look at me and question again, "Does he have a mole on his face by his nose."

"Yesum, he does"

"Oh Lawd have mercy!"

"What the matter Mama?"

"That you brother. You brother was askin you out for a date."

I started laughin.

"What's so funny, Ruthie?"

"Ain't my brother younger than me?"

"Yeh. He is."

"He told me he seventeen."

My aunt looked at me like she thinking real hard. "I should have showed you your brother and sister years ago. Land sakes, that why some brothers and sister end up marryin each other. They ain't been introduce to their sister or brother until it too late. It the old folks fault, not introducin dem to each other. You know what Ruthie? Not only is I gonna introduce you to you brother and sister but to you cousins too. I is gonna call a family reunion."

A few weeks after that, Mama had her family reunion. Everybody that came brought a dish of some kind. It was so many folks there that we didn't have enough room in the house for dem all. I didn't know I had so many folks livin so close to us. I met my Aunt Poppy, the one, my brother Wilson lived wit, and my Aunt May that my sister Tee lived wit. They was so happy to see me they couldn't stop huggin and kissin on me every time I past dem. My brother found out that day the I was his sister. When he was introduced to me, he look at me and said, "You sho nuff is ugly. You got those big old feet just like you sister Tee. Plus, you is as skinny as a stick."

"You didn't say that when you thought I wasn't you sister."

"I was jus tellin stories back then. Now I can tell you the truth since you is my sister."

"You even say you was seventeen Wilson, but you is fifteen. And, you know what Wilson? You is ugly too." I was a smilin as I pointed my finger in his face.

"Girl, let me take you to you sister Tee, so you and her can talk. Me and you ain't got nothin in common. I is the best lookin thang this side of the Mason-Dixie line. You and Tee is jus plain ugly." Wilson laughted and I laugh wit him.

Wilson took me over to my sister Tee and introduce her to me. Tee had a round face and her skin was the color of pecans. Her hair done up in braids that hung down her back.

"Hi Tee. This here is you sister Ruthie." Tee and I looked at each other. "So you is my big sister."

"I sho nuff am." We hug each other, and I was so happy to finally meet my sister and brother. Wilson left us to go find some other girls that wasn't family. After that day, Wilson, Tee, Alice, and I become good friends. Sometimes we would meet up together and take long walks and talk. We talk about our real mama and about being raise by our aunts. We all knew, except Alice, our real mama wasn't able to take care of us when we was little. She wasn't even able to take care of Alice, if it wasn't for my Aunt Flo.

One day Mama and I went to visit Papa grave. They was no headstone, jus a wooden cross. The grave was in the back of the church where so many people from that town was buried. I went to the grave and talk to it like Papa was livin.

"Papa, I is back home, and I met my sisters and brother. I was happy to see dem. Alice is my little sister and very sweet. I had a hard time Papa. I hate that you died, and sometime I feel like it my fault."

"It ain't you fault Ruthie." Aunt Flo put her arms around me. I look at her then back at the grave.

"I miss you Papa. I know you in heaven now, but someday I is gonna see you. I love you Papa."

After I git through talkin to Papa, Mama and me went back home.

CHAPTER TWENTY-NINE

I make enough money pickin cotton to take my real mama to the doctor. We found the reason she cold all the time was she had anemia. I bought her the medicine the doctor prescribe for her. After a while she stop actin like she cold, but her mind still the same.

It been nine months since I left Birmingham. I wrote to Ms. Mable from time to time jus to let her know how I was gittin along, and one day she sent me a letter about Miz Johnson. It say Miz Johnson is ill and want to see me. Some money was in the letter for a round-trip bus ticket. Miz Johnson was always thoughtful like that. I showed the letter to my aunt.

"Mama, she so very nice to me, and she the reason why I is here right now."

"Then you got to go and see her. But don't let that Beulah git to you, you got to stands up to her."

"Okay Mama."

I sent a letter to Ms. Mable telling her when I was comin so she could meet me at the station. A few days later I pack some of my clothes, kiss my aunt, Alice, and my real mama goodbye. My aunt ask Mr. James to take me to the bus station.

"Make sure to write you mama when you ready to come back, so I can come and git you," Mr. James said

"I will, sir."

He left me at the station and took off in his car.

When I finally arrives at my destination, Ms. Mable and Mr. Lester was there at the station waitin for me. I git off the bus and meet dem wit open arms. They both took turns huggin me.

"We is so glad you mama let you come," Ms. Mable said. "Let's git you suitcase so we can git you home and feed you, I know you hungry."

"I is hungry ma'am. I didn't have much on the bus to eat, jus a few pieces of fried chicken Mama fix for me. I ate that up an hour ago."

"Well come on child," Ms. Mable say, as she grab my arm leadin me out the station. "Lester, git her suitcase."

Mr. Lester grab hold to my suitcase. His body lean to the side where the suitcase was in his hand. Ms. Mable look over at him half-smilin, shakin her head, and said, "Don tell me dem suitcases is heavy."

"Girl must be packin bricks—this case is sho nuff heavy." He took hold of it wit both of his hands, holdin the suitcase in front.

"I can carry it." I reach for my case.

"I is gonna carry it ," Mr. Lester said, smilin.

"Lester jus jokin wit you, that suitcase ain't all that heavy. Come on hurry we got to catch the city bus." Ms. Mable hurried us out the bus station.

As soon as we git outside the station we seen a bus comin. We caught it and took a seat in the back. When we arrive at the house, Beulah the first person to greet us. She open the door for us, lettin her papa in first. Ms. Mable went in, then me. As I pass Beulah she let out a sigh.

"You again." Her voice dry in tone.

Ms. Mable heard Beulah speak. She stop walkin, turn around and look Beulah straight in the face. "Beulah, Ruthie is our invited guest. While she here, you treat her nice, you hear me?"

"Yes ma'am."

"I don't want to cause no trouble Ms. Mable, maybe I can find somewhere else to stay," I said. I was hopin she wouldn't say okay 'cause I only had a little bit of money. After that, they was jus lint in my pocket.

Ms. Mable look at me and say, "You stayin wit us. Now come on and unpack your things."

"Yes ma'am."

Ms. Mable started walkin in front of me toward Fanny Mae and Beulah bedroom. I look back at Beulah watchin us, and she licked out her tongue at me. Right then I wish I was back at home wit my mama and real mama. I knew I was gonna have a problem wit Beulah and her insults.

I wasn't the fightin kind, besides, I was the guest. I hoped by some little ounce of faith, Beulah had growed up, since she must be at least twenty. Sure didn't look like it. I follow Ms. Mable to the room, where she told me to hang my clothes up in the closet.

"Yes ma'am."

When I open the closet door I seen a most beautiful weddin dress hangin there. It was ivory white, cut low, wit pearl sewed in the front. The full skirt was made of white satin, and the dress had long sleeves made of white lace.

"Oh my, ain't tis beautiful."

"It Bealuh's. She is gittin married in about two weeks."

Jus then Fanny Mae ran in the room.

"Ruthie!" She scream.

She ran up to me and flung her arms around me huggin me tight. Seein her face, my heart leap for joy. I hug Fanny Mae back as tight as she helded me.

We release our grip and smile at each other.

"I is so happy to see you. Guess what? Annabelle brother ask me about you every time I see him."

"I is very happy to see you too Fanny Mae. But I don't know why he is a askin about me. He never gave me the time of day while I was here, although he did say somethin to me when I was leavin."

"You know how boys are. Sometimes they are so silly, afraid to show how they really feel until sometimes it's too late." Fanny Mae shook her head, half smilin.

"He not a boy, he a man. I think he older than Bealuh."

"Like I said, you know how boys are."

Ms. Mable left us alone to talk and catch up.

Fanny Mae and I both sat on the bed and face each other.

"I know you don't remember but there is another boy that likes you too, his name is Wilbert. He ask me about you too."

"What he look like? I don't think I ever saw him." I was tryin to remember.

"He brought some supply here once, but you was talking to my mama. That when he saw you. He never said anythin about you until you left. He is so easy to look at wit his curly hair and bedroom-eyes," Fanny Mae sighed. He's shore ain't like Oscar. Oscar got dem old snake eyes that dances all the time. He jus can't keep dem thangs straight. Sometimes I think he crazy. You know, I was talkin to him one day about Annabelle. I told him that I hadn't seen Annabelle for a while and where she at. You know that he won't look straight at you, he kind of look sideways when you talk to him. I guess, to keep you from seein those old dancin eyes. Well anyway, he look at me like I was somethin strange and said, I don know what you is talkin about."

I giggle because that jus seem funny to me. I could jus imagine him sayin that, lookin at her sideways.

"Girl, that ain't funny." Fanny Mae then giggle herself. "Nigger jus crazy. Well anyway, I found out that Annabelle jus git a job workin downtown cleanin in one of those big stores."

"I see Beulah is gittin married."

"Yeh. She lately been actin as mean as a rattlesnake on a hot rock. I be glad when she git married and move away from here."

"For a minute I thought it was you." I was still gigglin, I put my hand up to my mouth to keep from breakin out into a laugh.

"I see you is crazy too. Did you look at that big old dress? It big enough for two people, wit some room left over."

Fanny Mae walk over to the closet to show me the dress again. Jus as she open the door to the closet, Beulah walk in the room.

"Hi Beulah. I was about to show Ruthie you weddin dress."

"Humm." Beulah folded her arms in front of her, frownin at me and Fanny Mae.

Fanny Mae flung open the closet door, took hold of one of the sleeves, pull it around so I could see the front of it again.

"Ain't it purty?" Fanny Mae lift her eyes and give out a sigh.

"Leave my dress alone," Beulah bellow at Fanny Mae.

Fanny Mae take her hand off the dress like it hot. Beulah walk over to the closet, push her dress back in line, and close the closet door. Fanny Mae walk over to me and took me by the arm.

"Let's see if Mama through cookin."

She push me out the bedroom door, and I started toward the kitchen. I thought Fanny Mae behind me, but she had went back into the room wit Beulah. I hear Fanny Mae say, "Sure is a big old dress." The next thing I hear Beulah say was too bad to mention.

I hurry to the kitchen, and found Ms. Mable finishin the meal she was preparin. When she seen me, she smile and said, "Where is the girls? Beulah and Fanny Mae better come on and set the table." Ms. Mable put butter in the mash potatoes and start whippin dem.

I went to the cabinet and took out the dishes. I look at Ms. Mable. "They is gonna be comin, I guess, in a little bit ma'am."

"Put the dishes down and go git dem. Tell dem dinner ready."

"I hope you don't mine ma'am, but I think it best you go git dem."

Ms. Mable took one look at my face. She stop whippin the potatoes, pick up a heavy wooden spoon, and headed toward they room. She came back wit the both of dem rubbin their backsides and frownin at each other. I wanted to laugh but I knew better.

"Help Ruthie finish settin the table," Ms Mable said, as she went on back to her business of whippin the potatoes. We all set the table together, and I was careful not talk or look at Fanny Mae or Beulah. When supper was ready, Ms. Mable call her husband from the back door. Mr. Lester came in and look at the two girls.

"I see you two musta got your ass beat. Both of you got that ass-beat look on you faces."

He let out a chuckle and went over to the sink and wash his hands. Both of the girls look over at their papa then at each other and frown. They took a seat opposite of each other, and Mr. Lester sit at the head of the table. Ms. Mable said the blessin then took a seat at the other end. I sat by Fanny Mae. Nobody talk cept Ms. Mable and Mr. Lester.

After supper Ms. Mable spoke to Mr. Lester, "We be going over to Miz Johnson house Lester. I is takin Fanny Mae and Ruthie wit me. You don't mine stayin here, do you?"

"Don't mine at all. I didn't wanna take that long walk anyway. Make sure you tell Miz Johnson I said hello and I hope she feelin better."

"I sho nuff will."

Mr. Lester tell Beulah to wash the dishes—a job, that when I stay there before, all us girls had to do.

"Might as well git a start on what you will be doin after you gits married," he told Beulah, and went in the sittin room, sat in his favorite chair, and lit up his pipe as usual.

Ms. Mable, Fanny Mae and me took off walkin to Miz Johnson house. On our way there Ms. Mable told me a little about Miz Johnson condition.

"She got some sort of blood disease; it make her weak. She feel like she don't have long."

"Is her daughter there wit her?" I asked.

"No. Miz Johnson git a letter from her daughter and she say she is a comin soon."

Ms. Mable stare straight ahead, her face looking sad.

"I hope it won't be too late when she finally come. Well, at lease you here."

I felted a tightness in my throat. I couldn't imagine not havin Miz Johnson around.

When we arrive at Miz Johnson house we was met at the door by a young white lady wit blond hair. She dress in white, like a nurse. She smile at us and told us to come in.

"She told me that you all were comin. You are the people she was talkin about right?"

"Yesum, we is," Ms. Mable said.

"Follow me."

The lady lead us up to Miz Johnson bedroom. When we git there, the door already open, and Miz Johnson there sittin by the window.

"Miz Johnson, you have some folks here that want see you."

Without turnin around Miz Johnson said, "Come here Ruthie, you too Mable, and your daughter."

We all went over to Miz Johnson and seen her all tired and pale. Her face look as if she age maybe ten years more. When she spoke, her voice sound weary.

She look at Ms. Mable. " I am glad that you brought Ruthie and Fanny Mae, Mable."

"Ruthie would have came witout me Miz Johnson, wild horses wouldn't keep her or Fanny Mae away."

"Yesum Miz Johnson, I was a comin here anyway wit Ruthie or by myself," Fanny Mae said.

"How ou feelin today?" Ms. Mable eyes look concern at Miz Johnson.

"The same as yesterday, but I guess that's good I don't feel worse than yesterday—is that good Maggie?" Miz Johnson ask the woman that was dress like a nurse.

"Yes it is," Miz Johnson.

"Are you a nurse?" I ask Maggie.

"Yes I am."

The woman turn to Miz Johnson. "I have to go downstairs now but I will be back up in a few minutes. It's almost time for your medicine.

"Okay."

"Has you heard anythin more from you daughter?" Ms. Mable ask.

"No, not a word. But I know she's comin."

"Miz Johnson, we don't wanna tire you out too much, so you jus let us know when you want us to go."

"I stay tired all the time, Mable. Right now I need a little company."

"We don't want you neighbors talkin either. They might say somethin if us color folk stay at your house too long and not be workin."

"Do you think I care what they think? You know me better than that Mable. Stay a little while with me, I need to talk to people who know me."

Miz Johnson told Ms. Mable to sit in one of the chairs, and me and Fanny Mae sat on the floor. Ms. Mable and Miz Johnson talk for almost an hour before the nurse come wit some food for Miz Johnson along wit her medicine. Ms. Mable told Miz Johnson we be leavin, and Miz Johnson ask me to come back tomorra.

"I sure will, Miz Johnson, and I do some cleanin for you too."

She offer to pay me, but I say no. We bid her goodnight and left.

I went over to Miz Johnson house every mornin and stay until late evenin. We talk awhile and I cleans awhile. I even told Miz Johnson about my real mama finally sayin she love me.

"That's nice Ruthie. I thought that, in time, she would." Miz Johnson look at me like she thinking hard. "Ruthie have you forgiven Miz Williams for what she done to you?"

"No. I ain't never gonna stop hatin her for that."

"Hate is a strong word. One day you'll have to fogive her or you will become just like her."

I didn't understand what she meant by that 'cause it was no way I could be like Miz Williams. I let the thought go.

It was on Friday, one day before Beulah weddin. I went to Miz Johnson house and I talk about Beulah, and Miz Johnson was very happy for her.

"She really loves that boy."

"I know Miz Johnson; she should be happy, instead, every day she acts mean. She treat me and Fanny Mae bad. But I is still happy she gittin married."

"Are you goin to the weddin, Ruthie?"

"I wants to, but if you needs me Miz Johnson, I won't go. I will stay here wit you."

"Naw. You go and have fun. Tell me all about it on Sunday."

"I sho will, everythin from beginnin to end."

I left that day feeling happy that I could share so much wit Miz Johnson. On my way home I thought about Beulah gittin married, and I hope she be happy.

CHAPTER THIRTY

B eulah didn't wanna git married in the church. She want to git married in the back yard of her parents' house. On that morning, Ms. Mable, Fanny Mae, me, and some of the neighbors, decorate the backyard wit flowers, set up the chairs, and put the arch in place. Ms. Mable cook most of the food for the weddin but I help out a little. Some of the neighbors also brought in food for the weddin supper, and Ms. Mable done Beulah hair.

The weddin was schedule for six o'clock that evenin. At five-thirty Beulah need someone to help her git ready. Fanny Mae was in the bathroom stylin her hair, and Ms. Mable was tryin to git herself ready. I only had to put on my stockins, so I was gonna help Beulah git dress.

I walk in the bedroom where Beulah was. Beulah had her weddin dress on the bed along wit her stockins. Her gloves was on the dresser but she was on her hands and knees lookin in the closet. I ask what she lookin for.

"My shoes."

"Why don't you git ready? I look for dem."

"You probably hid dem, knowin you." She was lookin back at me from the closet and rollin her eyes.

"Girl, why would I do a thing like that? I want you to git married and be happy. I ain't seen you shoes."

"Maybe you jealous 'cause I is marryin Jeremiah. I remember that day when you two dance together. I remember when he said that you look purty and how you look at him. Maybe that why you hid my shoes. You might even like him yourself." Beulah git up off her hands and knees and stand up in front of me.

"That ain't true Beulah, and you know it." I went over and pick her dress up off the bed. "Come on now and put on you dress. The people is already coming in the yard."

"Git your hands off my dress!"

"I is jus tryin to help you, Beulah. Tis is suppose to be the happiest day of you life. Come on, let me help you wit you dress."

"Take you hands off my dress!" She command.

"Okay then, suit yourself."

I threw the dress back on the bed, only the top part of it actually touch the bed. The skirt part hung off the bed, draggin the rest of the dress to the floor. Beulah look at her dress on the floor and, witout warnin, hit me upside my head. I seen stars. I shook my head and without thinking, I hit her wit all my might in the mouth. She hit me again in the mouth, and I hit her in the eye. We started screamin, and hittin each other hard. I pull her hair and she pull mines. She pull my hair so hard I fell to the floor. When I fall on the floor, Ms. Mable, Mr. Lester, and Fanny Mae come in the room a runnin. They pulls me and Beulah apart, and I starts cryin. Beulah stood there breathin hard, lookin at me.

"What wrong wit you Beulah?!" Ms. Mable scream.

Beulah said nothin.

"I was jus trying to help her git dress Ms. Mable," I said between tears. "She think I hid her shoes."

Ms. Lester started chucklin as he looked at Beulah lip. "Beulah, I got you shoes, I took dem this morning. I'll bring dem to you. I seen they had some dust on dem from stayin in the closet so long and I was jus tryin to git the dust off. I guess I should have told you 'cause when your lip git through swellin, and you eye git through turnin black, you gonna be a sight for sore eyes." Mr. Lester Brown busted into a hearty laugh, shakin his head as he left the room .

Beulah ran over to the mirror. She look at herself and saw her lips swellin and her eye turnin dark.

"What is I gonna do?!" She screamed.

"You should have thought about that before you started fightin," Ms. Mable said. "I suggest you wear lots and lots of lipstick; you too, Ruthie.

For the rest, I got no suggestions," Fanny Mae snickers.

Fanny Mae took me by the hand. "Come on Ruthie, let's leave Beulah so she can git dress for *the weddin of the year*. Here, take you stockin wit you."

I pick up my stockin and look at Ms. Mable. "Can I finish dressin in your room Ms. Mable?"

Ms. Mable shook her head for yes and we left her in the room wit Beulah.

Fanny Mae and I went in her mama and papa room. Mr. Lester in the room wit Beulah's shoes. He left the room when we came in, headin toward the girls' room wit Beulah's shoes in his hand.

I looked at myself in the mirrow and saw I look terrible. I had a swoll up lip and a knot on the side of my head. I didn't wanna go to the weddin lookin like that, so I told Fanny Mae I wasn't goin.

"You got to go or Mama and Papa be mad at you. Come on, let's take care of that lip first."

Fanny Mae pile the red lipstick on my swollen lip, which made it look even larger. I comb my hair in front to hide the swellin on the side of my head. Fanny Mae git my stockins and rolled dem in little balls.

"What you doing? I got to wear those."

"You can either have bigger tits or stockins on you legs." She held dem up wit one in each hand.

I was almost flat chested. I look down at my chest and rub my hands across my breasts. I decide on bigger tits as I stuff the stockins in my bra, which in-turn fill out my dress in front

I wasn't in the weddin 'cause Beulah wanted it that way. For all that had happen, I was glad. I was gonna sit in the back row when the weddin start, but Ms. Mable made me sit up front wit her. I plan on runnin back to the house when the weddin was over 'cause nobody gonna miss me. Well, that didn't happen.

The weddin started, and Beulah came out the house wit most of the veil coverin her face. It work out okay 'cause Mr. Lester was guiding her wit his arm. Mr. Lester look like he holdin in his stomach, but every few seconds I see his stomach shake a little. I wonder if Mr. Lester was holdin it in to keep from laughin.

When they git to the alter, the pastor say, "Who giveth this woman away?"

Mr. Lester said, "I do."

Beulah and Jeremiah backs was facing the people. Mr. Lester Brown let go of Beulah arm and took a seat. Now, that weren't strange. But instead of sittin by his wife he took a chair and place it up close near the side of the alter. The chair was so close he be able to see the look on Jeremiah face as soon as he lift the veil.

At first I thought that he jus want to see Beulah face, one more time as being his daughter, before she become a wife. Then I thought Beulah face must have swoll up even more 'cause I could see he was laughin. When the pastor said "you may now kiss the bride," Mr. Lester started rockin in his seat and hummin. One veil, two veils, then three was lifted. Jeremiah and the pastor jerks they heads back. Mr. Lester bust out laughin but this time he cover his mouth.

Jeremiah eyes widen as he look at Beulah. "Damn, woman! What happen to you?"

I hear Beulah say, "Jus kiss me, but not on the lips."

She turn her head sideways and Jeremiah sort of gave a shiver, close his eyes, and gave her a quick kiss on the side of her jaw..

He quickly put the veils back on her face and hurry her down the aisle to the house before anyone could give dem any congratulations.

"I guess they must be in a hurry, for what I don't know," Ms. Ester said, as she eye the couple

The other guests seem bewilderd. Ms. Mable went in the house after Beulah and Jeremiah and wouldn't let nobody else in. I git up and stand by a tree hopin that no one would come over to me. I didn't want nobody to see my face. Finally, Jeremiah and Beulah came out the house hand-in-hand. They both walk up to me, and I didn't know what was goin to happen. I froze in my tracks. When they git to the tree, Beulah open up her arms and gave me the biggest hug.

"I is sorry, can you forgive me for treatin you like I did?" She look at me real sorrowful like.

I was shocked wit Beulah sayin sorry to me. I could have never dream she would ever say that, especially to me.

"I forgive you, but can you forgive me for messin up your special day?" I uttered, afraid of what might happen next.

"You didn't mess up my day. I got my man, and ain't he somethin?" Beulah look proudly at Jeremiah.

Wit those words they left me and went to talk to the other guests. I gave out a sigh of relief. I didn't know what Jeremiah had said to Beulah in the house, but she actin different. I look around to see if I could find Fanny Mae so I tell her about what jus happen. As my eyes search, I spotted Oscar a comin straight toward me. I cover my lip and think about walkin away, but he was too close upon me .

"No need to cover it, I know that your lip is swollen. I seen it as soon as you took a seat," he said, as he smile at me.

I took my hand away from my mouth. "I jus had a little fight wit somebody."

"Yeh, and could that somebody be Beulah?"

We both chuckle.

Oscar turn his head sideways as if he was lookin afar and said, "Ruthie, I wonder if you could go to the picture show wit me sometime?"

"I could ask Ms. Mable if she don't mind, I let you know what she say. Maybe she would let me go wit you next Saturday."

I looks around and seen Fanny Mae. "Oscar, I got to go and tell Fanny Mae somethin."

"Ok. Maybe we can dance later. Ms. Mable and Mr. Lester Brown got music, don't they?"

"Yesum, they does. I is gonna talk to you again in a few minutes."

I left him there by the tree and walk toward Fanny Mae. I look back at Oscar who was watching me.

I met with Fanny Mae and told her about what Beulah did and what Oscar said.

"I jus talk to Beulah too, she is actin different now. She should be sorry for treatin you so nasty. I hope she be happy now, since she got her man."

Fanny Mae stop talkin to me but she stood there lookin around.

"What is you lookin for Fanny Mae?"

"Before you go off to the picture show wit Oscar let me introduce you to Wilbert."

"I don't wanna see him wit my lip all swoll up."

"I don't see why, you talked to Oscar."

Fanny Mae spot Wilbert and call him over. I want to meet him and run away both at the same time. I put one of my hands to my swollen lip. As he git closer I could see that Fanny Mae was right, he was handsome. I drop my hand from my lip without thinkin, and swallow hard. Before he could git close enough for Fanny Mae to introduce him to me, another girl came up to him, took him by the arm and led him off. Fanny Mae and I jus stand there lookin in they direction. Finally, Fanny Mae spoke.

"I didn't know he had a girlfriend."

"Well that's all right. I didn't wanna meet him anyway, lookin like this." I start walkin back in the direction where Oscar was standin. Ms. Mable came out the house and call me and Fanny Mae.

Ms. Mable brought out a small table and place it in the yard. She hand Fanny Mae a tablecloth, and I help her put it on the table. Ms. Mable went back in the house and we follow. We came back out wit the plates, forks, and cups for the punch. I fix a plate of food and ate, and after a while, Mr. Lester set up some music on the music box. Oscar came up to me and we start dancing. We wind up dancin the evenin away.

The next day was Sunday, but instead of going to church I went over to Miz Johnson house. Maggie was still there and she open the door for me.

"Your Miz Johnson is feelin poorly today. I hope that seeing you will help her spirits. God, I wish her daughter would hurry up and come here for her mama's sake." She rubbed one of her arms and cast her eyes toward the stairs that lead to Miz Johnson room.

"I guess I better go on up." I start toward the stairs.

When I git to her room, I founded Miz Johnson on the bed. She was lying on her back, and her head face the window like she lookin for somebody to come through it.

"Miz Johnson , is you all right?" I walk over to the bed.

"I am about as alright as I can be, right now." She turn her head to me.

"Your nurse said that you was feelin quite poorly today." I pull up a chair close to her bed.

"I feel poorly every day, but enough about me. How was the weddin?" She smile as if she was expectin me to say something funny.

I started tellin her about the weddin. When I told her about the fight she said that she figure that me and Beulah would have it out one day. She said she hoped it would have been jus an argument and not a fight. The swellin in my lip had went down, and Miz Johnson thought I was the one deliver the most punches. I shooked my head. "Naw Miz Johnson. Beulah whip me real good."

I told her about Mr. Lester laughin at Beulah.

"Lester always had a good sense of humor. That kind of person will live a long time."

I told her about Oscar, and she remember him from the bus.

"I hope that he is right for you, since you like him. I would hope that you give yourself a chance to meet other boys before you decide on one. You have been through a lot in your short lifetime. Give yourself some time to know what you want and where you wanna go. Don't let anyone make that decision for you."

"I don't know if I like him that much now, Miz Johnson. Maybe I don't like him as much as I thought." Miz Johnson smile at me, then close her eyes.

"Ruthie, I am tired now, I need some sleep. You go on back to Mable and enjoy the day, but come back tomorrow."

"Okay, Miz Johnson."

I watch her drift off to sleep, and I whisper, "I will be back tomorra." I put the chair back where I found it, and left her house. I walked the road feelin sad that this woman, not too long ago, was full of energy and life. Now she barely had the energy to stay awake. Laughin even made her tired.

The next day I returned to Miz Johnson house. This time when I enter her room, her head was turn toward the door. She smile when she seen me.

"Come on in, Ruthie. Today I need to tell you somethin." Miz Johnson didn't look so tired and even her smile was different—like she had a wonderful secret. I was happy to see her voice seem stronger, and her whole body seem to radiate wit a positive attitude.

"Yes ma'am." I pull up a chair by her bed.

"Ruthie, have you given any thought to what I was tellin you the other day?" Miz Johnson began.

"Yesum. I decided not to go to the picture show wit Oscar,"

"That's not what I was tellin you. Anyway, are you still feelin that way about Miz Williams?"

"You mean, if I still hate her?" My smile disappear.

"That's what I wanna know." Miz Johnson eyes was searchin mine for the answer.

"Yes, I still hate her. Jus 'cause she was white and free to do what she want she felted that she could do anythang to me. At first I really liked her, but I didn't know she didn't like me. She seem like the most nicest person I had met but she change and kepted me like a slave. No white person helped me. Sure, they gave me some food every now and then, but they didn't help me git away from her. I could have died, and would they have cared? No. I was jus a little old color girl, no better'n a dog. Even after I am away from her, sometimes I still has nightmares about what she did to me. My papa die of a heart attack 'cause of her. My Aunt Flo was broken-hearted for years 'cause of her, yet she is still free to do whatever she please. I am not free to do anythang about it but I can have this hate for her. We live in a country that is suppose to be free for all people but I ain't free. Look at me, Miz Johnson, I is colored. The only freedom I have is in my mind. And, in there, I has the freedom to hate her."

I kepted my face turned away from Miz Johnson. In some strange way I didn't want her to see my face as I spoke about the hate I had for another white person. Maybe I was afraid she might start feelin hate for me because of it. Yet, I had to say what I felted. When I was finish, Ms. Johnson told me to look at her. She pull herself up on the pillows and spoke.

"You talk about freedom Ruthie, but none of us is truly free. Miz Williams thought that she was free to do whatever she wanted to you for, whatever reason. She is fooling herself. One day she will find out that she will have to pay for that. There is a judge who is watchin our every move and judging us, be us white, black or in-between. Do you think that I am free Ruthie because I am white? Did you know that there are places that I can't go. Things that I am not free to do. Something you said Ruthie that I truly agree with. That is, freedom began in your mind. The only thing you don't understand is that your mind is not free. No, you will never be free if you let hate rule you. Listen good to me Ruthie, you will never be free."

Miz Johnson relax back in her bed. "My daughter will be finally comin today after months of me waitin for her. Tell her that I waited until I couldn't wait no more. Remember this Ruthie, that I will always love you."

"I Love you too Miz Johnson." I smiled at her.

I did love her very much. She was not jus a person I work for, she was my friend. She close her eyes and went to sleep. Fear began to flow over my being as I watch her, for this seem to me as a different kind of sleep.

"Miz Johnson, Miz Johnson!" I screamed.

Maggie came a runnin up the stairs. She went over to the bed and grab hold of Miz Johnson wrist and took her pulse. She bend down and listen to her heart, and look at me.

"She's gone."

As soon as she spoke those words, my heart felted as if it was sinkin.

"Let me cover her face and get the doctor over here."

"Please don't cover her yet, Miss Maggie," I plead. "Let me stay wit her a little while ma'am. I wanna see her face jus a few more minutes."

"Okay."

Maggie left the room and went down the stairs. She left me in the room alone wit Miz Johnson, so I put my head on her chest and one of my arms around her. I listen to the stillness of her heart. My own heart felted heavy and empty. My head was filled wit darkness. My tears came down uncontrollable until the front of her gown was wet.

I heard footsteps runnin up the stairs, and a woman burst in the room. She look jus like Miz Johnson, jus younger. I figured she Miz Johnson daughter. I git up from huggin Miz Johnson and stood up by the bed.

"Mama !" She screamed, "No!"

Maggie was behind her, tryin to console her. The woman ran to the bedside. She lifted her mama in her arms. "Mama. Don't leave me!" She cried.

"She told me to tell you that she waited for you until she couldn't wait no more," I told the woman.

Miz Johnson's daughter look at me, still cryin. Then her eyes focus back at her mama. Maggie came over, still tryin to console her. I left the room and out the house. I headed toward my own comforter, Ms. Mable.

CHAPTER THIRTY-ONE

I stay wit Ms.Mable and her family for two weeks after the death of Miz Johnson. I thought about what Miz Johnson said and I tried prayin for the Lawd to help me not hate Miz Williams. I knew what Miz Johnson say was right. But in my heart I still wished I could somehow git even wit Miz Williams.

During those two weeks, Oscar was always visitin. The more Oscar came over, the more I wanted him to stay away. It took him too long to answer a question and he wouldn't look me in the face. He would turn his head and look at me out the corner of his eye when he talk to me.

Wilbert came around once and ask me out to the picture show. He and I had a very nice time that night, and he even held my hand as we walk back to Ms. Mable. He told me he really like me. I wanted him to kiss me, but neither him nor me was brave enough to go that far. When he left that night, I look for him to come around again 'cause he made me feel all tingly and light inside. But he never did. Later, I found out that Oscar told him not to come around me no more. Told him, if he did he would cut him wit his knife. When I was tolded that, it made me mad. I confront Oscar about it. He jus hung his head and say that he love me and he didn't wanna lose me.

"That why I did it Ruthie."

"Well you gonna lose me anyway. I is going back to Demopolis. I ain't never gonna see you again Oscar."

About six months after I git back to Demopolis, there was a knock at the door. When I answer it, to my amazement, there stood Oscar. He was smilin as if he had won a prize. I didn't open the screen door for him.

"Why, I mean, how, I mean, what, is the reason why you here?" I utter, feeling like an insect caught in a spider web.

"We all moved to this city 'cause we has other family members that live here. They said they is gonna help us find jobs. Nobody has a job cept Annabelle. You see, my papa died Ruthie."

I felted sad about that. I liked Oscar's papa.

"I is powerfully sorry, Oscar, about you papa. I hope you can find jobs here. I can't hardy find one cept for pickin cotton sometime. How did you find out where I stay?"

Ms. Mable give me you address, and it easy to find you." Oscar stood there lookin like he was expectin me to hug him or somethin.

"Who at the door Ruthie?" My aunt call from another room.

"It a boy I know, that came to visit me."

My aunt came out of the room and told me to let him in. I open the door for Oscar. He came in, gave me a quick kiss on my cheek, and went over to my mama. He greet her, tellin her he really like me and one day he hope I become his wife.

Oscar git a job workin in a small factory, and come to my house every evenin after work. He would talk to my aunt, but not my real mama 'cause sometimes it seem like she not all there. The more he talk to my aunt, the more she like him.

One afternoon as Aunt Flo, me, and, Alice was taking a walk, mama ask me about Oscar. "Ruthie. You don't never talk about Oscar."

"I don't like him."

"Why?"

"'Cause he has funny-lookin eyes."

Alice giggle when I said funny-lookin.

"Oscar is a good-lookin boy. I don't see nothang wrong wit him. He seem to like you a lot. He seem like a hard-workin boy. Maybe he be a good husband."

"I don't think so, Mama."

"But he a nice boy. That's what you want Ruthie, somebody that's nice and hard workin."

"I don't want him to be my husband. You suppose to love you husband, I don't love him."

"You might grow to love him. I didn't love you uncle when we first git married, but I knew he a hard-workin man. Later on, I love him. That what a woman need, a good provider."

I kept protestin about Oscar until my aunt dropped the subject, but I thought about what she said.

When I turned nineteen Oscar ask me to marry him, and I said yes.

Right after the weddin night, Oscar told me that I had to do somethang about the bag of bones I call a body.

We had a big argument that next day but by the next evening, I was eatin the food that Oscar said would make me the kind of woman he like. He cook the meal. We had fried fat back, fried potatoes, and fried okra, wit a large slice of chocolate pie for dinner. I had to admit that he was a very good cook.

Well, we ate all kinds of fattenin food. I gain so much weight, I had breasts as large as grapefruits, a butt as big as a large watermelon, and thighs so large they shook when I walks. I became a healthy, down-home, corn-fed, woman. When I come in the room at night, Oscar eyes light up jus lookin at my tits, butt, and thighs. Lucky I still had a small waist.

We was married for about five years when Oscar lose his job. He look for a job, for what seem about four months, wit no luck. After a while Oscar took to drinkin. When he drank, we fuss all the time. I decide to look for a job, not only to support us both, but also to git away from him.

I look in the newspaper and seen an ad for a live-in housekeeper. I only had to stay wit the person for five days a week and I would git the weekends off. I went into town to git the job. Strangely, where I had to go to apply, was at a lawyer office. When I git there, I was met by a kind-lookin middle-aged white man. He was muscular built, and tall, wit mix gray and brown hair. I figure the job was for his house, but I found out that it for someone else.

That person was a lady name Miz Thorten, and the lawyer was in control of her money. He told me where the house was and to start there the next day, if I wanted. I took the job.

I went home and told Oscar and we got into another argument. He didn't want me to take no job. We argues most of the evenin and into the night. By the next morning, I was runnin out the house wit a small suitcase. I needed the peace.

When I arrive at the house, it was eight o'clock in the morning. I look at the large white house. The porch was long, encirclin the whole front of the house, and they was four columns. They was four large windows facing the front and a large door to the entrance of the house. I was jus about to knock on the door when a colored woman open it.

"About time you git here, I is leaving. Good luck and goodbye."

The woman grab a small suitcase and left in a huff. She didn't give me no chance to ask her nothin. The last thing I saw was her behind bouncin it way on down the road. I went on in hopin the lady of the house was knowin I was a comin. I didn't see nobody.

"Hello, is anybody here? I is the new hired help." No answer.

"Hello?" I repeat myself, hopin I wasn't alone in the house.

"I hear you," a voice from another room answer me, "I'm in here."

I walk toward the voice. I came into a room wit two chairs, two sofas, and two wooden table that was the color of maple, both of dem shined from waxin. They was also two end tables, and a cabinet that helded figurines. Pictures of people and places that exist long ago was on the wall. I look around and found a white woman sittin in a wheelchair. She wore a white dress, and was thin and look in her sixties. Her lips was drawn close together and turn down into a frown. Her eyes kepted on me like an eagle watch a mouse. She was pale, like she ill. Her hair was thin and needed combin. She kept scratchin her head, and I see sores on her scalp. One of dem had crusted over.

"I is you new help." I said cheerfully.

"I know that." Her voice sound irritated

"My name Ruthie."

Her eyes widen.

"What you want me to do first?"

She didn't answer me, she jus scratch at the crusted sore. It bust open and pus ran from it.

"Do you need anything ma'am? Maybe I can put somethang on dem sores."

"No. I can take care of myself. Jus clean the house." She put both hands on the wheels of the chair and push off into another room.

"I went about the house lookin for anythang that need done. I found no dustin, washin, or cleanin to be done. The house was as clean and neat as a pin. I went back to Miz Thorten after a while and ask her if she wanted me to fix her somethin to eat.

"I want eggs and bacon for breakfast, and fix a small pot of coffee. For supper you fix chicken and dumplins. You know how to cook chicken and dumplins?"

"Yesum."

"Put on a pot of beans too."

"Yesum."

I went into the kitchen, she follow me and watch me as I fix her breakfast. I notice that Miz Thorten kitchen was all white wit everythang put away jus like Miz Williams. Nothang adorn her kitchen, and nothang of color except two pair of green curtains that covered the two windows in the kitchen. When the breakfast ready Miz Thorten left the room. When she came in the kitchen, she had a rag wit her. She took the rag and wipe off the table and her fork and knife, like they was dirty.

Miz Thorten ate her meal and watch me while I put on the beans and chicken for supper. Her watchin made me a little uneasy. To make myself feel at ease I thought to myself, "Maybe she is watchin me 'cause I is new and she don't trust me yet."

When she through eatin, I wash her dish. Miz Thorten stay in the kitchen wit me as I wash the dish and put it away. Every room I went in, she follow. When it was time for supper, I made some cornbread for the beans, and dumplins for the chicken. I waited until the dumplins was cooked. I ask Miz Thorten if she was ready to eat, and she said yes. I fix her a bowl of beans and a bowl of chicken and dumplins. I sat dem down in front of her along wit a slice of cornbread. She took a look at the bowl of beans and push it away.

"Why have you given me these beans?" She screamed.

"You told me to fix dem for you."

"Take them away!" She command.

As I was takin the beans to the sink, Miz Thorten look at me and said, "I told you to fix them beans 'cause those were for you."

I turn around and fix my eyes on Miz Thorten and very politely said, "Excuse me ma'am. I have eaten enough beans in my life. Ruthie is not eatin another bean. You have a lot of different food here, but if this is what I git to eat to keep this here job, I is leavin."

I took off my apron.

"Ruthie, don't go, please, I need your help. You can eat anythin you want."

I look at her pleadin wit me. I glance at the window and seen that it was already gittin dark, and I didn't like walkin in the dark by myself.

"Okay, Miz Thorten. But I ain't eatin no more beans."

I fix a bowl of chicken and dumplins, and put my bowl on the table.

"What are you doing?!"

"I is gittin ready to eat."

"Not at my table, you don't!"

"Where is I suppose to eat?"

"Take your food outside."

Suddenly I was not hungry, as I took the bowl outside. I sat on the front porch wit the bowl in my hand for a while, lookin at the road that I travel to come to tis house. I thought about Miz Johnson and how she let me eat at her table. It had been a long time since I had to eat my meals on the porch. I felted that I could find myself another job.

"I be leavin this here place in the mornin, this woman is impossible," I thought.

I sat out on the porch until Miz Thorten called me.

"Ruthie, come here. I am through eatin."

I pour the chicken and dumplins on the ground by the porch and went inside. Miz Thorten roll her chair away from the table. I took the bowls and wash dem and put dem away.

I wanted to know where I was gonna be sleepin for the night. She never told me. I had even left my suitcase by the front door.

"Where is the room where I is gonna be sleepin Miz Thorten?"

"I don know. I don't have a back porch that's closed in."

She wheeled herself toward her room and went inside, leavin me standin there in the kitchen. I didn't know what to do, but I knew I wasn't stayin up all night. I sat in the kitchen for a while thinkin. "What a horrible woman. Why did I picked this job? She must have treated the other woman the same way. That's why she left. Come morning, I is leavin too."

I git up and went peekin in each room. One of the rooms had a bed in it. I went over and laid on it witout botherin to undress. I went to sleep. The next day when I git up, I grab my suitcase to leave. Miz Thorten meet me at the front door jus as I open it.

"Ruthie, you leavin?"

"Yesum. I ain't stayin here. You want me to eat and sleep outside. I is goin home."

"Ruthie if you stay a least until I find somebody else, I will give you more money in addition to what my lawyer is gonna pay you. Three dollars—that will make six dollars a week."

"I can't be eatin on you porch and sleepin God knows where."

"You slept in a bed last night and you didn't eat nothin 'cause you poured the food out in the front."

She and me stop talkin for a second. I look at Miz Thorten, not knowin if I should stay or not. I wanted the extra money, but I didn't like being treated like she treat me.

Finally, she spoke, "You can sleep in that room as long as you wash the sheets every day."

"Okay Miz Thorten." I decided to stay but only because of the extra money she offer.

That rest of the week went well for the most part. I didn't work hard and Miz Thorten started treatin me nice.

When I git home that weekend, Oscar was laying on the floor, and the house was a mess, wit alcohol bottles all over the place. I git him up and helped him to the bed. Nothang had been done since I left. I was so mad at him as I started cleanin. I heard a knock at the door, it Oscar's mama. I open the door for her, threw my arms around her, and cried.

"Mama, I only been gone for a week and look at tis house. Oscar been drinkin and he ain't clean nothing since I left. Maybe I should jus quit my job."

"Don't quit your job Honey, somebody got to work. I didn't know my son was drinkin like this. When you at you job this week, I take care of him. I guarantee that when you come back here next week, you won't find him drunk."

"How you're gonna to do that Mama? He always wants to argue wit me."

"He ain't gonna argue wit me." She put her hands on her hips. "Honey go git me a bucket of cold water so I can sober him up."

" Mama, don't you mean some coffee?" I went toward the kitchen.

"No Honey. I said, a bucket of cold water."

I git Oscar mama a bucket of cold water. She told me not to follow her in the room where he was, but to stay in the kitchen. His mama went in the room wit the water. The next thing I heard was a bump and Oscar screamin.

" Mama, please don't!"

Squish was the next sound. Oscar came out the room wet, wit his mama right behind him hittin him on his head wit her fist. I wanted to laugh, but instead I kept it in—when she left, me and Oscar might jus fight because I was laughin at him.

She saw me tryin to hold in the laughter, and said, "You can laugh at this fool and he better not put his hands on you."

I bust out laughin. Oscar mad but he didn't say nothang to me. His mama made him clean up the house, wit those wet clothes on. She follow him as he clean, fussin and hittin him on the head. Oscar beg his mama to stop hittin him and let him take the wet clothes off. Only when the house was finally clean did she stop hittin him and let him change.

Before his mama left the house, she told him that he better not argue at me and that she is gonna come back every day to our house from now on. I didn't know that Oscar was scared of his mama. So from that day on, every time Oscar started doin somethang that I thought was wrong, I told his mama.

For the rest of that weekend everything was good well. Oscar and me had a good time talkin, goin to the picture show, and jus lyin around doin nothang. I felted a little sad when it was time for me to return to my job. He promise me he gonna be lookin for a job while I was away. We kiss, and I was off to Miz Thorten house again. When I git there, she open the door before I knock.

"Mornin, Miz Thorten."

She didn't say nothin. She jus stared at me.

"What wrong Miz Thorten?"

"Nothing's wrong."

"What you want me to fix you for breakfast?"

"I want pancakes."

"Okay then, pancakes it is."

She was wearin another white dress with a full skirt. She had comb her hair back and put some salve on the sores

I went in the kitchen to fix her breakfast, she went wit me and watch my every move. Her head turnin and swayin remind me of a snake watchin somthin to eat.

When I was through wit her meal, I set it before her. She left the room and came back wit the same old rag and wipe off the already-clean table and her utensils. I didn't eat breakfast that day 'cause I had already eaten at home. While she was eatin I told her that I was gonna wash her clothes. She said okay, and started eatin faster for some strange reason. I notice one sore on her scalp look a little worse. It was oozing blood along wit pus.

"Are you all right Miz Thorten? That sore look like it need a doctor."

"I am fine."

"Do they itch? Is that why you scratchin dem so much?"

She jus looked at me but said nothin.

"I could git you somethin for that and maybe it would heal."

"I said, it's fine." She stop eatin and narrow her eyes at me. I knew then to drop the subject.

"Ok. I'll jus go and git your dirty clothes. Where is they? "

"They are in my room."

"Okay ma'am."

I went to Miz Thorten room and found her dirty clothes on the floor beside her door. I gather the clothes up. She didn't have a washin machine, so I gits a wash board and two tubs and took dem outside to the back yard. The yard was large wit flowers and green grass. A few trees was in the yard, and a well was in the middle of it. It look jus like one that I seen in a storybook once. It was made of gray and brown stone wit a top that look like the roof of a house, jus smaller. It had two pieces of thick wood holdin up the roof. One piece of wood that went across the other two had a rope tied to it holdin the bucket. A lever held the rope in place.

I went over to the well and notice that it was not stable. The mortar seem to be crumblin around the stone, and the wood that held the roof up look dry like it was rotten. The rope looked old and dry.

I peep into the well and smell the most horrible stench. I pulled back, holdin my nose. I wonder if somethin had fell in the well and die. As beautiful as it look from afar, it was really a dilapidated thing, and I wonder why it was there. I went back and continue wit my work after I fill both of the tubs wit water from a faucet. One tub of water for washin and one for rinsin. As I was fillin the tubs, I notice Miz Thorten watchin me from a window. I act like I didn't see her. I git the soap and wash her clothes, but I felted her eyes on my every move. She remind me of Miz Williams.

When the washin was done I went back in the house and washed floors and dust tables. I iron the clothes as soon as they git dry. At every turn, there was Miz Thorten watchin me. Every day she watch me like I a thief. When the week was over she gave me three dollars, and another three dollars from her lawyer. I started not to take money she gave me out her own pocket. Then I said to myself, "From all the tension she gave me, watchin me—the money is for that."

That weekend when I git home, I told Oscar about the time that I had wit Miz Thorten. He told me to stay there wit her one more week and he, by the end of that week, gonna have a job. I went to visit my mama-in-law that weekend and told her about Miz Thorten.

"Honey you don't have to go back. I got some money you and Oscar can has. You don have to put up wit that woman."

I didn't wanna take Oscar mama money, so I went back to work for Miz Thorten the next week. When I git there, she met me at the door like she had done the week before. She wearin a white dress that had a full skirt, and the top of the dress had no sleeves. She wore a silver necklace wit a silver heart in the middle.

"Mornin, Miz Thorten," I address her.

"Mornin Ruthie."

"You look mighty purty today wit you white dress and all. Is you ready for you breakfast?"

"Yes. Fix me some bacon and eggs. I want one piece of toast with no butter, you hear? Just one."

"Yesum."

I fix her breakfast as usual, and she watch me as usual. When it was done I serv it to her and went to my duties. I remember that I had to clean her room, so I went there. As usual, the dirty clothes were at the door, and I move dem aside. I change her bed sheets, pullin dem tight, and put the spread back on the bed. I went over to dust the dresser wit the picture album was. As I was dustin, I accidentally knock the album off the dresser and I reaches down to pick it up. The album was lyin on the floor open to a picture of a little girl which remind me of Susie. I turn more pages and there was Mr. Williams and Miz Williams together wit little Johnny. I turn more pages and seen more pictures of the family.

"Why are you lookin at my album instead of cleanin my room?" Miz Thorten said from the doorway.

"You Miz Williams."

"Close my book and git back to work," she bellow. "I paid you good money to work, so do it."

"I should have known the first time you start watchin me. Only Miz Williams would watch me so close, but you in a wheelchair."

"Yes, I *was* Miz Williams. I git married again and I suffer a fall, that's why I am in this chair."

"Where is Susie now?"

"I don't know, she doesn't come around. She said that I was mean. She never acted right with me since you left. You ruined everything when you left. Little Johnny don't come here either. I sometimes think that maybe his papa keeps him away from me."

Miz Thorten face had an expression of sadness.

"I got to go," I said in disgust. I didn't wanna stay there another moment.

"The last time you left, it hurt me Ruthie. You made a mockery out of me with my neighbors."

"Hurt you. What about me? Remember what you put me through?"

"Ruthie stay, don't go, I need you." Her voice sound sincere.

"Naw, Miz Thorten. Not after the way you treat me when I a child. I really liked you but you treated me like a dog. You were the 'cause of my papa's death. You told the most worse lies. You told my family I was dead, even sent dem ashes, tellin dem that they was mine. Why Miz Thorten? Why?" I said, between tears and anger.

"You never like me Ruthie, but you and your parents liked the money that I gave you. Remember that figurine that I showed you. If it wasn't for the love of money you would have ran for your life, but you didn't because of greed. If your parents really loved you they wouldn't never let you go with me. They would have come and got you after the time that I promised to sent you back. They didn't Ruthie, they wanted the money. They weren't your real parents anyway. It was greed, Ruthie, that made them do what they did to you. I saved you Ruthie. I gave you a home, a nice home, and food in your stomach when other people were starvin. I saved you."

"From what? The love of my family. They really loved me and they missed me. You see MizThorten, I know you change the wordin of my letters. Even at times you didn't even mail dem. You kepted me as a slave. You jus a hateful, controllin woman. Why you hate me? I bet you don't know, cept that I is colored. You had a husband and a family that loved you. You lost dem because of the hate that drove you. You know what, I hated you too after I founded out what you done. A person that I loved very much told me not to hate you but to feel sorry for you."

"She was probably some old niggard. I don't need no niggard, feelin sorry for me."

I bend down and looked Miz Thorten in the face. "Naw she wasn't no niggard, but a white lady. Her name was Miz Johnson. She even told me what a niggard was. You know what MizThorten, I ain't no niggard. I is a colored woman and a proud one."

I stood up from her and started walkin away.

"Ruthie you come back here!"

I stop walkin. Lookin straight ahead, like the door been hypotizing me. I spoke again.

"In the country, we had a well. One day a sore-headed chicken fell in it and drown. My papa took it out. I was only six years old then. I knowin the chicken had died in it and I didn't wanna drink the water, it was posion to me. I swear I could see a bit of pus from the chicken on the top of the water. But a river ran under the well. Later that day, the water rose up in the well and went over the top, cleanin that old well. When it was through, that well water were again crystal clear and cold. The well you has in back seem to be dried up. It serve no purpose cept be a grave for anything that happen to fall in its grip."

I started walkin again, wit Miz Thorten following me as I headed out the door. She kept tellin me to stop, but I continue walkin down the steps. Finally, she stop the wheelchair on the porch. She started moanin in pain like somethang was hurtin her. I stop walkin and turn around. She was slump over to one side in her wheelchair. One of her hands was on her chest. The other hand was holdin tightly on the arm of the wheelchair. Her eyes was shut, the muscles in her forhead was all press together to form wrinkles between both eyes. She press her lips together and let out another moan, louder than the first. I walk back over to her, wonderin what was wrong. She open her eyes and look up at me.

"Ruthie, please, before you go, please get the medicine on my dresser and a glass of water and give it to me. I need my medicine, I is feelin mighty bad right now like I might be having a heart attack."

"I is gonna git you the medicine, then I is gonna leave. You understand, Miz Thorten?"

She shook her head for yes. I put my suitcase down and left her. I went back in the house headin for her room. I looked on her dresser for the medicine but I din't find any. I searched in her dresser draws. Still no medicine. My mind began to race, trying to figure out where it could be. I ran back to the porch where I had left Miz Thorten, hoping that her illness hadn't gotten worse. When I reach the porch, she was gone. I went back in the house and call for her, hopin she had came back inside and went in one of the rooms. No answer, as I search from room to room. I ran back outside to the backyard, and I spot her sittin on the ledge of the well.

"Git on off that well!" I shouted. I walked towards her direction.

I guess you know by now that I didn't need no medicine."

"Git off the well MizThorten. It ain't safe!"

"Don't come no closer Ruthie."

I stop in my tracks. I was jus a few yards away.

"Remember what I told you when you was a little girl? Remember that I was gonna hide my jewery and tell the police you stole it if you left me? Well, this here necklace should do."

Miz Thorten snatched her necklace off her neck and held it over the well.

"Please MizThorten, don't do this."

MizThorten let the necklace go. It fell silent into the gapin hole, and my heart sanked. I looked at the woman that now held the rest of my life in her hands. The look on her face let me know that I didn't have a prayer.

"You see Ruthie, you can't talk to me like that and get away with it. You disrespected me, gal. Now I am gonna get up and call the police."

She move her hips slightly, and I seen the stones move beneath her.

"Please Miz Thorten, let me help you git off the well!"

I move toward her again, fearin that she might fall.

"I told you to stay away from me!"

She shifted her hips an inch more off the stone. Some stones crumbled, sendin dem, along with Miz Thorten, headin into the Well. Miz Thorten scream, and her arms reach frantically for the rope that held the bucket. She grab the rope, and the levy that helded the rope in place shifted. She, wit the bucket, began to move into the gapin hole. I ran to the well grabbin hold to her white dress, near her knees. Her body laid arched wit her back over the well. The stones crumbled violently as I pulled her body towards me. Before my eyes could blink, the stones beneath her collaped. Now her whole body was in the well. White dust erupt in my face as the levy shifted again. The moaning sound of the wood enter the air. I held on to Miz Thorten dress as her body fell a few more inches into the well.

Miz Thorten scream, "Help me Ruthie. I don't wanna die!"

I clinged tighter to her dress only to find it tearin across her waist. I pulls harder. My body was leanin up against the wall of the well. The stones that I lean on began to crumble. Her weight along wit mine was too much for it to bear. My body slid closer to the openin as the stones moved out of place. A stone fell over but it didn't hit Miz Thorten. Sheer terror grip my mind as I inch toward the evil opening. I knew right then that if I continued holdin on to her, Miz Thorten and me would enter into the foul dark hole. Why should I? She is jus as hateful as this well. I knew If I let her go I would be free of her, even if I had to go to prison. Suddenly the words that Miz Johnson said jus before she died flashed in my mind: *you can never be free if your mind is not free from hate*. The words echoed through my most inter being. Was I jus as hateful as Miz Thorten? Was this the final fate that hate had to offer?

"No, I ain't like you!" The words bellowed out my mouth.

I began to pull wit all of my might. The well was ready to take another life. My fate as well as hers look me dead in the face wit a gratifying smile. I look towards the sky and in desperation I cried out "GOD, OH GOD, PLEASE HELP ME!" as a tear rolled down my eye. At that very moment, hands grasp my waist.

I hear a man voice say, "I gotcha. Now hold on to her!"

The man pull me back as I helded on to Miz Thorten's dress.

"Keep holdin on. I see her. I am gonna let you go. You steady yourself. Put one foot in front of the other!"

I did as I was told. The man turned my waist loose, and wit two steps he was in front of the well; I saw that is wast her lawyer. He steady himself and took hold of her waist and pulled her out the well to safety. Only then did I let go of the dress.

Miz Thorten laid in his arms a sobbin. He lifted her up and place her back in her wheelchair. He looked at us both.

"What happen here? Miz Thorten, I was just comin here to give you these papers to sign when I hear Ruthie scream." His face question what had jus happen. Miz Thorten or me didn't'say a word to him.

My legs collapse under me and I plumbered to the ground on my knees in relief. I hung my head and say, "Thank you Lawd!" I took a deep breath and let the air enter my lungs, and I finally felt free. I git up from the ground, and started walkin toward the house to git my suitcase. Then I started walkin down the road for home. I could hear Miz Thorten call to me.

"Ruthie, Ruthie, I'm alone here! I don't wanna be alone! What can I do?"

I shouted back to her, "TEAR THAT DAMN WELL DOWN!"